DIRECTORS IN PERSPECTIVE

General editor: C.D. Innes

Ingmar Bergman

TITLES IN THIS SERIES:

Ingmar Bergman: Lise-Lone and Frederick J. Marker

Peter Stein: Michael Patterson

FUTURE TITLES:

Adolph Appia: Richard Beecham

Roger Blin: Martin Esslin

Bertolt Brecht: John Fuegi

Peter Brook: Albert Hunt and Geoffrey Reeves

Joseph Chaikin: Eileen Blumenthal

E. Gordon Craig: Christopher Innes

Jerzy Grotowski: Nicholas Sales

Max Reinhardt: John Styan

Constantin Stanislavski: Peter Holland

Ingmar Bergman
Four Decades in the Theater

LISE-LONE MARKER   FREDERICK J. MARKER
University of Toronto

CAMBRIDGE UNIVERSITY PRESS
CAMBRIDGE
LONDON   NEW YORK   NEW ROCHELLE
MELBOURNE   SYDNEY

Published by the Press Syndicate of the University of Cambridge
The Pitt Building, Trumpington Street, Cambridge CB2 1RP
32 East 57th Street, New York, NY 10022, USA
296 Beaconsfield Parade, Middle Park, Melbourne 3206, Australia

© Cambridge University Press 1982

First published 1982

Printed in the United States of America

Library of Congress Cataloging in Publication Data
Marker, Lise-Lone and Frederick, J.
Ingmar Bergman, four decades in the theater.
(Directors in perspective)
Bibliography: p.
1. Bergman, Ingmar, 1918–
2. Theater–Production and direction.
I. Title. II. Series.
PN2778.B4M3   792'.0233'0924   81-7719
ISBN 0 521 22441 1   hard covers   AACR2
ISBN 0 521 29501 7   paperback

PN
2778
.B4
.M3
1982 Contents

List of illustrations	*page* vii
Preface	xiii
Introduction: The statue of Thalia	1
1. Talking about theater: a conversation with Ingmar Bergman	5
2. First seasons	31
American realism	44
Savage comedy	49
3. The Strindberg cycle	54
Early Strindberg productions	55
The Ghost Sonata: three productions	67
Dream plays	97
Toward a new Damascus	113
4. A theater for Molière	132
Portrait of a misanthrope	145
5. The essence of Ibsen	172
The airless world of Hedda Gabler	178
An actors' theater	201
6. Talking about tomorrow	220
7. Bergman's world: a chronology	235
Notes	249
Selected bibliography	256
Index	259

Illustrations

Opening scene of *Macbeth,* Hälsingborg City Theatre, 1944.
Photograph by Olle Lindberg. *page* 33
Stage setting for *Macbeth,* Gothenburg City Theatre, 1948.
Courtesy of Teaterhistoriska museet, Göteborg. 35
Stage setting for *Twelfth Night,* Dramaten, Stockholm, 1975.
Photograph by Beata Bergström. 38
Scene from *Twelfth Night,* Dramaten, 1975. Photograph by
Beata Bergström. 39
Scene from *Caligula,* Gothenburg City Theatre, 1946.
Courtesy of Teaterhistoriska museet, Göteborg. 42
Stage setting for *A Streetcar Named Desire,* Gothenburg City
Theatre, 1949. Courtesy of Teaterhistoriska museet,
Göteborg. 46
Stage setting for *Who's Afraid of Virginia Woolf?,* Dramaten,
1963. Photograph by Beata Bergström. 48
Stage setting for *Divine Words (Divinas palabras),* Gothenburg
City Theatre, 1950. Courtesy of Teaterhistoriska
museet, Göteborg. 51
Scene from *The Ghost Sonata,* Malmö City Theatre, 1954.
Courtesy of Theatre and Film Dept., University of
Lund. 68
Scene from *The Ghost Sonata,* Dramaten, 1973. Photograph
by Beata Bergström. 70
Naima Wifstrand in *The Ghost Sonata,* Malmö City Theatre,
1954. Courtesy of Theatre and Film Dept., University
of Lund. 72
Scene from *The Ghost Sonata,* Dramaten, 1973. Photograph
by Beata Bergström. 74
Scene from *The Ghost Sonata,* Malmö City Theatre, 1954.
Courtesy of Theatre and Film Dept., University of
Lund. 77
Scene from *The Ghost Sonata,* Dramaten, 1973. Photograph
by Beata Bergström. 78
Scene from *The Ghost Sonata,* Malmö City Theatre, 1954.
Courtesy of Theatre and Film Dept., University of
Lund. 81

vii

Final scene from *The Ghost Sonata,* Malmö City Theatre,
    1954. Courtesy of Theatre and Film Dept., University
    of Lund.   84
Stage setting for *The Ghost Sonata,* first scene, Dramaten,
    1973. Photograph by Beata Bergström.   89
Stage setting for *The Ghost Sonata,* third scene, Dramaten,
    1973. Photograph by Lennart E. Halling.   89
Arrangement of the stage for *Woyzeck,* Dramaten, 1969.
    Photograph by Beata Bergström.   103
Scene from *A Dream Play,* Dramaten, 1970. Photograph by
    Beata Bergström.   107
Scene from *A Dream Play,* Dramaten, 1970. Photograph by
    Beata Bergström.   107
Scene from *A Dream Play,* Residenztheater, Munich, 1977.
    Photograph by Jean-Marie Bottequin.   108
Scene from *A Dream Play,* Dramaten, 1970. Photograph by
    Beata Bergström.   110
Max von Sydow in *A Dream Play,* Dramaten, 1970.
    Photograph by Beata Bergström.   111
Final scene from *A Dream Play,* Residenztheater, 1977.
    Photograph by Jean-Marie Bottequin.   112
Scene from *To Damascus,* Dramaten, 1974. Photograph by
    Beata Bergström.   119
Scene from *To Damascus,* Dramaten, 1974. Photograph by
    Beata Bergström.   120
Scene from *To Damascus,* Dramaten, 1974. Photograph by
    Beata Bergström.   121
Scene from *To Damascus,* Dramaten, 1974. Photograph by
    Beata Bergström.   123
Anders Ek and Jan-Olaf Strandberg in *To Damascus.*
    Photograph by Beata Bergström.   124
Scene from *To Damascus,* Dramaten, 1974. Photograph by
    Beata Bergström.   125
Scene from *To Damascus,* Dramaten, 1974. Photograph by
    Beata Bergström.   127
Scene from *To Damascus,* Dramaten, 1974. Photograph by
    Beata Bergström.   129
Scene from *Tartuffe,* Residenztheater, 1979. Photograph by
    Jean-Marie Bottequin.   134
Stage setting for *Don Juan,* China Theatre, Stockholm, 1965.
    Photograph by Lennart E. Halling.   136

Scene from *Criticism of the School for Wives,* Dramaten, 1966.
Photograph by Beata Bergström. 136
Scene from *Tartuffe,* Residenztheater, 1979. Photograph by
Jean-Marie Bottequin. 137
Scene from *Tartuffe,* Residenztheater, 1979. Photograph by
Jean-Marie Bottequin. 138
Scene from *Tartuffe,* Residenztheater, 1979. Photograph by
Jean-Marie Bottequin. 139
Scene from *Yvonne, Princess of Burgundy,* Residenztheater,
1980. Photograph by Jean-Marie Bottequin. 142
Stage setting for *The Misanthrope,* Danish Royal Theatre,
Copenhagen, 1973. Courtesy of the Royal Theatre. 145
Stage setting for *The Misanthrope,* Malmö City Theatre, 1957.
Photograph by Alice Stridh. 147
Scene from *The Misanthrope,* Danish Royal Theatre, 1973.
Photograph by Rigmor Mydtskov. 150
Scene from *The Misanthrope,* Danish Royal Theatre, 1973.
Photograph by Rigmor Mydtskov. 152
Max von Sydow in *The Misanthrope,* Malmö City Theatre,
1957. Photograph by Alice Stridh. 153
Scene from *The Misanthrope,* Danish Royal Theatre, 1973.
Photograph by Rigmor Mydtskov. 159
Scene from *The Misanthrope,* Malmö City Theatre, 1957.
Photograph by Alice Stridh. 162
Scene from *The Misanthrope,* Danish Royal Theatre, 1973.
Photograph by Rigmor Mydtskov. 167
Scene from *The Misanthrope,* Danish Royal Theatre, 1973.
Photograph by Rigmor Mydtskov. 168
Final scene from *The Misanthrope,* Danish Royal Theatre,
1973. Photograph by Rigmor Mydtskov. 170
Scene from *Peer Gynt,* Malmö City Theatre, 1957.
Photograph by Georg Oddner, Stockholm. Courtesy
of Theatre and Film Dept., University of Lund. 177
Christine Buchegger in *Hedda Gabler,* Residenztheater, 1979.
Photograph by Jean-Marie Bottequin. 182
Stage setting for *Hedda Gabler,* Dramaten, 1964. Photograph
by Beata Bergström. 185
Scene from *Hedda Gabler,* Residenztheater, 1979. Photograph
by Jean-Marie Bottequin. 187
Scene from *Hedda Gabler,* Dramaten, 1964. Photograph by
Beata Bergström. 190

Scene from *Hedda Gabler,* Residenztheater, 1979. Photograph
    by Jean-Marie Bottequin.   192
Scene from *Hedda Gabler,* Dramaten, 1964. Photograph by
    Beata Bergström.   194
Scene from *Hedda Gabler,* Residenztheater, 1979. Photograph
    by Jean-Marie Bottequin.   200
Stage setting for *The Wild Duck,* Dramaten, 1972. Photograph
    by Beata Bergström.   202
Stage setting for *The Wild Duck,* Dramaten, 1972. Photograph
    by Beata Bergström.   203
Scene from *The Wild Duck,* Dramaten, 1972. Photograph by
    Beata Bergström.   204
Scene from *The Wild Duck,* Dramaten, 1972. Photograph by
    Beata Bergström.   209
Scene from *The Wild Duck,* Dramaten, 1972. Photograph by
    Beata Bergström.   212
Rehearsing *Miss Julie.* Photograph by Jean-Marie Bottequin.   213
Rehearsing *The Misanthrope.* Photograph by Rigmor
    Mydtskov.   214
Rehearsing *The Three Sisters.* Photograph by Jean-Marie
    Bottequin.   215
Rehearsing *The Wild Duck.* Photograph by Beata Bergström.   216
Rehearsing *Twelfth Night:* portrait of a director. Photograph
    by Beata Bergström.   219

FIGURES

1. Floor plan, *The Ghost Sonata,* act 1   86
 2. Floor plan, *The Ghost Sonata,* act 2   87
 3. Floor plan, *The Ghost Sonata,* act 3   88
 4. Plan of the stage (Lilla scenen) for *A Dream Play*   99
 5. Floor plan, *A Dream Play*   99
 6. Blocking plan, *A Dream Play,* scene 1   100
 7. Blocking plan, *A Dream Play,* scene 1   101
 8. Blocking plan, *A Dream Play,* scene 3   104
 9. Blocking plan, *A Dream Play,* scene 4   105
10. Blueprint of the stage (Dramaten) for *To Damascus*   116
11. Plan of the stage (Danish Royal Theatre) for *The
    Misanthrope*   146
12. Blocking plan, *The Misanthrope* (V.i)   148
13. Blocking plan, *The Misanthrope* (III.iii)   149
14. Blocking plan, *The Misanthrope* (I.i)   155

15. Blocking plan, *The Misanthrope* (I.iii)   160
16. Blocking plan, *The Misanthrope* (II.iv)   164
17. Blocking plan, *The Misanthrope,* final scene   169
18. Plan of the stage (Residenztheater) for *Hedda Gabler*   184

Other photographs of Ingmar Bergman in the text are by Rigmor Mydtskov (pp. 7, 10, 13, 227) and by Jean-Marie Bottequin (pp. 19, 229, 233). Cover photograph by Mydtškov.

Preface

High above the streets of Munich, in a spacious, well-lighted, and scrupulously neat rehearsal room at the top of the Residenztheater, Ingmar Bergman is awaited by his crew, his actors, and a trio of nervously expectant visitors. This, as the director's young assistant, with a knowing twinkle, has told the visitors, is the very *Zauberküche* itself – the magical kitchen where the sorcerer perfects his mighty art.

Bergman himself, laughing and breathless as he makes a running entrance, uses no such metaphysical terms to describe this place and the process that is about to begin here. "Now," he explains to his visitors (one of whom is his wife) eagerly, "now you are in the laboratory. We are still trying different ways and different solutions, and so you must be very understanding."

As the rehearsal of the play (in this instance Bergman's new stage adaptation of his own film, *Scenes from a Marriage*) gets underway, the validity of both these viewpoints quickly emerges. The force of Bergman's presence *is* magical, virtually mesmeric; and yet the precision of his method is as clean and analytical as any laboratory scientist's.

Creative sorcery leavened with clinical clarity – yet there is clearly something else in the atmosphere as well, some additional dimension that accounts for the sense of ease and affectionate collaboration at a Bergman rehearsal. Very soon the actors have forgotten that outsiders are present and begin instead to test their control of their very first "audience." Their director – seated less than ten feet from them, leaning forward with his elbows resting on his knees – follows every word and every move with an alert, almost boyish excitement. There is a faint smile on his face. And all at once his attitude calls to mind an earlier remark of his. "The reason why I am much more a man of the theater than a man of the film is because to work in the theater is a way of living," he had observed. "To go to the theater in the morning, to go to the rehearsal room, to come together with the actors and sit down, and to work with them . . . learning to listen to the playwright's words and to his heart together with the actors . . . that is a way of living; that is the best of all."

If rehearsing a play is at once both a magical and a scientific

xiii

undertaking in Bergman's theater, it is assuredly, to a very significant degree, a process of collective collaboration as well. His art is
intimately bound up with an ability to establish a close and intensely
creative personal contact with his actors. This ability springs in turn
from his unwavering conviction that, in the last analysis, it will be
the actor and the actor alone who must bring the text to life in the
hearts of the audience. "And so one learns more and more about
how to free the actor and liberate those powers, the magic that will
work this miracle."

A miracle, by its very nature, has a way of obscuring and rendering
invisible the process by which it was achieved. We are concerned in
this book chiefly with the detailed critical analysis of finished productions and the directorial interpretation that finds expression in each of
them. At the same time, however, we hope that some sense of the
intricate and methodical creative process underlying the completed
production is also conveyed. At least a glimpse, as it were, into the
wizard's magical kitchen.

A study of a contemporary theater artist who is still at the height
of his powers and productivity is, in a number of ways, a special
sort of undertaking. On the one hand, the productions discussed
here have already become, from the moment the final curtain has
fallen on each of them, part of a defined and describable historical
context. The artistic world of Ingmar Bergman is, however, a continually expanding universe ruled by the twin forces of fertile curiosity and creative energy. With him, the germ of an idea has a way of
becoming a reality with truly startling speed. Barely a year ago, for
example, he talked hypothetically about the effect that might be
produced if Ibsen's *A Doll's House,* Strindberg's *Miss Julie,* and a
stage version of his own *Scenes from a Marriage* were to be performed
simultaneously, either in the same theater at different times of day
or else in separate theaters on the same evening. And now, virtually
as these lines are written, intensive rehearsals for that bold and
demanding trilogic experiment are already in high gear in Munich.
And, by the time this book actually reaches print, Bergman will have
long since moved on to a new and entirely different challenge – the
making of *Fanny and Alexander,* a film that promises to be one of the
most remarkable of his career.

Although the writer of contemporary history is by no means less
dependent upon the primary evidence and objective documentation
that provide the only reliable foundation for all theater research,
there are supplemental approaches to a contemporary subject that
are not open to the student of the more distant theatrical past. The

most obvious and potentially most useful of these is firsthand observation – the vivid recollection of rare and exciting moments in the
theater that will, one senses, not soon fade from memory. Yet even
the richest, most vivid of these received impressions is selective and
thus seductive. Hence, we have tried in every instance to fortify our
own personal recollection of particular Bergman productions with as
much documentary evidence as possible. In particular, every effort
has been made to allow contemporary newspaper critics (as will-
ingly from Eskilstuna or Örebro as from Stockholm, Copenhagen, or
Munich) to speak frequently, in their own voices, as descriptive
seismographs registering the impact that a given theatrical moment
had upon its first audiences.*

A second and very different approach to a contemporary subject is
afforded by the possibility – in some cases only a hypothetical possibility at best – of direct consultation. In this respect, as in many
others, we have been greatly helped by Ingmar Bergman's generos-
ity. Introducing and concluding this work are edited transcripts of
two lengthy conversations with him; they make available, for the
first time in English, his theoretical views on theater – on actors and
acting, directing, critics, and the nature of the theatrical experience
in general. Precisely because of his well-known reluctance to set
down his creative ideas in abstract or critical terms, these informal
notes and counternotes, steeped in the wit and the convinced humanity of the speaker, illuminate the landscape of his art, both as a
stage director and a film maker, in a unique way.

The writing of a book such as this has obviously depended upon
the active assistance and cooperation of a large number of individuals and institutions. The kindness with which our persistent and
occasionally frantic calls for help were invariably received has been a
lasting source of both encouragement and astonishment. We would
be sorely remiss, however, if we did not specify certain particular
debts of gratitude that we feel deeply.

Our work in the library and archives of the Royal Dramatic Theatre in Stockholm was made immeasurably easier and more pleasur-
able by Dr. Tom J. A. Olsson, Sten Rodin, Nea Cleve, and their
congenial colleagues at that wonderful theater. At the Residenztheater in Munich, we have also been shown continual hospitality and
cooperation at every juncture. We are very grateful to Eva Zankl

---

*Because of the large number of newspaper articles cited in the text, dates have
been specified (in the notes) only in those cases in which confusion might arise. As a
general rule, the newspaper reviews of a performance have appeared on the day
following the date given for its opening.

and her predecessor Christine Kabisch for their swift and able assistance on so many occasions. We are indebted to Johannes Kaetzler, the assistant director for many of Bergman's Munich productions, for the time he has generously taken out of a busy schedule to consult with us. Our special thanks go to the actors at the Residenz, in particular to Gaby Dohm and Erich Hallhuber, for tolerating our presence at rehearsals.

At the Danish Royal Theatre in Copenhagen, librarians Niels Peter Jørgensen and Ida Poulsen, stage manager Cyril Glynn, and in particular Ulla Elmquist, another of Bergman's capable assistant directors, have all been generous with their aid. Sidsel Jacobsen, Palle Prehn, and Norma Bøgedal of Danmarks Radio were helpful beyond the call of duty in making relevant videotapes available to us. We wish to thank also, for their help and courtesy, Olof Halmgård, archivist of the Malmö City Theatre, Åke Pettersson, director of Teaterhistoriska museet in Gothenburg, Lars-Owe Carlberg of Cinematograph, Stig Nahlbom of *Expressen* in Stockholm, Frau Dezsy of the Neues Festspielhaus in Bregenz, and Gerd Lindquist and the Department of Drama, Theater, and Film Studies at the University of Lund – Isaac Borg's old alma mater.

Photographers Beata Bergström (Stockholm) and Rigmor Mydtskov (Copenhagen) have been especially kind in granting us unlimited access to their work, which, going far beyond publicity photography, forms a permanent documentary record of the scenes and settings in a given production.

Portions of this study appeared in abridged form as the special Bergman issue of *Theater* (Fall/Winter 1979), and we are indebted to Dr. Joel Schechter and his staff at Yale for their enthusiasm and helpful editorial guidance on that occasion. Also on the editorial side, Professor Christopher Innes deserves an expression of thanks for his constructive counsel and suggestions. In preparing the manuscript for publication, we have been greatly aided by the expert and sympathetic editorial advice provided by Donna McIvor and Sarah Stanton of Cambridge University Press.

In a very tangible sense, this study owes its very existence to the generous financial support and encouragement of the Social Sciences and Humanities Research Council of Canada.

Most keenly felt of all is our deep sense of gratitude toward Ingmar Bergman and his wife Ingrid. For her patient cooperation and gracious forbearance, we remain profoundly in her debt. For the many delightful hours spent with Ingmar Bergman talking about theater, we can find no adequate expression of our appreciation. To admit that this study has been thoroughly and irrevocably influenced by his ideas and by the echo of his infectious laughter may perhaps, in certain quarters, cause its sober objectivity to be called into question. We shall gladly take that risk.

Toronto   LISE-LONE MARKER
                                                             FREDERICK J. MARKER

Introduction: The statue of Thalia

A close critical study of the stage productions and related theatrical theories and methods of Ingmar Bergman has long been overdue. His richly productive career in the living theater has tended to be unjustly overshadowed, at least outside of Europe, by his prodigious accomplishments and renown as a film maker. Yet Bergman himself attaches the utmost importance to his continuous activity as a theater director, and an understanding of this side of his work is indispensible to a completely balanced assessment of his art. "There has always been a short distance between my work in the theater and my work in the film studio," he has reminded interviewers more than once. "Sometimes this has been an advantage and sometimes it has been a burden, but the distance has always been small."

For nearly four decades, Bergman has continued to belong among the most exciting and innovative directors active in the European theater. Today, his reputation in this respect looms larger than ever, and his formidable creative energy shows no sign of slacking.

Almost from the beginning, during his years of apprenticeship in the 1940s, the forceful and fiery young director's experiments at the city theaters in Hälsingborg and Gothenburg aroused the curiosity and then quickly won the respect of the major Swedish critics. Then, during the 1950s his six luminous seasons at the Malmö City Theatre began to attract the same sort of wider international notice that came, during these same years, to such films as *Smiles of a Summer Night, The Seventh Seal,* and *Wild Strawberries.*

During the 1960s – the decade memorable for such cinematic masterpieces as *Through a Glass Darkly, Winter Light, The Silence,* and *Persona* – the vigor of Bergman's involvement in the theater rarely abated. For three and one-half onerous years he even found time to serve with distinction as chief executive officer of Dramaten (the Royal Dramatic Theatre in Stockholm), Sweden's national theater. As the 1960s drew to a close, it seemed for a while that he might be ready to retire for good from the Scandinavian theater scene and its vicissitudes. Happily, however, the new decade – which holds special interest for the student of Bergman's theater – brought with it a whole succession of new productions that must be counted among Bergman's finest and most permanent theatrical achievements. In-

1

novative stage interpretations of Strindberg's *A Dream Play* and *To Damascus*, Ibsen's *The Wild Duck*, and Shakespeare's *Twelfth Night* mingled during this period with major revivals of such Bergman classics as Strindberg's *The Ghost Sonata*, Molière's *The Misanthrope*, and Ibsen's *Hedda Gabler*.

Although Dramaten has remained Bergman's true spiritual home as a director, this lasting and fruitful relationship was abruptly altered by his clash with the blundering Swedish tax bureaucracy in 1976. Without warning, Swedish police descended upon the theater in the midst of a rehearsal of Strindberg's *The Dance of Death*, and Bergman was peremptorily taken in for questioning in connection with allegations that were later proven to be utterly groundless. The Bergman *Dance of Death* was never completed. Instead, this rash and shocking action on the part of the tax authorities resulted in his self-imposed exile in West Germany, where he has directed regularly since then at the Residenztheater in Munich.

Before this unexpected move, Bergman's directing activity had, with only a single exception, been restricted to theaters within Scandinavia. Hence, his newer German productions of Strindberg, Chekhov, Molière, and Ibsen have introduced a distinctly new and by no means less interesting phase in his artistic development. With his confidently stylized and wildly caricatured staging of Witold Gombrowicz's tragifarce *Yvonne, Princess of Burgundy* in 1980, he served clear notice that his fifth decade in the theater would be as open to experiment and change as the preceding four have been. This was a performance that, to the enthusiastic German critics, revealed Bergman from an entirely new angle; yet its ancestors could be discerned among his savagely ironic and grotesque productions of the 1940s and early 1950s.

An ample, annotated chronology at the back of this book should provide the interested reader with a sufficiently detailed synopsis of Bergman's astonishingly productive and versatile career as stage director, film maker, playwright, and more. The approach adopted in the book itself, however, is neither biographical nor strictly chronological. Rather than attempting a comprehensive and correspondingly less detailed account of Bergman's entire oeuvre, we have focused chiefly on his key productions of the works of three playwrights. Each of these writers has continued to hold a central place in his theater poetics. These practical production analyses represent different aspects of his directional syntax and interpretative genius. Taken together, they should convey, we hope, something of the range and depth of his mastery.

The playwrights chosen – August Strindberg, Molière, and Henrik Ibsen – represent Bergman's own preferences as fairly as they do ours. His deep affinity for Strindberg has remained one of the essential features – perhaps even the *most* essential feature – of his artistic physiognomy. His impressive cycle of Strindberg productions – particularly of *The Ghost Sonata, A Dream Play,* and *To Damascus* – has continued to strengthen the lasting bond between these two kindred spirits. Bergman's successive reinterpretations of Ibsen's plays – especially of *Hedda Gabler* – have already been recognized as milestones in the stage history of that playwright's work in the modern period. Finally, Bergman is in a very basic sense a classical director – someone with a remarkable gift for assimilating the reality of past styles and traditions in staging a classical play. As a result, perhaps no director outside of France has had greater success than he has in translating the essence and the inner, spiritual reality of Molière's darkly comic vision to the contemporary stage.

The art of the theater, seen from Bergman's perspective, is both a popular and a collective art, arising out of an intensely collaborative creative process. This attitude predicates his familiar assertion that only three basic elements are ultimately necessary "for a theatrical production to function": a text, actors, and an audience. Above all, he likes to remark, "a theater's basis in reality is its audience. Otherwise, the theater lives with surface roots, and becomes a staggering colossus, heavily subsidized, with no basis in reality." Accordingly, a discussion of Bergman's theatrical vision and methods invariably finds itself returning often to the unique and dynamic interplay of these three basic elements of his art: the informed clarity of his conceptual reinterpretations of particular texts; his (implied) philosophy of acting, characterized by his exceptional ability to mold and influence an acting ensemble; finally and not least important, the often radical techniques he has adopted to reshape the audience's imaginative response, thereby forging an ever stronger bond between the performer and the spectator, the stage and the auditorium.

As to the question of whether the reader may expect to deduce from Bergman's stage productions a single unifying philosophy or even a theory of the theater, Bergman himself, as steadfastly opposed to theatrical formulas as he is to ideological dogmatism of any kind, would undoubtedly reply in the negative. He describes his art as intuitive and utilitarian ("I make products for use") and, in the theater, he is as fervently convinced as Reinhardt was that there can be no single method for staging all plays, that each play faces the director with a new and completely distinct interpretative problem.

Yet, the perceptive reader will quickly begin to notice recurrent technical devices, compositional patterns, and interpretative choices that together add up to something like a Bergman "style." Underlying it, there is a hopeful vision, rather than a theory, of theater as he believes it ought to be. "I wonder whether any of you has seen the statue of Thalia in the lobby of the Malmö City Theatre?" he asked a group of writers a number of years ago.

It is a large, well-developed, gorgeous female figure with generous contours; she has an insolent, merry face with a large mouth and a big nose, and she comes toward you with sweeping strides, holding both the tragic and the comic masks in an easy grasp. She is indomitable and free, and an incredible laughter is painted all over her face.

That is how I see the theater when it is best and truest.

1 Talking about theater: a conversation with Ingmar Bergman

Although few artists of the modern period have been more reluctant than Ingmar Bergman to discuss creative methods in an abstract or hypothetical fashion, statements made by him in major interviews and occasional public appearances over the years have often yielded invaluable substantive insights into his art as a film maker. The same cannot be said of his luminous career in the theater, however, which has rarely been the subject of more than a passing reference or two in most of these earlier interviews. The one exception, a lively and informative "Dialogue" with Bergman conducted by Henrik Sjögren, appeared in Swedish more than ten years ago, well before Bergman's epoch-making productions of Strindberg, Ibsen, Shakespeare, and Molière during the 1970s. Until now, in fact, no interview in English has, to our knowledge, concerned itself exclusively with the subject of Bergman's attitudes toward and lasting contributions to the development of the modern theater.

Consequently, we have attempted, by means of the two conversations with Bergman that frame this study of his scenic art, to offer the reader as direct an impression as possible of his ideas and assumptions about the nature of the theatrical experience and its effect upon a modern audience. The first of these conversations – excerpted from a much longer interview conducted in the autumn of 1979, just before Bergman began shooting his new film *Aus dem Leben der Marionetten*, in his offices at Bavaria Film Studios outside Munich – introduces a wide variety of topics and concerns that are intrinsic to an understanding of his theatrical style. His views are rich in insight, invariably laced with humor, and steeped in the experience of some forty years in the theater; they touch on subjects ranging from the nature of the actor's art to the relationship between film and stage in his own work, from the current state of the German theater (in which he has been actively engaged since 1977) to such key creative principles of his art as rhythm, choreography, and suggestion. As he talks about his own productions and those of others, a great deal about his directorial vision and method becomes much clearer – everything, perhaps, except the magician's innermost technical secrets ("a few small tricks"), over which the master has always carefully and purposefully drawn a veil. "By all means, borrow my machines and duplicate what

5

I am doing," he once remarked, some thirty years ago. "Take your time. Learn to be agile with your fingers, learn how, just at the right moment, to divert the attention of the audience with your spiel, learn speed, and the mysterious illumination! You will still not do what I am doing, you will still fail. You see, I perform magic. I conjure!"

TALKING ABOUT THEATER

LLM.   In writing about your long and richly productive career as a stage director, we're naturally very interested to know where you yourself would like to see the emphasis placed. Which performances are your own favorites? You have said before that you dislike looking back at any of your work from the past. But which stage productions do you feel are the ones you like best?

IB.   It's very difficult. I don't know. It has nothing to do with the result; it has to do only with the atmosphere – the time we had together when we worked on the play. The reason why I am much more a man of the theater than a man of the film is because theater is to me always . . . to work in the theater is a way of living. To make a picture is a heavy job, it really is. But to go to the theater in the morning, to go to the rehearsal room, to come together with the actors and sit down, and to work with them . . . learning to listen to the playwright's words and to his heart together with the actors . . . that is a way of living; that is the best of all. And if you are together with actors who share the same way of thinking, the same attitude toward their job, it's wonderful. I think I will make one or two or three more pictures – and then I will stop. But I hope I will have the chance to work with the theater until they carry me out. [Laughter.]

LLM.   I hope you don't mean that about your films.

IB.   Oh yes, oh yes, oh yes. That's very simple. Because film making is physically very, very heavy – it's a lousy job – physically. One day you feel very tired, you don't want to . . . and when you are tired physically, you need an enormous vitality every day to come through, to be on top. Do you understand? You make about three minutes of the picture every day, and those three minutes must be on top, on the very top. You start at nine o'clock in the morning and then you work eight hours, very hard. And everything comes from you . . . it comes from me, everything, at every moment. And the whole crew depends on your feelings, on your most irrational reactions. And it's *very* difficult.

FJM.   Different from the theater in that respect?

IB.   At the theater, if you don't feel well, you don't feel well . . .
and you can say to the actors: Today I don't feel well, let's go out
for a walk in the park or go to the museum and see an exhibit or
just sit down and have a chat. Or . . . today it was not so very
good, but perhaps tomorrow or the day after tomorrow or next
week it will be better. Film making is very neurotic – you're obsessed – your work is very neurotic; but the creative work of the
theater, made together with the actors, is a very healthy way of
creating.

FJM.   You often speak of the theater as a collective, in the sense of
working together with the actors.

IB.   Yes, it's a wonderful way of coming together and being in
contact with other people.

FJM.   As a director it must be difficult to reach that stage of being

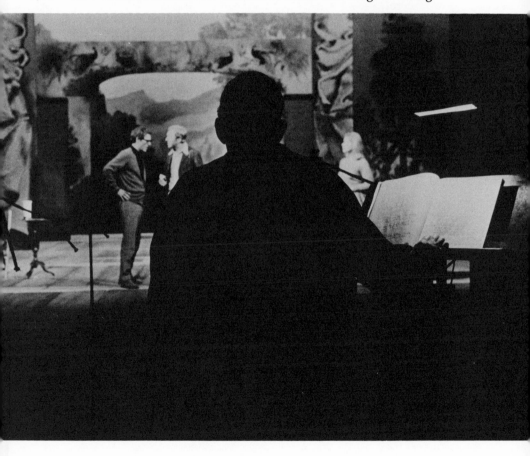

able to be relaxed enough to take it that way. Do you know what I
mean? Isn't the young director who is starting out much more
tense . . .

IB.   That's different. Of course. Every day, every morning while
you are rehearsing, you wake up very, very early in a kind of
tension, and the tension is always there; but you have to use it as
a battery. You must not infect the actors, because if you infect
them with your tension, they will be very unhappy. So you must
simply tell the actors to sit down and then say to them: Children,
let's relax; let's just take it easy. Let's listen to each other. Because
acting is never – and that is a great misunderstanding – acting is
never an *I*, it is always a *you*. Because the minute two actors forget
themselves and take everything from the other one, then you
have the great moments of performance. And that is the whole
secret.

FJM.   What I meant before about tension is also related to our earlier discussions of the director's script, which you always prepare
and then put aside. You have often said that improvisation is
dependent upon careful preparation. But what *is* the relationship
between pre-preparation and then being able to put it all aside?

IB.   You must be absolutely certain when you go to rehearsals.
When you go to the first rehearsal, you must be absolutely sure;
you must have prepared precisely and you must be absolutely
sure – that *this* is what Strindberg has meant. And you must be
happy with it. You must have made it your own experience – your
own spiritual experience. And then you can relax in the material,
you feel you are there. There are no longer any acts of violence,
not against the text, not against the actors. Rehearsing in the
theater has to do with contact, with listening, with tenderness,
with love, with security. And then if, together with the actors,
you can produce this atmosphere, it is a creative atmosphere –
then it starts. It's a miracle. It starts. Yes, it is alive. Because I get
things from the actors and I give things back to the actors.

FJM.   Without worrying about what you had planned beforehand.

IB.   Yes. But I have to prepare precisely for every little moment, in
every little detail. I must know that *this* is what I want to do, and
then I can improvise.

LLM.   You don't have the sounds of their voices in mind, then,
before you go in?

IB.   Yes, sometimes. But not always. Sometimes very clearly . . . I
have the actors in mind, always, when I prepare; I always have
actors in mind. What can this actor do, and what can he not do?

What are his limitations? What are his difficulties? What is his strength?

LLM. Do you ever read lines for them?

IB. No, never. Never. I can tell them the rhythm. We can talk about the rhythm of a line, but I never tell them how to play it. We can talk about the choreography and we can talk about the rhythm and the pauses, but I never tell them how to say it.

FJM. Rhythm is very important to you, isn't it.

IB. Rhythm is the most important. That is the most important of all. Also in film.

LLM. Do you see a connection between film and theater in that respect?

IB. No. Not very much. But rhythm is always the most important thing that exists. Because everything is rhythm. At every moment of our lives, without ever thinking about it, we live with different kinds of rhythm – breathing, the beating of the heart, the movement of our eyes, the cycle of day and night, of destruction and creation, everything in the world is rhythm. And therefore our artistic work must also be built on the fact that we work with it – we must listen our way forward to the specific rhythm of the play, to the specific rhythm of the text. And this is precisely the difficulty when you work so much with translations; if the translator has not captured the rhythm of the original – which happens very rarely – then we are caught in a hell, because you sense that you are working against the text, going against the play. It is very difficult.

FJM. What about your German production of *Hedda Gabler?*

IB. A marvellous translation – [Heiner] Gimmler's translation is almost perfect. I read about ten different German translations, and they were all bad. So we had to commission a new one.

LLM. This past summer we saw no fewer than three Bergman productions in a single month – *Hedda Gabler* in Munich, *Twelfth Night* in Stockholm, and *Tartuffe,* which we managed to see when it played in Bregenz. And in all three places, the audience reaction was simply astonishing. Especially for *Hedda Gabler,* which is usually not a play that inspires explosive enthusiasm.

IB. No, it's a dark play. Very difficult for the audience.

LLM. Your production of it is really the only one I've ever seen that brings the *whole* play to life on the stage, rather than just a single role. So many actresses have reduced the play to a psychological study of a neurotic woman . . .

IB. Oh yes, I've seen them. [Laughter.] But, you see, it's essential that you have all the right actors. Just as in Chekhov. If you don't have the actors for the other parts, the whole play will fall into pieces. Even if the maid is wrong, a lot of the sense will be lost. And I had the actors here at the Residenztheater. Of course, our Tesman [Kurt Meisel] was too old for the part, but he has the right imagination, the right approach to the character. He is perfect because he creates the impression of a great child.

LLM. For *Tartuffe*, too, there were ten curtain calls, a tremendous ovation, at the Bregenzer Festspiele.

IB. *Tartuffe* is a less successful production, I think. I'm not entirely happy with it. I had wonderful ideas about how to do it, how to make it work; but something happened during rehearsals – I don't know exactly what it was. I don't think the actors were used to my . . . at any rate, we didn't find the right tune. In Molière, you see, you must be very precise–at every moment, at all times you must be absolutely precise. And at the same time you must be very open, direct, vulgar, brutal, and sensitive. It has to be all of that. And you must forget about psychology; everything comes from the choreography, from the rhythm–Molière is almost impossible to translate, you know. When you translate Molière you have to be very free.

LLM. In order to capture the precise rhythm of the original.

IB. Yes.

LLM. When you talk about rhythm, you don't mean merely speech rhythm and textual rhythm, do you. You mean visual rhythm as well.

IB. Yes, everything. The entire arrangement of movements, the whole rhythm of the performance. That to me is essential. To go faster, to go slower, to stop, all those things.

FJM. I wouldn't presume to contradict you–but I do think that the *Tartuffe* did work.

LLM. I think I understand what you mean about choreography and precision, though. Especially when I compare it . . .

IB. To the Danish production.

LLM. Yes, to your production of *The Misanthrope* in Copenhagen six years ago.

IB. It was the second time I did *The Misanthrope*–and I could do it again and again for no matter how many times, because it is one of the plays I love most. I had planned to direct it at the Royal Dramatic Theatre while I was head of the theater, but then I had no time and I had to leave it to Bengt Ekerot. And it was no success. But the Danish actors had this absolute, complete discipline–self-discipline–and they enjoyed the precision of Molière. Because they have a tradition–here you have no such tradition. The actors here resisted it.

LLM. *The Misanthrope* was a performance you could talk about almost in balletic terms. The movements were as clearly and precisely choreographed as they would be in a ballet.

IB. Yes, because you must do that with Molière. It is absolutely necessary. I also directed a very unsuccessful *School for Wives* at the Royal Dramatic Theatre a year after I had left as head of the theater. We did *The Critique of the School for Wives* as a prologue, and that was very successful. But the actor who played the main part in the play itself disliked that kind of choreography, and he protested utterly and completely against it. We were unable to find any solution together; and so it fell to pieces.

FJM.   What do you mean when you say choreography?

IB.   Choreography is movement, the moves – I don't know the word in English.

FJM.   An ugly word: "blocking."

IB.   The movements of the actors, going from a sofa, moving to that chair, coming back, stopping, turning the head toward the audience – all that is what I call the choreography.

LLM.   It is much more than simple "blocking," though. You describe it almost as a ballet choreographer would; you talk not only about moving from one point on the stage to another, but also about gesturing, about the slightest turn of the head . . .

IB.   Yes, everything.

LLM.   You must literally demonstrate to your actors what you want, almost the way the choreographer of a ballet does. Do you do that?

IB.   In a way, yes.

LLM.   One is so struck by the precision of their gestures, their movements . . .

IB.   Yes, I tell them . . .

LLM.   . . . what you want.

IB.   Yes. But sometimes the actor himself begins, and then I can say to him: Try to do it that way – and that may be better. It's a kind of collaboration. Very close. Very close, very erotic. It's very intimate. You are very close to actors when you work with them, at creative rehearsals.

LLM.   Before you go in to rehearsals, do you know precisely, in visual terms, how the actor is to move, gesture, and so on?

IB.   Yes, in a way. In a way. Especially the place where they are – the different positions of the actors. So I know exactly where they are. Where I have them. And – whether they have contact or no contact. Whether they look at each other or do not look at each other. That is all-important. The relationship [demonstrating] between an actor here and an actor there – how they relate to each other is extremely important. In Chekhov, it is the most important thing of all – to place all the actors in relationship to one another. To have them relate to one another – or not; and have them listen to each other – or not listen; and have them react – or not react. The whole secret of Chekhov is in the listening – in what the various characters hear, what they don't hear, what they pretend not to hear.

FJM. Your concern with physical relations and pictorial composition would seem to make you an ideal ballet choreographer. Have you ever wanted to choreograph a ballet?

IB. No, I can't dance a step, you know. I cannot take a step as a dancer.

FJM. You did one ballet, didn't you—*Skymningslekar* [*Twilight Games*]?

IB. *Skymningslekar* [laughs]—I didn't do it, I only wrote it. But I'm extremely fascinated by ballet. I have always been fascinated by it.

LLM. I once sat in on some of George Balanchine's rehearsals at Lincoln Center. He dances very little himself by now. You would naturally have someone beside you to assist and demonstrate, as he does.

IB. Yes. There must be some kind of intimate collaboration. But—I think there are people better able to do it than I am.

FJM.   Speaking of attending rehearsals, your idea of holding open rehearsals for the public is a fascinating one.

IB.   Yes. I like that very much. I-almost die-and the actors, too, almost die, but we have found it is very healthy. Because- slowly-the actors acquire an unneurotic relationship to the spectators, to the audience. And that is very, very good.

FJM.   For whose sake is it done? For the sake of the actors?

IB.   Oh yes, always for theirs.

FJM.   Not for your sake?

IB.   No.

LLM.   Not so that you are able to judge . . .

IB.   No. No, I know exactly. But I just want the actors . . . I also want the audience to come to us and see what we are doing. To see that there is no magic in our work, and that there is nevertheless a magic in it. That is very good for all of them, for the audience too.

FJM.   Sometimes in costume, sometimes not.

IB.   Yes. Most interesting for the audience, of course, is without costumes and without settings.

LLM.   Do you ever conduct an open rehearsal as an ordinary rehearsal?

IB.   No. I did with *Woyzeck,* but I don't think it is a good idea. Because if we do it as a rehearsal, with the audience there, then I play the director and the actors play the actors.

LLM.   And the audience comes to watch you, no doubt.

IB.   [Laugh.] Yes. So you see, that would be a sort of performance. I always refuse to allow people to watch our rehearsals when we are still in the rehearsal room. Once we are on the stage, it doesn't matter so very much, because we don't know that people are there looking at us-if a few people are there, it doesn't matter. But the moment we know at rehearsals, we start playing, we begin playing our parts. And that is not good.

LLM.   Do you usually say something to the audience at the beginning of an open rehearsal?

IB.   Oh yes. I always bid the audience welcome, and I explain that they must help us, that now we must work together. A theater performance is to an exceptional extent a matter of give and take. It is in their hearts, in their imaginations that the performance must take place. Because there are only three things necessary for a performance to work: the play-the words-the actors, and the audience. Everything else is absolutely unimportant. But if you have those three elements, there will be a performance. Nothing else is needed.

LLM.   By that you mean settings, for example?

IB.   Theater, settings, directors, tickets, money, costumes, everything. Everything else is unimportant. It's wonderful to think about.

FJM.   But surely the director – I suppose, if you could go back to the nineteenth century or the eighteenth century, to another kind of actor entirely, you wouldn't need the director. The director as such wasn't there. But today there is no way one can eliminate – or wants to eliminate – the influence of the director. He has to be there, doesn't he?

IB.   No. I don't think so. If there are chamber orchestras playing without a conductor –

LLM.   That was, of course, Strindberg's idea. Strindberg thought the actors ought to be able to do it on their own.

IB.   Yes. Sometimes it is very good to have a director, but sometimes it is not necessary.

LLM.   But if there had been no direction of your *Hedda Gabler* or *The Wild Duck,* for instance, the actors setting out to do these plays would in all probability simply have followed Ibsen's stage directions, furnished a living room, placed the attic at the rear in *The Wild Duck,* and you would get . . .

IB.   No, that's something else entirely. For those plays you need a director. But if you play O'Neill's *Long Day's Journey into Night,* it isn't necessary; or if you play, shall I say, Albee's *Who's Afraid of Virginia Woolf?;* or if you play a piece by Marivaux, and the actors are *experienced* actors, there is no reason to have a director.

LLM.   But for Molière and Ibsen?

IB.   For them you must have a director, I think.

LLM.   Strindberg, too?

IB.   Yes.

FJM.   But if you perform *Who's Afraid* without a director, you won't get a Bergman production of *Who's Afraid;* you won't achieve the same rhythm and intensity.

IB.   No, if they are very good actors, they will find it, they will find a rhythm of their own. I am sure of that, I am convinced. It's not so difficult. You can read it – and it's all there. Everything works out quickly and easily, because there is no depth of dimension. It's no problem. There are lots of plays you can perform without a director. The actors soon start giving everything and holding nothing back. The last rehearsal weeks get a trifle boring, in fact.

LLM. I remember something you said when you spoke to the Royal Theatre acting school back in 1958 or so: that there is a difference between directing younger actors – in an ensemble that you yourself have in a sense created – and handling older, more experienced actors, who must be dealt with in a somewhat different way. Do you still feel that is true?

IB. Well, I have worked in this business – this profession – for about forty years; and I have had real difficulties with actors – *real* difficulties – three or four times. That's not very much. Because you always find some way to communicate with an actor. It's not difficult.

LLM. They should surely be eager to communicate.

IB. But you must understand: They stand there, they expose themselves, they are very vulnerable. You sit there and you are not vulnerable; you're always protected. But they stand there with their faces and bodies terribly exposed. And so you have to be careful, listen to them, take care of them, respect them. It is most important.

LLM. To continue talking about your work with the actor, I wonder if you could say something about your concept of the so-called focal point of energy – the magnetic point where the actor is best located in a particular stage space?

IB. Yes, of course, the magic point. It has nothing to do with the shape of the setting, only with the particular theater. It is there on every stage. You have to look for it, and you have to find it – the point where the actor is best and most effectively located. Approach and withdrawal effects are all created in relation to this point. That is the difficulty when you come to a new stage: You don't yet know where the magic point is located. The first time I experienced that, in a conscious way, was at the enormous theater in Malmö. You had to locate, very consciously, the point on the stage where the actors are strongest. And I remember it very well: It was a small rectangle, six meters by four meters, about two and a half meters from the front. After that, there was no problem.

FJM. And then everything is choreographed in relation to that point?

IB. Yes. At our Royal Dramatic Theatre in Stockholm – it's a wonderful house – you can be anywhere on the stage and it is magic all over. So close, so intimate.

FJM.   Do you like the new Residenztheater here in Munich? It's rather unlovely compared to Dramaten.

IB.   The acoustics are very good. But it is wrongly built, isn't it. The relation between stage and auditorium doesn't exist – because the stage never starts.

FJM.   There is no clearly defined proscenium, you mean.

IB.   No, it is terrible. And the elevation of the stage is too low, so that when you sit in the auditorium, you must continually crane your neck to see; you can't sit quietly and watch the stage. For short people it's a very great problem. So for the first time in the history of this theater, I brought everything forward in *Hedda Gabler.* We acted the whole thing in front of the fire curtain. Behind the setting was the iron curtain.

LLM.   You may have been the first one to do that at the Royal Theatre in Copenhagen, too. Didn't you build the stage out over the orchestra pit for *The Misanthrope?*

IB.   Perhaps we did it that way. I can't remember.

FJM.   The often unusual way in which you light the stage is closely related to this technique of thrusting the action forward, isn't it? I'm thinking now of the special lighting equipment installed at the Royal Theatre for *The Misanthrope* – what have by now come to be known as Bergman lamps.

IB.   No [laughs] – Bergman lamps. Yes, I see. They have arranged some Bergman lamps at the National Theatre in Oslo too, I think. And here as well, finally. [Laughs.]

FJM.   They used them here for *Hedda Gabler,* didn't they?

IB.   Yes, they had to.

FJM.   Hung on battens, along the whole front of the balcony.

IB.   Yes – it was a big fight.

FJM.   You like strong frontal lighting very much, don't you.

IB.   Oh yes, yes, I do.

FJM.   Because of the faces?

IB.   Yes, of course. It's – look now [pointing to sunlight striking the interviewer's face] you have it now. And then, you know, suddenly the actors are . . . The actors' relation to the stage is also a part of the rhythm of the performance, and if you change the angle at which the light strikes the stage, you achieve a completely new rhythm. For the eye. And it becomes a little bit of a shock, if you change the light like that.

FJM.   You achieve very interesting frescolike effects in *Hedda.* The impression created by that very strong, amber-colored front lighting is almost like a fresco or a frieze.

IB. It's very strange, because it looks as though the actors are float-
ing; they lift themselves off the floor.

LLM. But they are lights that evoke a certain kind of *emotional*
response in the spectator. As a spectator, you're not supposed to
notice the changes very much, are you?

IB. No, no, no, it's unconscious. For the spectator, of course, it has
to be completely unconscious. I hate it when the spectator says:
"Aha! *Beautiful!* – he changed the lights." [Laughter.]

FJM. Because the lighting is not – horrible word – "symbolic," the
sort of thing where suddenly a spotlight . . .

IB. No. I hate that. I hate it when the director intrudes, when he
reaches out and touches the spectator like this and says: "Look
what I have done! See, how symbolic all this is!" Here in the
German theater, you know, when they play Kleist's *Prince of Homburg* – the whole stage is filled with potatoes [laughter], and you
ask: "Why? Why is the stage filled with potatoes so that the actors
have to walk around falling over potatoes the entire time?" "Yes,
because you should know that the intention of the director is to
make it clear that Prussia was an agrarian society, a farmers' country at that time." With that, you see, the director has mixed himself into the play, and he addresses himself not so much to the
audience as to the critics. He has a conversation with the critics
over the heads of the actors and the audience. That is very, very
modern here in Germany today – that kind of neurotic conversation. They love it.

LLM. Why are the critics taken in by it?

IB. The critics love it, too. Theater tradition is so strong here, you
see; every theatergoer has seen *Tartuffe* five times, *Faust* ten times,
The Prince of Homburg six times. And so, as the Germans say, *man
muss sich was einfallen lassen.* [Laughter.] You have to dream up
something. And the critic sits there saying: "Aha! I saw this very
thing in 1943 in Berlin or in Kassel or wherever" – they have 110
city theaters here, you know. It's incredible. But the vitality is
enormous.

  The Germans can have trouble with Ibsen or Molière – and they
cannot play Strindberg; they don't understand him. They perform
him without humor, very, very serious, very profound. Heavy.
But they play the Russians beautifully. They do marvellous performances of Shakespeare; they have an enormous Shakespearean tradition. And, of course, they make their own classics seem
so new and wonderful and fresh – not always, perhaps, but very

often – at least the talented ones do. There is much to learn from the way they play their own classics. Not to mention the Austrian classics – I love those, they were something almost completely new to me. To see Nestroy, to see Grillparzer, to see Schnitzler and Horváth – it was all new. Not to mention Raimund!

FJM.   One is struck by the very strongly conceptual orientation of much contemporary German theater, don't you think? The fondness for the explicit directorial comment.

IB.   Oh yes, yes. Garbage on the stage, for instance. The Germans love to clutter the stage with garbage – to demonstrate the rottenness of the bourgeois world. [Laughter.] But they're hysterical, you see, because they have the feeling that everyone has done everything already. They don't always understand that what you have to play – is the play. And if you play it, it will always be new – if it's alive. If it is alive, it will always be new because there are different people directing and acting and watching.

LLM.   The other sort of thing is not the renewal of tradition – it is only making something that will seem popular, flashy.

IB.   Of course, there are some who are very cynical about it; they are fully aware that they are what the Germans call *mittelmass* – mediocre – and they know that if they take ideas from here and ideas from there and put them on the stage, the critics will sit back and say: "Ah! Always something new. *Semper aliquid novi.*" Do you know that they are going to perform *Hamlet* here at the Kammerspiele with an actor who weighs 240 pounds? Oh, yes.

LLM.   For the sake of doing it.

IB.   Why not? If you have no idea how to do it otherwise . . .

LLM.   You yourself *have* been a renewer of the traditions of staging the classics, in the true sense. I am thinking now not only of Strindberg and Ibsen – but also of Molière, though perhaps less radically so in his case.

IB.   No, not at all. My intention is *not* to be a renewer. I want only to present the plays and to make them live in the hearts of the audience. That is my only intention. I read the play, it lives in me. I infect the actors with my intentions, and they give me back many things in return. During a certain period of creativity and of intimate relations, we develop a creation that is, I hope, fully alive. And the only reason why it has been made is in order to infect the spectator – so that it may be alive in his heart, in his mind. And that is everything.

LLM.   I was thinking of something so absolutely wonderful as your

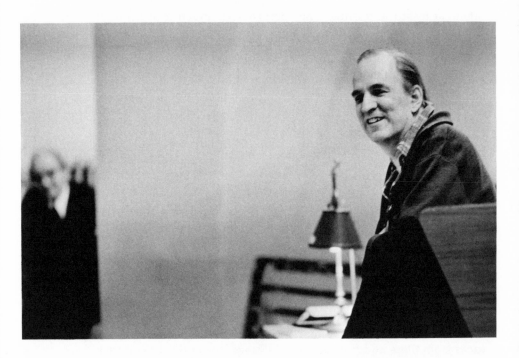

production of *The Wild Duck,* with the inspiration of placing the attic at the front instead of at the back. That is what I mean by renewal.

IB.   But it is very simple. To me, it's absolutely logical. Once you agree that the only important things are the words, the actors, and the audience, then it isn't the setting that matters. The actors must materialize, before the eyes of the audience, the magic of the attic. And they cannot do that at a distance; with their eyes, their way of walking and standing and moving, they create it in front of you. So you can see it. That is the magic of the theater.

LLM.   Perhaps, but few have recognized it so clearly.

IB.   But it's really very simple; it's completely logical. My experience has taught me the importance of simple suggestion in the theater. You are an actor and you take this terrible chair [demonstrating] and you put it up here on the table, and then you tell the audience: "My dear friends, you may think this chair looks terrible but you are mistaken. This is the most expensive and most beautiful diamond-encrusted gold chair ever created. It was made for a small Chinese empress six thousand years ago; she died sitting on it, and it was buried with her. Now it's here – and it is very, very fragile. But now take care of it, for I must leave you for a few moments." Then you come back as a scoundrel, and you begin to knock the chair around – and the entire audience will hate that scoundrel. They will become anxious because they have accepted the suggestion and have developed feelings about the chair. And *that* is theater.

FJM. And any chair, even a rehearsal chair, will do?

IB. Of course! It can be anything, everything, whatever you want. Shakespeare realized that. Shakespeare never tells you about anything, what is going on, how a scene looks; it is a street or a mountain or another part of the forest. But, suddenly, the actors would come on to his stage in the sunlight – because they always performed in broad daylight – carrying burning torches, and four oboes in the orchestra would play a small, small melody – and the whole audience knew at once that it was night. It can't be more fantastic than that!

LLM. Is that why in *A Dream Play*, for instance, you choose to eliminate the entire environment of the play?

IB. Of course, of course.

LLM. Again, that's what I mean by innovation in a positive sense – an absolutely wonderful way of making the audience relationship to Strindberg so much closer.

IB. But Strindberg himself realized it. He wrote about it to August Falck at the Intimate Theatre: "Couldn't we play *A Dream Play* with just a curtain?" And of course we can play it that way. That was my enormous mistake when I presented the play for the first time here in Germany.

LLM. For that production you seemed to be using the same type of screens you have used before in Stockholm, but in the background there seemed to be a great deal more – a complete structure.

IB. I was new here, and an old, famous master of settings [Walter Dörfler] asked me . . . he wanted to design the settings and I couldn't . . . I said, of course, that will be fine. Then I started work on *The Serpent's Egg*, and when he came back to me he had made the *most* wonderful wall. You can see it here. [Dörfler's sombre, massive stage design for *A Dream Play* hangs in one of Bergman's offices.] We built the whole thing. And when it came up on the stage, it dwarfed everything else. I tried different ways, but it dominated the entire space. I knew when I saw it that I should throw the whole thing out. But he was a very nice man; I liked him very much, and he had worked very hard on it. So I felt we had to try it – but it was a great mistake. The performance itself was not so bad—in a way it was very good, because everything was completely new to the actors, the manner of rehearsing, everything.

FJM. *Three Sisters,* your second German production, adopted a much simpler approach.

IB. I staged that with almost no setting at all, only some furniture. The setting could be either outside or inside; it remained the same the entire time.

FJM. Chekhov is not a dramatist you have directed often. It's been seventeen or eighteen years since your only other Chekhov production, *The Seagull,* appeared in Stockholm.

IB. That was very unsuccessful. At the time I was [chuckles] so very confused, and I didn't have the patience. And the girl who played Nina [Christina Shollin] was a very talented young girl, but she was not very experienced. If only one actor in a Chekhov play is not on the same level, the whole thing falls to pieces. Otherwise I had a fantastic cast for that production—but Nina was a little bit inexperienced and new and a little bit dry. And so it all fell to pieces. Did you see *The Ghost Sonata* at the Royal Dramatic Theatre? That was one of my good ones, I think.

LLM. To an audience the play suddenly became crystal clear; one suddenly understood it completely.

IB. Yes. I had Gertrud Fridh playing both the Mummy and the Young Lady, and that was—very good.

FJM. It brought a fascinating kind of unity to the play.

IB. *A Dream Play* and *The Ghost Sonata* and *To Damascus*—I like all of those productions very much.

FJM. What about *The Dance of Death?* You were just going into rehearsal for it when we were at the theater [Dramaten] last autumn.

IB. That was a terrible time. Let's not talk about it—because Anders Ek is one of my closest friends. . . . He had this illness, you know, this blood cancer, for perhaps two years, but we thought it would have been possible. Then, a month before we started, he had such terrible pains in his back that every step nearly made him cry. So we had only a week of rehearsals—then I had to tell him it was impossible.

FJM. That was the second time you started *Dance of Death,* wasn't it.

IB. [Barely audible] Yes.

FJM. We were looking at some photographs of the model for the set; it looked like a fascinating concept.

LLM. You were going to reverse Strindberg's arrangement, weren't you? By placing the outside toward the audience.

IB. Yes.

FJM. With the sentry parading past . . .

IB. Yes, we–don't talk about it. You know, for ten years Anders Ek and I had talked about doing *The Dance of Death* together–and now, I don't want to do it with anyone else.

FJM. Are you planning to do more with *To Damascus*?

IB. I am very attracted by the idea of returning to certain plays. As a director I have plays that follow me, that pursue me through the years, and my view of these changes. I discover new attitudes toward the text, and create new performances. Next time I will try to do all three parts of *To Damascus*. I have been planning for a long time to do all three parts together, but I didn't have the chance this time. It was impossible for me to make the cuts.

LLM. It must be an enormously difficult play to cut.

IB. Yes, *To Damascus* is particularly difficult–because I love the play so much. You know, you have grown up with it. I saw it for the first time under the direction of Olof Molander [in 1937], and I will never forget it.

FJM. That was Part One, wasn't it?

IB. That was Part One.

FJM. Has anyone else ever done Parts One and Two together, other than you? I don't think so.

IB. No, not Parts One and Two–but all three parts together. Per Lindberg did it in the thirties.

FJM. It would be a fascinating project for you.

IB. Yes

LLM. When I remember *To Damascus*, I think of those striking visual images from the performance. One remembers the emotional impression of the whole, of course–but above all those marvellous figure compositions. Do you feel that your work as a film maker and your work as a stage director overlap to some extent with that kind of thing?

IB. No. It is so different.

FJM. The question is a central one, though. And a very difficult one as well. In film interviews, you have stated that "there is a short distance between my work in the theater and my work in the film studio" and that a "mutual relationship" exists between the two kinds of work. But exactly what sort of relationship?

IB. Did you want to say something?

LLM.   I only wanted to ask whether you yourself feel that the question is worth discussing, or not.

IB.   Yes. Let us try. I do not think there are many connections; but let us try to find them. I have never discussed the problem in this way before, but let us try. For the moment, I can find only one connection. There are perhaps more, but I find only this one. When I work together with the actors in the studio, in front of the camera, I always place the actors in relation to the camera so that they feel they are at their best. They feel – not that they are beautiful, but that the magic of their faces and their movements will be registered by the camera. And they like that. They sense that, because I like them, I wish them to be as powerful and multidimensional as personalities and actors as possible. On the stage I do exactly the same thing. I position them, as we talked about, according to the principle of the magic point. I place them on the stage, in relation to each other and in relation to the audience, so that they feel they are effective – that their charisma will work on the audience. And then they feel secure; they know they can do their best. Some actors, you know, have to fight against the settings, against the lighting, against the choreography, against the director – they have a need to fight. And that *can* be very good – with talented actors it can work marvellously – but they never feel secure.

And there you have one relationship. I must always function as a kind of radar, you see: I can tell whether an actor feels well, whether he feels secure, or whether he feels tense and unhappy. And I feel it faster than he feels it, I can tell before he says so, because my intuition is always at work and tells me at all times what is going on inside this man or this woman. That is, of course, an important connection between my film making and my work in the theater – the relation that must be established between camera and actors or stage and actors, seen in conjunction with the audience.

FJM.   What about technical things . . .

IB.   Don't you think this could be true?

FJM.   Yes definitely. [Laughter.]

IB.   I have never thought about it, but perhaps that is the way it is. I don't know.

FJM.   It's a very convincing point. But what about more technical relationships? When you choreograph on the stage, for instance, are the same or similar impulses at work as when you choreograph a film? In other words, your films are renowned, among many other things, for their astonishing use of closeup photography. Do you consciously or unconsciously try to incorporate that impulse toward the closeup into your theater work? Or, to take a different example, you have talked about the sense in which distance will tend to intensify whatever is horrible or terrifying; when Bertil Anderberg [as Raval] is smitten by the plague in *The Seventh Seal,* for instance, he lies screaming out in the forest, behind a woodpile, out of sight. What I'm asking is, does that kind of thinking about camera shots and spatial compositions find any specific equivalent in your theater work?

IB.   No, no, no.

FJM.   Not at all?

IB.   No. There are some tricks in common – but they are just details. A few small tricks. [Pause.] You know, there is a play by Sartre called *The Unburied Dead;* there is a schoolroom where a torture scene takes place before the eyes of the audience. The head of the theater in Gothenburg [Torsten Hammarén] staged it, and it was fantastic. But in this torture scene, the actor cried and screamed – and it looked just like an actor crying and screaming. A kind of *Grand Guignol,* not very impressive. Then one day he stopped to ask whether he could do it in some other way. So he piled up the chairs and desks for the school children in a straight line, and behind this mountain of tables and chairs the torturing was done. You didn't see it, you only saw some of the movements and heard the screams. And it was so terrifying that people couldn't take it. That is one of the secrets of our business – not to show everything.

FJM.   And in that, in the use of suggestion, film is like theater?

IB.   Yes. Yes, in that they are alike. Some years ago I made a film called *Persona.* There is a small scene in which the nurse tells the actress about a sexual experience she had had together with a girl friend of hers, with two boys. She tells her about it in detail, and the only thing we see, practically the entire time, is the face of Liv Ullmann [in the role of the actress, Elisabet Vogler], who eats the scene. She eats with her lips what she is being told – and it is a very erotic scene. If you had tried to re-create the scene with the two boys and the two girls, it would have been merely disgusting. Now, it's very erotic. It's strange, isn't it.

LLM.   I would like to ask you about something else; in fact, I would like to ask you about two things. In many of your more recent theater productions, you seem to be very attracted to the idea of using a low platform stage set up on the stage itself. Does that go together with your concept of the magic point, the focal point of energy on the stage?

IB.   Yes, exactly. It's very–I like it very much because when the actor is standing outside the platform, he is private; the moment he takes a step toward the platform, he is an actor playing a part. He's someone else; it is a great magic. The platform is ancient. The platform is absolutely the archetypal theater, the very oldest form of the theater. You have a wagon or a platform or the steps of a church or some stones or an elevation of some sort or an altar–and the actor stands there waiting. Or a circus ring. And the actors stand there and then they climb up onto the wagon or the platform or whatever it is–and suddenly they are powerful, magical, mysterious, multidimensional. *And that is immensely fascinating.*

LLM.   The one thing, apart from everything else, that stays in my mind from the performance of *Tartuffe* is the presence of Tartuffe's servant, that strange, heavy figure in black.

IB.   Yes.

LLM.   Often he just stands beside the platform watching; but what is he watching–all those mad people?

IB.   Yes, exactly. It is very fascinating, very interesting . . .

FJM.   The actor then becomes spectator.

IB.   Exactly.

FJM.   And a kind of bond is then established between the actor and the spectator in the auditorium.

IB.   And that is truly magical.

LLM.   Yes, it is. But is he, then, a sort of comment on these mad people in *Tartuffe?*

IB.   Of course.

LLM.   It's astonishing, because you never forget him–[laughter] even though he is a very minor figure.

IB.   But he is there in Molière's text, he is talked about; it's just that Molière does not keep him on the stage throughout.

LLM.   Basque, Célimène's servant in *The Misanthrope,* was so amusing, too; that was also a completely new idea, using him to link the scenes.

IB.   But the Basque I had in Malmö [Lenn Hjortsberg] was the most brilliant Basque I have ever had, he really was. The Basque I had in Copenhagen was not that amusing; but my Basque in Malmö was so funny that people nearly split from laughing. He was amazing, unforgettable.–Yes, this Basque is a strange character; he is fantastic. In that incredible scene, the love scene between Alceste and Célimène, suddenly this fantastic figure of Basque turns up with his unbelievably complicated tricks and business.

FJM.   In the Copenhagen production, you kept the actors who weren't involved in a particular scene in view, seated on chairs placed on the outskirts of the stage. They sat watching the action, casually awaiting their cues. You didn't do that in Malmö, did you?

IB.   No.

LLM.   How did the idea occur to you?

IB.   It occurred to me because, not so very long ago, it was actually the practice. During the 1940s it was still the custom that the actors at the Comédie Française did not go to their dressing rooms during the course of a performance, but sat on the stage behind the scene and read or knitted or just sat. It was a kind of tradition that they should do so; each and every one had his own chair, with his name on it. I find that an intensely fascinating idea, that the actors should be there the whole time. What is more, you can glimpse them there in the background, like shadows, as a presence.

LLM.   When they sat in the wings during your production of *The Misanthrope*, what did you tell them? Were they listening to what was happening on the stage, or . . .

IB.   It isn't necessary for them to listen. They have to sit down, they have to relax, and they are there. They are involved in the play.

LLM.   And in the atmosphere.

IB.   The entire time. They can't escape it. They cannot get out of it, because they have it in their bodies, in their nerves. I find it fantastic that you have them there on the stage; that seems so powerfully magical. Because theater is always magic, all the time.

LLM.   And the presence of these actor-spectators then reinforces the impression of theater within the theater?

IB.   Yes, of course. And besides, it's good for the actors not to go off to their dressing rooms and sit there drinking coffee.

LLM.   It helps to sustain concentration, you mean.

IB.   Yes. And that is enormously good for them.

LLM.   In Molière's own time, spectators were actually seated on the stage. Was that something that influenced your thinking about this idea?

IB.   The audience sat there on the stage, it is true, and Molière disapproved of that enormously. He was terribly angry about it, and that emerges continually in such works as *L'Impromptu de Versailles*. There you can really find his undivided hatred directed at that audience of nobles. And, after all, he had been subjected to some horrible experiences when he had written and acted in *Dom Garcie de Navarre*, his tragedy about jealousy. The story is told–

even though it may not be confirmed as absolutely true – that one evening some noblemen seated on the stage forced him and black-mailed him to play that deeply serious role – the main role of the jealous protagonist – as comic. And he did so with an unbelievable sense of humiliation.

FJM. Your deep immersion in the Molière tradition goes back a great many years, doesn't it. Which productions did you see when you went to Paris for that famous first visit, back in the autumn of 1949?

IB. Everything.

FJM. And what do you remember?

IB. Everything.

LLM. Jouvet?

IB. Yes, yes, yes. I went to the theater every night. It was an unbelievable, completely overwhelming experience. It was my first experience. I had never been outside of Sweden before. Of course I had been to Berlin, in the summer of 1934, but that was only as a schoolboy.

When I was in Paris, the Comédie Française was doing productions both on the main stage, the old stage, and at the Odéon, and they were fantastic experiences. In particular I remember *The Misanthrope,* which was like a revelation to me.

LLM. Who played Alceste?

IB. Jean Meyer, I think it was, and I remember it as a totally astonishing production – staggering so far as hearing French was concerned because – brrrrt – they went through it just like that! It was one of those performances that seemed to – it was such a great revelation, a great personal experience to encounter the French theater tradition. One of the most incredible things of all was to see Feydeau on the stage of the Comédie Française – that was the most astonishing experience of all.

LLM. Haven't you ever thought of directing Feydeau yourself?

IB. Oh yes, many times, but first I must wait until I become old. [Laughter.]

LLM. Why?

IB. Because, you see, you need immense experience, you have to have enormous experience to direct Feydeau. I am not really very good as a farce director. Perhaps I'll get to be eventually, in due time. But I can't do it right yet. Maybe I can learn to do it eventually.

LLM. But is that really true? What about the farcical elements that made your *Tartuffe* so entertaining, for instance?

IB.   Oh yes. But I lack the self-confidence. I don't really feel confi-
dent about farce yet. Unfortunately. Perhaps it will come in time.
But I find it wonderful. And the thing I found most wonderful at
that time was the amazing brutality of the French when they play
farce. Their incredible brutality and power and tempo and then
that black, savage humor that suddenly becomes absurd. – Well,
then I saw Jouvet and Barrault, naturally. And, what is more, I
also saw a thing called *L'Arlésienne* [*The Girl from Arles*].

LLM.   It's from the story by Alphonse Daudet, isn't it?

IB.   Bizet wrote music for it. It was one of the strangest theater
experiences of my life, both in the auditorium and during the
intermission. We were at a matinee at the Odéon, and the part of
the girl was played by one of the *sociétaires*, who must have been
sixty – decked out in curls and dressed like a young girl and
smartly made up and all, but very old. And the setting looked like
it must have been a hundred years old at least. You've never seen
the play or read it?

FJM.   No, never.

IB.   Well, it's unbelievably sentimental trash. A real old stinker,
you see. The acting was astonishingly sloppy, and in the pit a
forty-man orchestra sat and played those splendid pieces by
Bizet, that golden music. The thing dragged on and suddenly I
heard a peculiar sound beside me and, looking aside, I discovered this French bureaucrat – a little fat, a little bald – and his
entire family dissolved in tears. They were all crying like mad
people. [Laughter.] And then I heard the same peculiar sound
again, and, turning round in my seat, I saw that practically the
entire audience was in the grips of a hysterical sobbing attack.
And then to watch this sixty-year-old battle-ax, you know, just
standing there at the footlights going through the part. Frightful
old hag. Later, during the intermission, I walked around a little –
I was alone and was at that time young and handsome – and
strolled in the lobby and took a glass of wine or something of the
sort; when suddenly one of the attendants rushes over and says:
"Come here. Yes, you, come on. Hurry up." So off we went,
walked backstage and through an enormous corridor, until we
came to a door. Here was a whole queue of handsome young
men, and so I took my place in the queue. Then one went in
and, after two minutes, out he came again, and then the next
went in and, after two minutes, he too was back. Then came my
turn; I went in and there, stretched out on a divan in some sort
of outlandish dressing gown, was our battle-ax, made up like an

Easter egg and holding a glass of champagne in her hand. The entire dressing room was filled with laurel wreaths and photographs. And then she grabs my program and scribbles her name and hands it back to me and the attendant ushers me right back out again. [Laughter.] That was their job, you see, to keep her in a good mood, and so the attendants had to go out and round up whatever young men might serve the purpose.

It is really marvellous how much the French love their old actors. So this old diva had to be treated as she had always been. And if young men were expected to be there, as they had been all her life, then young men would be there, waiting for her autograph. Isn't it charming?

FJM.   Wonderful.

IB.   For *that*, too, is theater. I love it – as incredibly confusing as the experience was, it was at the same time truly marvellous.

Geiselgasteig, October 1979

2   First seasons

By the time Ingmar Bergman embarked on his professional theater career, at the age of twenty-six, as the artistic director of the Hälsingborg City Theatre in southern Sweden, he had already established a solid reputation for himself as a director and, to a lesser degree, even as a playwright. Half a dozen years before being called to Hälsingborg in 1944, he had already begun to attract critical attention with his imaginative amateur productions of Strindberg, Lagerkvist, Shakespeare, and others at Mäster Olofsgården, a religious settlement house located in the old part of Stockholm. By the early 1940s, his abilities had been strikingly and conclusively demonstrated in his student-theater productions, in his organization of an experimental children's theater in Medborgarhuset (the Civic Center), and in several successful productions that he directed for the enterprising Swedish Playwrights Studio, a professional group formed to foster new Swedish drama. "If you want to see something truly interesting right now and need to have your faith restored in the fact that Thalia still lives, it is clearly to the Student Theatre you must go," Nils Beyer proclaimed in *Morgon–Tidningen* early in 1943. "The credit is due, above all, to the principal director of this small academic amateur theater – one of the most remarkable young directing talents we have in this country at the moment – Ingmar Bergman."[1] No promising young artist could have wished for a clearer mandate.

Much earlier, during those otherwise so traumatic adolescent years of remorseless psychological warfare in his father's rectory at Uppsala (a period that Bergman has looked back on as "a life and death struggle: either the parents were broken or the child was broken"[2]), the embryonic director had practiced and perfected his craft through the traditional medium of toy theaters – in this instance, sophisticated scale models that were eventually equipped "with lighting boards, turntables, elevator stages, and everything conceivable: big, solid affairs that filled my whole room so that no one could get in."[3] The young enthusiast drew upon "all of world drama" for his solitary productions: "I staged *Lucky Per's Journey* and *Master Olof* – I performed a great deal of Strindberg in my theater, and even did Maeterlinck's *The Blue Bird*. Above all, though, I

31

wanted spectacular shows that required a lot of work with stage machinery and lighting effects," he recalls in another interview.[4] As he began to see more and more live theater and opera in the Stockholm of the 1930s, his miniature stages grew in direct response to the influence exerted on him by the productions of Sweden's two foremost directors of the period, Olof Molander and Alf Sjöberg.

The Hälsingborg engagement meant that Bergman could begin to try out the ideas and methods he had acquired in a professional theater of his own – albeit a modest one, venerable in its traditions (it had been established in 1921) but possessing distinctly limited technical and financial resources. When he became the fourth artistic director of the Hälsingborg City Theatre in the autumn of 1944 – during the same period that his first original screenplay, Hets [Torment], was released under Alf Sjöberg's direction – his principal mission was literally a rescue action. The institution's state subsidy had just been withdrawn and morale was low, but the town of some eighty thousand inhabitants had made up its mind not to let its theater die. Bergman and his young company set out to infuse new life into the staid municipal playhouse by making it a meaningful, even controversial forum in the community. "The town's unquiet corner" was the spirited phrase adopted by the young manager in one of his frequent program declarations.

During two vigorous seasons at Hälsingborg, Bergman directed an astonishing total of nine productions himself. All but three were works by modern Swedish dramatists (including Hjalmar Bergman, Olle Hedberg, Björn-Erik Höijer, and Brita von Horn) – a fact that in itself reflects a commitment to native Swedish writing that has remained characteristic of his work in the theater. (On the other hand, one should perhaps emphasize at the very outset Bergman's outspokenly pragmatic attitude toward the whole question of the choice of repertory: "I have never had a program in my selection of plays, rather I have directed whatever I have had a desire to direct or have been invited to direct or have felt obligated to direct. I have never adhered to any rigid principle."[5]) Probably the single most interesting production to emerge out of these first formative seasons, however, was the pictorially expressive and politically engaged version of Macbeth, which he presented as his third bill in November 1944. His earlier amateur production of the play at Mäster Olofsgården had attracted widespread interest when it coincided with the German invasion of Denmark and Norway in April 1940. Now, the time was the last autumn of the war, and Bergman once again saw in the figure of Macbeth the embodiment of Nazi totalitarianism – the personification of those fascist qualities that also color the character of Caligula, the Latin teacher, in *Torment,* and that he had seen infect the attitudes of his family and his teachers in Uppsala. The young director – if one is right in seeing his hand in the unsigned program note for the production – viewed Shakespeare's play as "an anti-Nazi drama, a ferocious confrontation with a murderer and a war criminal. Remorselessly and with psychoanalytical logic, the mighty dictator is torn apart. With an increasing, incomprehensible power his crimes multiply, one giving birth to the next, until at last they annihilate him."

Technical resources at Hälsingborg were minimal ("some foots and twelve spotlights and four floodlights for the backdrop"), but with them Bergman and his designer, Gunnar Lindblad, created for the play a simple but effective visual framework that depended chiefly on a ramp of stairs, scattered suggestions of scenery, projected silhouettes, and a threateningly red or black sky in the background. This *Macbeth* was no elaborate historical saga of bloodshed and ambition played out against a background of brooding granite castles and wind-whipped stretches of heath, but rather a concise, modernized indictment of the "curse of usurped power, the over-

The opening scene of *Macbeth,* Hälsingborg, 1944. Setting by Gunnar Lindblad.

whelming force of evil" that the young director saw as its real subject. Interestingly enough, even at this early point one critic applied the term "chamber play" – a designation that has since become virtually a critical cliché in discussions both of Bergman's films and of his stage productions – to his simplified approach. ("It was plenty aestheticized with the resources we had, but without the possibilities to aestheticize," Bergman himself has remarked with typical frankness. "Sometimes it worked, but more frequently it didn't work at all.")

It is worth pausing over a few of the more startling textual modifications introduced in this production, particularly because of the piquant foretaste of Bergman's mature style that they provide. The witches – Macbeth's "secret, black, and midnight hags" – become a more concrete and more persistent influence. The heath on which they first appear was now evidently a battlefield where the bereaved wives of the fallen gathered; the most talkative of the weird sisters was translated into a fortune-teller figure who reappeared at intervals throughout. Herbert Grevenius, among the first major critics to make the pilgrimage from Stockholm to review the activities at Bergman's "unquiet corner," painted a vivid verbal picture in *Stockholms–Tidningen* of a subsequent pantomimic interpolation:

The witches have obsessed Macbeth's mind, and as he writhes on his bed beside his wife in a gaping black chamber with quivering fever-shadows on the walls and an immense crucifix glimpsed in the haze of the background, the fortune-teller and her sisters from the battlefield appear in a ragged group at the foot of the bed, and the room is filled with the sound of disembodied voices. This is poetry on a level with the poem.

During Lady Macbeth's illness, Grevenius continues:

Macbeth carouses with endlessly laughing girls and sinister men, hushed for a moment by the physician in his black cape who glides like a shadow down a winding stairway. Then he shouts and the motley crowd rouses itself again in a drunken and possessed gavotte, which becomes doubly grotesque as they dance out of the darkness of the room past a blood-red spotlight.

Sune Ericson's performance in the title role added its full share to the grotesque and macabre atmosphere of the final acts. His "Life's but a walking shadow" speech (V.v) was delivered, for example, not in reaction to the cry that proclaims Lady Macbeth's death, but seated and cradling the corpse of his dead wife in his arms! Even these few glimpses from this production – the orgy with the laughing girls, the drunken danse macabre, Macbeth spiritually impaled

Multiple-level setting for *Macbeth,* designed by Carl-Johan Ström.
Gothenburg, 1948.

between the crucifix and the witches – indicate clearly enough the
propensity for simplified but boldly suggestive visual concepts and
emphatic figure compositions that we have come to identify with
Bergman's style.[6]

His third attempt at *Macbeth* represented a contrast to the modest
Hälsingborg performance in almost every respect. By the autumn of
1946 Bergman had been hired as resident director at the larger and
more important Gothenburg City Theatre, where he remained for a
three-season engagement that taught him to master one of the most
technically advanced stage facilities in Europe. His controversial
revival of *Macbeth* at Gothenburg, which opened on the main stage

on March 12, 1948, was a picturesque visual spectacle that seemed to many critics, however, to overwhelm both Shakespeare and the actors with what one of them called its "numerous periphrastic flourishes around the heart of the drama. . . . The sensations keep our attention alive, but they distract our gaze from the faces of the actors, which ought to be the true focus of our attention" (*Göteborgs Handels–och Sjöfartstidning*). It is a point that the mature Bergman would not lose sight of again in his later work. At this juncture in his career, however, a critic like Karl Ragnar Gierow was inclined to observe that he had

a good grasp of and eye for the external things: corpses hang from ropes above the stage almost all the time; the witches, far from being half-real presences conjured up out of terror, take part in the celebrations for King Duncan and stretch forth their highly corporeal legs and arms at every opportunity from start to finish. Drums are banged, trumpets blare, gongs are sounded. Processions and magnificent stage pictures are provided as frequently as occasion allows. But the rhythm of the play tends to be obscured by the theatrical coups (*Svenska Dagbladet*).

One major aspect of the problem was obviously the stage setting itself. "The scenes emerge with unprecedented wildness and energy in their composition," Grevenius declared, but even he was obliged to add that "eventually the ceaseless raising and lowering of stage machinery and the whole weight of the scenic apparatus served to dissipate the ability to listen with real attentiveness." The enforced simplicity of the Hälsingborg set was now replaced by a massive Wagnerian apparatus that included an elaborate playing area on two levels, connected by a perilously steep spiral staircase. It could incorporate at various times a two-story drawbridge capable of being raised and lowered; a hall in reddish purple tones for the banquet scene and Banquo's apparition; and even a small, stylized arcade for two interpolated dance sequences, "which established the mood of dour Scotland and of the lighter, more airy Renaissance festivities of the English court" (*Göteborgs–Posten*). Carl-Johan Ström, who designed the majority of Bergman's productions in Gothenburg, found full scope for his customary technique of placing dark, neutral foreground silhouettes against a contrastingly bright, vivid background.[7] In this case Ström framed his stage between the dark outline of a brooding watchtower and the winding stairs on one side and the silhouette of an ancient, towering oak tree on the other. Bergman being Bergman, he lost no opportunity to exploit the visual potentialities of Ström's gargantuan tree. Carcasses of roasted oxen were suspended from it during the fateful banquet; sinister silhouettes of hanged men dangled ("like overripe fruit") from its branches during the more diabolical scenes; and the omnipresent witches – who by now had become young, lascivious wenches seductively draped in ragged shreds of black, red, and green costumes – climbed decoratively among its limbs.

Bergman always utilizes the plastic and visually expressive aspects of the physical theater to their fullest extent, but the more flamboyant experiments of his Gothenburg period eventually taught him to mistrust effects that are not organically integrated or motivated. "Superimposed trappings always hang loosely and rattle," he remarks drily. "One hears and sees from them that they hang on the outside and are dead, no matter how unusual or tasteful they may otherwise be. I've done a lot of that kind of thing, too." In terms of the use of stage space, for example, the contrast between this early Macbeth and his production of *Twelfth Night* at Dramaten three decades afterwards is startling. In the later production, designed by Gunilla Palmstierna-Weiss, the entire play was acted on a small, rough-hewn platform erected in the shadow of an encircling Tudor framework of beams and gables – suggestive of an Elizabethan playhouse, perhaps also of a Tudor hall, maybe even an innyard. Across the back ran a musicians' gallery, from which six costumed players accompanied the action. Kept to a bare minimum, the furnishings on the small platform – chairs, a pair of screens, a benchbed – were carried on and off by costumed stagehands. The characters – even the twin brother Sebastian, whose presence alone is needed to resolve the comic confusion in *Twelfth Night* – stood awaiting their entrances in full view of the audience. At the back of this miniature stage, a picturesquely stylized painted hanging was used to announce the location – the utopian realm of Illyria. Nothing more was needed to convey the intrinsic sense of theatricality, of a game of illusion and make believe, that infused Bergman's conception of the comedy. At the height of his apprenticeship some thirty years before, however, the young director was still taken up with the idea – not an unusual one for 1946 – of a much more ponderous version of an "Elizabethan" stage, shaped (as he proclaimed in an interview in *Ny Tid*) "entirely in the style of the theaters of Shakespeare's time, that is, with an inner space that can be closed off by doors."

Bergman has also alluded in later interviews to another difficulty that must obviously have compounded the confusion caused by the top-heavy physical staging of his Gothenburg *Macbeth* – the fact that he and Anders Ek, who played Macbeth and who has remained one of his closest associates through the years, held diametrically opposing views about the nature of the central conflict:

Anders was a socialist, and I regarded the drama as one of moral conflict. Anders saw it such that the murderer is driven to his crimes, yet nevertheless retains his innocence. In that sense the production became very unclear because we started out from different assumptions. I had staged a work at the center of which stands a character who is, little by little, morally broken; Anders created an individual who is unyieldingly innocent, who remains pure from start to finish.[8]

Perhaps the anecdote is of interest chiefly because it illustrates another of the lessons that the young Bergman had begun to learn in "the strict school" at Gothenburg, where Torsten Hammarén and a skilled ensemble of strong actors "demanded of me that I account for what I did – why are you doing it? Why have you imagined it

Unit setting for *Twelfth Night*, designed by Gunilla Palmstierna-Weiss. Dramaten, 1975.

Bibi Andersson as Viola (*right*) and Lil Terselius as Olivia in *Twelfth Night*. Note the stylized depiction of Illyria in the background.

that way!"[9] For the first time, the young director found himself obliged to adopt "a certain intellectual consciousness in relation to the playwrights and their works." For a man whose gifts as a director of actors are legendary and perhaps unequaled in modern theater or film, he is engagingly candid about the slow process by which he arrived at one of his cardinal rules as a director – that "compulsion won't work":

When you start out as a director – at least when I started out – you're terribly afraid. If you are afraid and insecure, then you must not say you're afraid and insecure and you adopt the opposite attitude – you become decisive, you insist, become ruthless. . . . Now I am completely open. The other way was such a strain, so terribly exhausting. But you young people have a different climate and a different point of departure. And we mustn't forget either that fashion changes. I was born and grew up in the age of the big guns, and naturally I wanted – even though I was only a little peashooter – to be a big gun too, to behave like a big gun. All those manners are something you pick up damned quickly.[10]

Behind Bergman's education as a director looms invariably – by his own admission – the ambivalent figure of Torsten Hammarén ("he was Sweden's most prominent farce director of all time, that remarkable man"). Above all, this indomitable manager of Gothenburg City Theatre taught him the significance of methodical preparation as an indispensable prerequisite for fruitful improvisation – "the whole technique of working calmly and clearly and methodically, of preparing carefully what you intend to do." Bergman today is more firm than ever in his conviction that, for a director to be able to "relax in the material" and establish an atmosphere of mutual creativity with his actors, he must first prepare himself for the first rehearsal so intensively that the text becomes virtually his "own spiritual experience." "To do anything effectively and with a purpose, it is necessary to be well prepared. If you are, then you can improvise," he is fond of insisting. "If you are unprepared and improvise, you end up in utter formlessness."[11]

Some of Hammarén's other practical, straightforward principles of theater management also left a deep and lasting impression on his most famous disciple – so much so that they formed the basis for the laconic statement that Bergman himself chose to issue when he assumed the onerous headship of the Royal Dramatic Theatre in Stockholm in 1964. This terse but revealing document, printed at the front of Dramaten's first program for the 1964–5 season, takes the form of "Three Questions" posed by the new managing director to his old teacher. The first concerned choice of repertory, and the answer came back crisply: "I can play only those plays that I myself like – and want to see. Anything else is hypocrisy." The second lesson dealt with the hiring of actors, and here the reply was even terser: "There are two kinds of actors – those who should walk on, and those who should walk out." The third and final question asked for the most essential characteristic of a theater manager, and Hammarén answered: "Trust. In your co-workers, in your audience. And perhaps even, to a certain degree in spite of everything, in the press."

As a director, Bergman has been strongly attracted to the idea of returning to certain plays, almost in the way a conductor returns to a symphony many, many times during the course of his career. "I have plays that follow me, that pursue me through the years, and my view of these changes," he says. "I discovered new attitudes toward the text, and create new performances." Although he has consistently ranked *Macbeth* among these favorite plays, he has not, however – at least not yet – returned to it for a third professional production (as he has with such key works as Strindberg's *A Dream Play*, Ibsen's *Hedda Gabler*, and Hjalmar Bergman's bittersweet fantasy, *The Legend*). Until quite recently in fact, with his two successful productions of *Twelfth Night* at Dramaten in 1975 and again in 1979, *Macbeth* had also been his sole Shakespearean venture – a circumstance that appears to be related directly to his high regard for Alf Sjöberg's epoch-making Shakespearean productions at Dramaten during the 1950s and 1960s.[12] (He has remarked more than once that "Sjöberg's performances of Shakespeare's plays have been so outstanding, so overwhelming, so crystal clear that I have not had anything different to offer."[13]) Instead, it was Molière, Ibsen, and, above all, Strindberg who were to become the classical dramatists in whose work Bergman has found special inspiration, and in whose service he has forged a new theatrical style.

The foundation for this impressive program of classical revivals was laid very slowly, however. For a long time, Bergman declares, "all theater was to me simply suggestions, atmosphere, situations. But the fact that a stage play had an intellectual intention – I arrived at that much later. And the fact that I myself might have an intellectual intention with a stage production – that came later still."[14] In Gothenburg, where *Macbeth* was really the only classical text that he had an opportunity to direct, the majority of his other productions (three on the main stage, six in the theater's intimate studio) reflected the popular repertory and tastes of postwar Scandinavia – that is, French existentialist plays (Camus, Anouilh); recent American drama (Tennessee Williams); and contemporary Swedish works (including another Björn-Erik Höijer premiere and two of Bergman's own so-called moralities, *Dagen slutar tidigt* [*Early Ends the Day*] and *Mig till skräck* [*To My Terror*][15]).

The production of Albert Camus's existential drama *Caligula*, which marked Bergman's debut as a director on the demanding Gothenburg stage (November 29, 1946), has also remained, in retrospect, one of the most striking of his early achievements. In this instance, an almost ideal coordination was achieved between Ström's carefully controlled setting for the imperial Roman palace and the grotesque, surreal, at times even acrobatic conception of Camus's somewhat

Scene from Camus's *Caligula*, with *right*, Anders Ek in the title role.
Gothenburg, 1946.

cerebral play that the young director presented to the startled
burghers of Gothenburg. "A genuine *angst* is always there behind his
commitment to form," observed Grevenius in *Stockholms–Tidningen*,
"and this has induced even so placid a temperament as designer
Carl-Johan Ström to work up a palace room which, with its leaning
red columns, its huge Egyptian portals, and its masks grinning in the
darkness, draws, so to speak, a magic circle of barrenness and death
around the drama's central character." Seen from various angles on
the turntable stage and dominated by an obligatory Ström silhouette
of a quadrangular roof pattern projected against a bright horizon, this
expressive vision of Caligula's palace (also called by one critic "a cross
between a modern hatbox and an Aztec temple"!) won high praise
from Elis Andersson in a perceptive review in *Göteborgs–Posten* for its
spaciousness, perspective depth, and brilliant colors. "The setting
facilitates entrances and groupings; with its stairways and its multiple

divided planes it affords the ideal conditions for accentuating the action," he declared. Individual critics might complain about the use of "movement for its own sake" in Bergman's dynamic and explosive choreography or (even more absurdly) about his disregard of historical accuracy, but most agreed with Andersson's view that, in this case, "it is well worth the risk that the pictures themselves can sometimes take the wind out of what is being said."

Often enough, Bergman's "pictures" – the bold visual accents with which he punctuated his production – did just that. In the first act, Caligula (who earlier has told his friend and aide Helicon of his desire for "the impossible" – "the moon, or happiness, or eternal life") summoned his staff by hammering on an immense gong "suspended like a glowing full moon against the night sky" in a vivid moment that seemed, to critic Ebbe Linde (in *Ny Tid*) "a brilliant impulse both in symbolic and in visually functional terms." Gigantic, glowering masks hung in corners and between the pillars of Ström's constructivist set, and, as they caught the light from various angles, they made their own silently mocking comment on the vision Caligula reads in his mirror of "an end of memories, no more masks."

The violent second-act banquet at which Caligula displays such wanton cruelty toward his enemies became, in Bergman's hands, a surrealistic "orgy of loathsomeness" that reached a crescendo in an "equilibristic" murder scene. Acrobatics played a large part in the production as a whole, particularly in the physically and psychologically intense performance of Anders Ek as Camus's obsessed protagonist. "He dances and crawls, he makes fantastic leaps, he strikes the most unusual plastic poses, he is – with the exception of a few quiet moments – a whirlwind of unrest throughout the performance," Elis Andersson noted. "In fact he fulfills all the physical demands of the role in a manner that should leave even an adherent of Meyerhold's biomechanics satisfied." *Expressen* too, described Ek's characterization as "an unbroken series of virtuoso acrobatic numbers, but acrobatic numbers that were transformed into dazzling metamorphic art, even in the facial expressions." The chiseled countenance of this Caligula was not that of "the beautiful and familiar marble bust, but of an inwardly consumed individual with sleepless eyes and tense facial features," remarked another observer. (Surely no one who has ever seen Ek's face as Frost, the tormented circus clown in Bergman's film *The Naked Night,* will ever forget its supple expressiveness.)

Caligula's desperate pursuit of some point of logical certainty in

an illogical universe took its most radically grotesque turn in Bergman's third act, when Ek appeared as a nightmarishly distorted
Venus – wearing a flame-red fright wig, false hips, and enormous
breasts. "Venus strikes a highly unflattering acrobatic pose atop a
pillar, and turns toward the audience that part of the body on which
one usually sits," reported the critic for *Aftonbladet* with propriety.
"Around the pillar of Venus storms the clown-show of life, with
harlots, dancing skeletons, and all the curiosities that could ever be
imagined on life's fairgrounds." In general, the Caligula conceived
by Bergman and Ek – for, unlike their *Macbeth*, there was no hint
here of any discrepancy between the director's concept and the actor's performance – was a warped, sardonic *Stürmer* of immense
physical powers who thumbs his nose at a meaningless world (or, to
be more exact, thrusts his backside in its face). In his malice and
violence, however, one ultimately detected little of that terrifying
methodical "logic" that drives Camus's complex protagonist – his
determination, as Sartre puts it, to "choose to be the man to persuade other men of the world's absurdity."[16]

AMERICAN REALISM

No doubt for a variety of reasons, *Caligula* has remained Bergman's
only encounter as a director with the philosophical nihilism of
French absurdist drama – although he had been preparing to make a
film of Camus's novel *The Fall* shortly before the French writer's
death in 1960, and had been in lengthy correspondence with him.
(The two popular plays by Jean Anouilh that he directed in Gothenburg, *La Sauvage* and the delightful *Le Bal des voleurs*, can hardly be
said to fall into the absurdist category.) In terms of the sharp distinction that Sartre draws, in his essay "Forgers of Myths," between a
psychologically preoccupied "theater of characters" and the existential "theater of situation and choice" represented by his own work
and that of Anouilh (specifically his *Antigone*), one is inclined to
suggest that the young Bergman was constitutionally much more
attuned to works in the first of these two classifications. Perhaps for
this reason, the more concrete, psychologically grounded emotionality of modern American drama held a much stronger attraction for
him – for a period, at least – and found provocative, at times even
explosive articulation in the increasingly more direct, uncluttered,
actor-oriented style that he gradually developed. Tennessee Williams was in high favor throughout Scandinavia during the years
around 1950, and Bergman staged three of his plays in that period –

A Streetcar Named Desire (1949), a radically altered version of *The Rose Tattoo* (1951), and *Cat on a Hot Tin Roof* (1956). During the 1960s, Bergman's interest shifted briefly to the plays of Edward Albee, and he presented probing and erotically intense interpretations of both *Who's Afraid of Virginia Woolf?* (1963) and a partially rewritten and demystified version of *Tiny Alice* (1965) – the latter so sexually explicit that one critic observed "hardly ever have we come closer to seeing the sexual act performed on stage" than in an interpolated copulation scene between Alice and the Lawyer.

Although Bergman's production of *Streetcar*, with which he concluded his three-season contract at Gothenburg in 1949, was naturally considerably tamer in this regard – the 1940s were not the 1960s, after all, even in Scandinavia! – it represented a critical sensation in almost every other way. The choice of the play itself was anything but unusual, of course – *Streetcar* seemed to be de rigueur for theaters throughout Scandinavia at that moment[17] – but the approach that he took to it was wholly personal and original. The result was a veritable theatrical paraphrase and intensification of the inner spirit of Williams's drama, "held together by a clarity and with a forcefully conceived totality of vision that actually made the play finer than it is in the text by itself."[18] The acrobatic Anders Ek was an appropriately athletic Stanley Kowalski; the superbly self-possessed and authoritative actress–director Karin Kavli was Bergman's Blanche Dubois. (Because he is nothing if not a genius in the art of casting actors, his choice of these two performers for other roles in the subsequent plays of his American series is worth noting in passing: Ek was later seen as Brother Julian in *Tiny Alice*; Kavli was both Serafina in *Rose Tattoo* and the formidable Martha in *Who's Afraid*.)

As a framework for the focal life-and-death struggle between Blanche and Stanley, Bergman created a highly concrete, pliable atmosphere of light, shadow, and sounds to intensify the mood of desperation that prevails in the play. "He has coordinated all these thousands of sounds that flow through the house and around it – the clatter from the street, the vendor's cry, music from the movie-house, the creaking and grinding from the train station, thunder, rain, and church bells, a mighty arsenal of sound effects – with the neon lights and the rather dilapidated interior to form a suggestive background for Blanche's fate," Elis Andersson recorded in *Göteborgs–Posten*. Both the passing of time and Blanche's vicissitudes of fortune were suggested by "a small symbolic apple tree that lives its life in Desire, from its flowering to the falling of its leaves." The

A Streetcar Named Desire, the setting for 632 Elysian Fields. Gothenburg, 1949.

chant of the blind Mexican flower vendor in scene nine was carried as an echo through the entire last movement of the play.

In turn, the director chose to delete most of the playwright's own very specific instructions for staging and stage effects. "He quite simply has no need for them," Andersson remarked, "given the way in which he has built up the house in Desire and the street and his utilization of the turntable stage." As this comment suggests, it was above all in its free, fluid use of the remarkably flexible stage space at Gothenburg that Bergman's version of *Streetcar* departed most radically from the familiar pattern so firmly established by Elia Kazan's direction and Jo Mielziner's design concept for the Broadway production of the play. Carl-Johan Ström, himself a disciple of the style represented by American designers like Mielziner and Boris Aronson, created in this instance a setting that, in a sense, transformed the tactile values that are suggested in Williams's stage directions—but were only indicated in Mielziner's painted street backdrop – into a three-dimensional environment.[19] Desire, for Bergman and Ström, was first of all a place. Blanche's entrance opened the play, as she seeks (*"with faintly hysterical humor"*) to explain to Eunice the directions she has received, and on Bergman's stage she found a very specific source for her hysteria in the bewildering street scene into which she was suddenly thrust. "To the left a large boarding house, to the right a place called Desire or the Pleasure Garden, conceived of here as a nonstop movie house," wrote Ebbe Linde in *Dagens Nyheter*. "People stream out past a black doorman in red uniform, sailors and girls; bicycles are mounted, a real automobile roars into the street and races out." In the midst of this raucous neighborhood scene, the shadowy precincts of 632 Elysian Fields swung slowly into view on the revolving stage; but even when the Kowalski apartment occupied the stage, the shape and the flashing lights of Desire, Bergman's surrealistic picture palace of dreams, continued to be visible in the background.

"It is always my intention to be exact, to be concrete," Bergman told John Simon in an interview (in a reply that referred to the final striking image of the Dance of Death in *The Seventh Seal,* but which applies with at least as much validity to his work in the theater). "My intention is always to be very simple."[20] By "simplicity" Bergman, here and elsewhere, means "clarity," the absence of metaphysical topsyturvydom. Understood in this manner, his early production of *Streetcar* – with its battery of exact, specifically directed visual and aural effects (or "suggestions," as Bergman would call them, that together "create a dimension") – was "simple" and typical of one stage in his artistic development. Step by step, as the actor in Bergman's theater has gradually become his undivided focus of attention ("the actor is always the most suggestive of all, provided he has something to offer"), the concrete physical effects or "suggestions" in a production of this kind have been steadily and drastically reduced in number and in apparent randomness. This steadily increasing physical simplification was clearly in evidence in the subsequent productions of his American series, for example. In the production of *Who's Afraid* at Dramaten in 1963 (the European premiere of the play), one saw only an uncompromisingly bare gray room that consisted of a primitive wall-screen at the back and an absolute minimum of furnishings – an omnipresent bar wagon, a fringed, bourgeois sofa and armchairs – around which the scenes of Albee's dance of death were choreographed in acrobatic contortions. "His entire objective has been to enclose and transfix – in a milieu of rat-gray furniture and dishcloth-colored cretonne covers – a model

marriage of hatred and humiliation, a relentless battle of the sexes,"
wrote Per Erik Wahlund in *Svenska Dagbladet*.[21] The physical presentation of *Tiny Alice,* which Bergman took on after the play's intended
director fell ill, was starker yet–a stage enclosed by drapes, furnished only with two formal chairs and (for the scenes in Miss
Alice's mansion) a stylized, man-sized model of a castle. Dimly visible on two luminous hanging globes that flanked the proscenium–
and that find no origin whatever in Albee's stage directions–were a
list of author's names and an outline of the various branches of
science (including both magic and ethics), scrawled in a schoolgirl's
handwriting.

The thrust of such extreme and suggestive simplification is certainly not toward abstraction, however, but toward greater concentration and emotional intensification–animated, in Bergman's own
words, by a growing "need for clarity":

an awareness that a suggestion that aims at many targets reaches none of
them. But a suggestion that is single and directed, that always strikes home.

The bare, gray room designed by Georg Magnusson for Albee's *Who's
Afraid of Virginia Woolf?* Dramaten, 1963.

If you set up a series of suggestions like that beside one another, all of which are directed at the same target but each of which has a different coloring, you will get an immensely faceted spectrum. But if the suggestions go toward different targets, then you get no unity and merely become exhausted. It is on this theory that my productions build.[22]

Most would agree that, in this regard, the seasons in Gothenburg were crucial years (if perhaps not entirely contented ones) of experiment and growth for Bergman, during which the place of this discipline and formal clarity in his art was established – years during which "he coaxed from the great theatrical machine its secrets, tested the possibilities, and learned to control them."[23]

SAVAGE COMEDY

During the eleven months that elapsed between *Streetcar* and his next stage production – an unprecedented respite for a man like Bergman, who had been used to directing at least three or four productions a season – he found his first opportunity, at the age of thirty-one, to travel outside of Sweden and to experience modern European theater at first hand. In Paris in the autumn of 1949, he discovered Molière and the performance traditions of the Comédie Française ("an unbelievable, totally overwhelming experience," he calls it: "It was such a great revelation to encounter the French theater tradition"), and this discovery has, as we know, had a profound and lasting effect on his art. When he came back to the Gothenburg City Theatre to stage a guest production early the following year, however, it was not yet a Molière comedy but one of the most savage of the so-called *comedias bárbara* of Ramón María del Valle-Inclán that he presented.

In itself, the bold decision to produce Valle-Inclán's sprawling and complicated tragicomedy *Divine Words* (*Divinas palabras,* February 3, 1950) inevitably confronted the director with great formal and organizational difficulties – and yet, Grevenius declared in *Stockholms–Tidningen,*

it couldn't be done more simply. Already in *Caligula,* Ingmar Bergman succeeded in creating artistic mass effects with a small number of actors and sparse scenery. The austerity of that play almost automatically provided for such a solution. To find a simple and contained shape for a play as chaotic as Valle-Inclán's is considerably harder. But this clearly shows how it ought to be done.

Although not all the Swedish critics agreed with this assessment of Bergman's success in taming this wild and brutal epic of human depravity in the lower depths of rural Spain, the production is central to his development as a director in several respects. The monochromatic visual effects and arresting figure compositions that he created within Ström's stylized highway setting stood out with a clarity of definition that seems to predict some of the film maker's most memorable works of the 1950s:

The sun's red eye flames in a coal-black heaven. A procession of glittering torches moves brilliantly across the night sky. Frequently, entire scenes are built up as long frescoes of figures set against black space. The small, white rustic church around which the events are occasionally drawn together glows against a sky of thunder (*Götesborgs–Posten*).

Valle-Inclán's concept of *esperpento* – a truthful vision arrived at by systematic deformation, achieved by "the mathematics of a concave mirror" – found concrete scenic realization in the steady rhythmic progression of harsh black-and-white (or, more exactly, black-and-red) contrasts created by Bergman. The play's strange collection of vagabonds, bandits, and beggars (exhibiting in the production a "resplendent, gypsylike wretchedness, with much naked flesh and much undisguised shamelessness") was juxtaposed with a particularly vivid, Bergmanesque counterimage – pious pilgrims hurrying along the highway past this valley of sin, displaying their crucifixes, icons, and stigmatized hands. Not surprisingly, perhaps, the director himself has apparently admitted that this production provided the direct inspiration for the grotesque procession of howling, twisting flagellants in *The Seventh Seal*.[24]

The character of Mari–Gaila, the adulterous wife of the village sexton and the chief focus of interest in *Divine Words*, represents a severe challenge to the abilities of any actress. In the play she is a callous, lascivious figure with few redeeming actions to her credit. Among much else, she derives profit (and sadistic pleasure) from exhibiting her dead sister-in-law's hideously deformed idiot child, a hydrocephalic dwarf, as a freak; she drives her humiliated husband to drink and even attempted incest because of her flagrantly licentious behavior; in the end an angry crowd discovers her copulating in an open field; they proceed to strip her and drag her naked atop a wagon to her husband's church. Only the sexton's intonation of some randomly chosen "divine words" of unintelligible Latin, as he leads his naked wife into the safety of the sanctuary, succeeds in dispersing the superstitious mob. (It is perhaps self-evident that this graphic sequence of humiliation and counterhumiliation strikes a chord that is fundamental not only to a specific motion picture like *The Naked Night*, but indeed to the entire corpus of Bergman's films.)

Karin Kavli's intense performance as Mari-Gaila directly anticipated her even more defiantly unrepentant and demonic interpretation of Kersti in Bergman's first major Strindberg production, *The
Crown-Bride*, less than three years later. As Mari, she developed
swiftly from a blond, gentle, essentially naive peasant wife to a
woman who, once seduced into evil ways, remained possessed by
and exultant in her sensuality and carnality. Confronted by the mob
in the field, "she tears off her own blouse and stands there in her red
slip like a triumphant sinner and a witch," one observer declared. "A
wonderfully directed scene acted with compelling ferocity."[25] (Those
inclined to smile a little at the commotion caused by the degree of
Kavli's "nakedness" in this scene should be reminded that the innocent bucolic nudity of Harriet Andersson in *Summer with Monika*
[released in 1953] had caused that film to be banned in Nice and Los
Angeles, to run a year in Montivideo, and to enjoy wide circulation in
pirated underground prints. Had Bergman chosen the supremely
erotic Andersson to play Mari-Gaila, Gothenburg might well have
had a riot on its hands!) The stripping and elevation of the adulteress
became, in Bergman's handling of this–otherwise precariously oper-

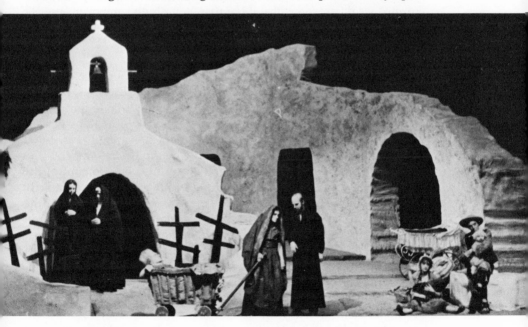

The stylized monochromatic setting designed by Carl-Johan Ström for
Valle-Inclan's *Divine Words*, Bergman's last production in Gothenburg,
1950.

atic–scene, a mystical ritualistic act that exposed the true subject of Valle-Inclán's tragicomedy–the latent paganism and thinly cloaked moral hypocrisy of the Spanish populace:

When the adulteress trapped in debauchery is lifted up onto the hayrick by the furious and enthusiastic harvesters, the doubleness of their action suddenly becomes clear. Behind outraged moral feelings one detects the echo of an age-old fertility rite, mixed with fear and lust, as the half-naked sinner (completely naked in the original) becomes both human victim and divine symbol. And it is not until the biblical words are uttered in Latin that the church reasserts its power over the primeval demons and their awakening recedes. That this scene works must be called a triumph for the director (*Göteborgs Handels– och Sjöfartstidning*).

In his review of *Divine Words*, Herbert Grevenius, Bergman's staunchest critical supporter during the 1940s and a frequent collaborator on his early films, tried to formulate a broader judgment that, in retrospect, supplies an apt and prophetic summary of the outcome of these first formative seasons in the director's long career:

It is usual to call Ingmar Bergman possessed. That has become the cliché. If by it one is trying to describe his artistic passion, then it must be accepted – provided we do not forget that it is a passion for truth and not an aesthetic passion for beauty. But the time has come to take notice of the control, the method, a search for form that is, for once in a Swedish director, . . . more Gallic than Germanic (*Stockholms–Tidningen*).

It is, Bergman himself declares, "only through experience, through my mistakes and to a certain degree through my successes, through an increased self-confidence, that I have little by little taught myself artistic selectivity."[26] Out of his score of early productions at Hälsingborg and at Hammarén's stricter school in Gothenburg, however, the "demon director" quietly and methodically extracted the most important lessons of all–the ability to use and to control the technical resources of the theater, the preeminent value of simplicity and suggestion, the basic and focal significance of the actor in the scheme of things, the need for that painstaking preparation without which improvisation becomes mere amateurish self-indulgence.

Two more seasons were to elapse–seasons of bitter frustration during which the Swedish film industry was shut down, and Bergman supported himself by making one-minute advertising films for Sunlight and by directing a few unremarkable stage productions in Stockholm and Norrköping–before he transformed the newly built 1700-seat Malmö City Theatre into one of the most vigorous and innovative theater centers in Europe during the mid-1950s. But by that time, of course, Bergman had already become Bergman. He had by then begun to gather around him a group of such "favorite" actors as Anders Ek and Gertrud Fridh, and his six-year stay at Malmö as director and artistic adviser enabled him to build and train a veritable Bergman ensemble of performing artists–Bibi Andersson, Harriet Andersson, Ingrid Thulin, Gunnel Lindblom, Naima Wifstrand, Max von Sydow, and others–who were to appear with regularity both in his stage productions and in his major films. He had taught himself to master the considerable complexities of the theater machine at Gothenburg, but the Malmö engagement represented a challenge of quite another magnitude. The vast open stage at Malmö had been completed in 1944 in response to Per Lindberg's vision of a democratized "people's theater"–a flexible, classless space in which there must be "no definite borderline between stage and auditorium, no frame around the stage." The auditorium, Lindberg had insisted, "must be of such dimensions that a ticket need not cost more than a cinema ticket," and the very shape of the theater itself "must make the audience feel its participation in the play and stimulate the actors into becoming the audience's guide to the goals they are both striving to reach."[27] It took Bergman to prove that the gargantuan theater that resulted from this vision could be used effectively for normal dramatic productions, and its special demands exerted in turn a profound effect upon the maturation of the aims and methods of his scenic art.

Most significant of all, however, was the change in Bergman's repertory that clearly heralded a new and more important phase of his directing career. During the Malmö years of excitement and experiment between 1952 and 1958, be began for the first time to devote himself in earnest to that succession of brilliant classical revivals–of Strindberg, Hjalmar Bergman, Ibsen, Goethe, and, in particular, Molière–that has since grown to form the keystone of his contribution to the modern theater. It is above all in his numerous productions of Strindberg, Ibsen, and Molière during the past quarter of a century that we find that unique and exciting union of tradition *and* innovation in Bergman's style most startlingly revealed–that functioning of a historical sense that, as T. S. Eliot once put it, "involves a perception not only of the pastness of the past, but of its presence."

3 The Strindberg cycle

What the hand, dare seize the fire?

William Blake

That Ingmar Bergman and August Strindberg are, in a great many ways, kindred spirits has long since been enshrined amongst the most hallowed critical commonplaces of Bergman criticism. "I have been reading him since I was twelve or thirteen," Bergman has told more than one interviewer. "Strindberg has generally been my companion throughout life, alternately repelling and attracting me" – not, he adds, because of any temperamental affinity, but "simply because he expressed certain things in the same way that I experienced them but could not myself describe them."[1] Seizing avidly upon this clue, critics eager to lay bare the mystery of Bergman's art have set off along one of two broad paths in search of bigger game. The one path has led them into the archetypal Forest of Shared Attitudes – toward women, Original Sin, a strict Lutheran upbringing, lost innocence, the search for identity, and much more.[2] The other path ends in the Grove of Parallels, where selected thematic similarities between certain of Bergman's films and certain of Strindberg's plays – *Persona* and *The Stronger*, *A Passion* and *The Ghost Sonata*, *Wild Strawberries* and *A Dream Play*, *Through a Glass Darkly* and *Easter*, to pick four pairs at random – are erected and revered.[3] But although Bergman himself has readily recognized the Strindberg resonances in, for example, *Wild Strawberries*, few film critics seem prepared to heed the remark that is intended to clarify the nature of such resonances: "There is naturally theater work going on alongside all the time. Much could be said about the mutual relationship between my work in the theater and my work in film."[4] It is precisely in terms of this "theater work" – specifically, the productions of the fourteen or more Strindberg plays that Bergman has directed, often more than once, for radio (*Playing with Fire*, *The Dutchman*, *Mother Love*, *Crimes and Crimes*, *Easter*, *The First Warning*), television (*Storm Weather* and *A Dream Play*), and the stage (*The Pelican*, *The Crown-Bride*, *The Ghost Sonata*, *Erik XIV*, *A Dream Play*, *To Damascus*) – that we can most profitably begin to consider the concrete stylistic, formal, and theatrical characteristics that together define the real consanguinity of these two artists. At the heart of such an inquiry is the cycle of six plays by Strindberg, which the director and his ensemble have performed in the presence of their most important collaborator – a live theater audience. (*The Dance of Death*, which was in preparation when Bergman was picked up by the Swedish police on allegations of tax evasion in 1976 and rehearsals for which were resumed and again interrupted in the autumn of 1978 when Anders Ek fell ill, would have made seven. Instead, the 1981 production of *Miss Julie* in Munich will now become the seventh in this cycle.)

EARLY STRINDBERG PRODUCTIONS

Even in the toy theaters of Bergman's youth, Strindberg productions had figured prominently. By the early 1940s he was directing highly regarded amateur productions of such difficult works as *Lucky Per's Journey* and *Swanwhite* at Mäster Olofsgården in Stockholm.[5] The first real notice of what was to come was served in 1945, however, when he directed a guest production of *The Pelican*, Opus Four of Strindberg's Chamber Plays, on the intimate studio stage of the Malmö City Theatre. The program for this production (November 25, 1945) contains a brief article by the director that provides an unusually direct and revealing personal comment (unusual for Bergman, at least) on Olof Molander's approach – and hence, by implication, his own preferred approach as well – to the staging of Strindberg:

At first, Strindberg's inferno dramas put the strangest visions into the heads of Europe's directors, who felt they were out after Freudian deep-sea fish and began to throw themselves into levels, projections, and other devices for all they were worth. It was director's theater, display theater, but it wasn't Strindberg. Molander has made us see the magic in Strindberg's dramaturgy. We have begun to understand that the strange fascination of the stage itself and the Strindbergian dialogue are compatible. Molander gives us Strindberg without embellishments or directorial visions, tunes in to the text, and leaves it at that. He makes us hear the poet's anxiety-driven fever pulse. It becomes a vision of toiling, weeping, evil-smitten humanity. We listen to a strange, muted chamber music. And the dream play emerges in all its grotesqueness, its terror, and its beauty. . . . I want only to express my debt of gratitude to Molander.

First it was *A Dream Play*. Night after night I stood in the wings and sobbed and never really knew why. After that came *To Damascus, Saga of the Folkungs,* and *The Ghost Sonata.* It is the sort of thing you never forget and never leave behind, especially if you happen to be a director and least of all if, as one, you are directing a Strindberg drama.

At the core of this generous *hommage* is the unmistakable consciousness of being part of a tradition – a consciousness that is one of the most characteristic features of Bergman's artistic physiognomy, both as a film maker and as a stage director. "I don't think that somebody just becomes a director, you know. We are like stones in a building, all of us," he has said repeatedly. "We all depend on the people coming before; I am just a part of this."[6] In the case of Strindberg, as Bergman quite rightly observes, it was Molander's impressive cycle of productions at Dramaten in the mid-1930s that ultimately succeeded in forging a fluid, responsive scenic form that was perfectly attuned to Strindberg's associational, mutational dramaturgy. "It was Max Reinhardt who discovered the unique scenic music of *The Ghost Sonata,* and Olof Molander who transposed that music into Swedish," one reviewer of Bergman's 1954 production of that play was prompted to remark.[7] The observation is as apt as it is concise. In Scandinavia, Reinhardt's touring productions of Strindberg had been seminal events that, in the words of the Swedish reformer Per Lindberg, "opened our eyes to the visionary, musical power in Strindberg's last dream plays." His boldly expressionistic *Ghost Sonata,* which came to Stockholm in 1917, made Hummel into a ghastly personification of evil and transformed the play itself into a grotesque and terrifying "nightmare of marionettes." Even the young Olof Molander found in his virtuoso interpretation of *The Pelican,* which played in Gothenburg and later in Stockholm in 1920, "a scenic masterpiece that is not even suggested by a reading of that chamber play."[8] One year later, his strange, starkly dematerialized Swedish-language production of *A Dream Play* at Dramaten contributed even more provocatively to an overall vision of a Strindberg in which, to borrow Siegfried Jacobsohn's words, "a shivering, desperate, shrieking humanity" struggles in an atmosphere "so distorted, so gloomy, so full of fantastic life and motion, that it might be Van Gogh's."[9]

On the same stage fourteen years later, in October 1935, the first of Molander's seven very different productions of *A Dream Play* – which Bergman singles out again and again as a "fundamental dramatic experience" in his own career – became a pivotal event in Scandinavian theater and culture. It was a turning point because it established a deliberate and, in the minds of many, a more authentic alternative to the Germanic Strindberg of Reinhardt and his followers. In direct contrast to the Reinhardt experiment, Molander's pioneering production reaffirmed a lucid undertone of resignation and consolation, a recognition of the humanity that so often seemed absent in the German *Schrei*-versions of Strindberg's plays. Both Molander's identification of the Dreamer, in all three of his voices, with Strindberg himself and the use of specific, recognizable projections of *fin de siècle* Stockholm to which he attached the action served to restore a relevance and a Swedishness to the work. Most important of all in terms of its influence on Bergman, perhaps, was the surrealism, or "fantastic realism" that this director applied to the staging of Strindberg. His style depended on a fluid progression of suggestive, dreamlike settings, each one composed only of fragmented bits of sharply etched reality (a table, a portion of a wall, the cloverleaf door) suspended in a void of darkened space and supplemented, in this instance, by the projected views of Strindberg's Stockholm – the old Dramaten with Jacob's Church in the background, the Horse Guard Palace, a corner of the old Royal Opera where the Officer waits a lifetime for his Victoria.

Not long after Bergman had published his program declaration apostrophizing this method and repudiating the empty European (read German) "director's theater" that it had replaced, Molander himself appeared in print to renounce, in notably similar terms, even his youthful flirtation with the Reinhardt formula for Strindberg:

The German, Reinhardt-inspired romantic expressionism, which during the years between the world wars came to characterize theater art in Germany, has always been alien to me. I also felt that *The Pelican* was a grotesque manifestation of this romantic expressionism, and was completely foreign to Strindberg's surrealistic dreamplay dramaturgy. It is certainly true that nightmares are often its subject, but the nightmares of everyday, of life as we live it, not a nightmare life in any higher sense, not caricature.[10]

Indirectly, this comment speaks to Bergman's production of *The Pelican* as well, which, although it was in no sense merely a Molander imitation, derived its power from his method – from the preservation of a cold, relentlessly concrete sense of reality in which the play's more mystical signs (the creaking of the rocking chair, the mysterious Maeterlinckian sounds outside, the final holocaust) could be resolutely anchored.

A severe, cheerless interior, designed by Martin Ahlbom, was steeped in the cold whiteness of its essential elements – the rocking chair, a tiled stove, a row of windows – and decorated with a sprawling potted palm and a crepe-hung portrait of the recently deceased father, which bore the unmistakable features of Strindberg himself. Within the stark confines of this domestic wasteland, Bergman worked to create a performance from which all extraneous "symbolic" overtones were expunged, and that concentrated instead on the central thematic action of the play – the unmasking, to which the Mother makes explicit reference at the end of the first scene, of Strindberg's blind and suffering self-deceivers. "As the play was now given, it depicted a series of awakenings on the part of those who had previously been sleepwalkers," the critic for *Dagens Nyheter* observed. "The Son, anxious from the outset to find reality, awakens when he reads the letter that his father left, with its revelations about the Mother. Gerda awakens when she reaches clarity – or certainty – about her husband's deception of her with the Mother. Even the Mother sees herself, at least in a glimpse, in her confrontation with Gerda. There is less oversized evil but deeper human insight in this interpretation. We see a dreamplay about bewildered and suffering humanity." At the heart of Bergman's interpretation was an intelligent, Oswald-like portrayal of the Son by Anders Ek, "a frightening portrait of an individual stricken to the heart and sick to the very marrow. The bent knees and head held at an angle, the stammering speech and discreetly suggested imbalance – all of this gave us in a nutshell the tragedy of someone doomed from the outset" (*Morgon–Tidningen*). The critics were by no means uniformly favorable toward the production, however, and this particular comment on Anders Ek's performance might well suggest a reason why some, Herbert Grevenius among them, argued that suspense was lost because "the characters never do walk in their sleep: they are already awake, and hence the play is robbed of the tension that lies in the fact that they are injected, one dose at a time, with truth and with black perspicacity" (*Stockholms–Tidningen*).

As could be expected, the climactic fire scene in which this drama of suffering and purgation culminates ("a domestic Götterdämmerung," Evert Sprinchorn has called it, which "announces the bankruptcy of the family as an institution and the end of bourgeois drama"[11]) presented the director with his severest challenge and called forth some of his most interesting and most controversial antinaturalistic moves. No sounds of burning wood or puffs of smoke accompanied this inferno – much to the regret of a few literal-minded reviewers who admitted that they would have liked "a more violent crescendo accompanied by crackling sound effects." (After all, even Molander had nearly caused a panic when, during his first production of the play in 1921, clouds of smoke had billowed out into the auditorium!) Instead, Bergman suggested the fire by the simplest possible means, with a flickering red glow that played over the background. Also eliminated in his simplified scheme of things was the perilously melodramatic moment when Strindberg's demonic vampire–mother leaps through a balcony door to escape the flames; here, she was seen instead collapsing in the doorway to the dining room – ironically, the place of nourishment from which she had just been barred by the rebellious Gerda and her husband. Perhaps Bergman's most expressive visual comment was the image with which he chose to clarify the Son's closing summer-poem of serenity and peace. At the moment of death, the "fire" was extinguished and a translucent white curtain was lowered behind the door and windows in the background, with the result that the room stood bathed in light as brother and sister sank to the floor together. " 'Now summer vacation is beginning,' was their last reply, and they were engulfed in the light of liberation," wrote Ragnar Josephson in *Svenska Dagbladet*. "It was very beautiful." One might well be inclined to suppose that the director had not forgotten the tone and the luminous atmosphere of that famous speech when he came to create his own cycle of "summer" films a few years later.

The Crown-Bride, Bergman's first major Strindberg production and also the work with which he made a sensational directing debut on the immense main stage at Malmö in 1952, has often been called a national-romantic folk drama – the playwright himself regarded it as the most Swedish of his plays. It has also been viewed by critics as an example of Strindberg's post-inferno mystical theater – a Damascus drama transposed into a folksong key, linked thematically both to *Swanwhite* and *A Dream Play* (which were published together with it) by a renewed sense of spiritual peace and of the redemptive power of certain characters. In its simplest outline, the complicated action of the play supports either view – or both, for they are not mutually contradictory. Kersti, a young peasant girl in the idyllic province of Dalarna (Dalecarlia) who has secretly borne a son with Mats, drowns the baby to be able to marry her lover as a legitimate "crown" (i.e. virgin) bride. Tormented by the demons of a guilty conscience, she confesses her crime at her own wedding feast. In the midst of her despair and disgrace, the penitent shepherdess meets a Child in White – the image of the Christ child – and gains spiritual solace. Meanwhile, the ancient feud between Mats's family and hers has now flared up again. On Easter morning, as she is making her way from prison to the church to perform penance, Kersti falls through the ice on Krummedikke Lake as the quarreling parties fight, and her "sacrificial" death works their reconciliation. In Bergman's theatrical paraphrase, however, the action of *The Crown-Bride* was presented in an entirely new and often surprising perspective. Not only was the play's superstructure of romantic folklore and fairy tale dismantled and its use of traditional Swedish folk melodies discarded. The consoling facility with which the sinner moves toward atonement and redemption from the powers of darkness (through the epiphanic device of the Child in White) was also drawn into serious question. In what a program note for the Bergman production (November 14, 1952) referred to as "a world where the powers hold sway and a dreaded God drives man to penance and destruction," Kersti's destiny seemed, almost to the final moment, "a Damascus pilgrimage" toward a very ambiguous salvation at best. "A paroxysm of somber nocturnal and fertility rites, a cross between Garcia Lorca's Spain and Bergman's own Barjärna" was how Ebbe Linde chose to describe the atmosphere evoked by the production – an atmosphere that indeed had much in common with the mood of darkness and evil prevalent in Bergman's own "passion play," *The Murder at Barjärna,* which he had staged in Malmö eight months before.

The intense, defiant performance by Karin Kavli as Mari-Gaila in the Gothenburg production of *Divine Words* had given only a foretaste of her deromanticized, virtually demonic characterization of the title figure in Strindberg's play. The traditional perception of this character's development – from the selfish and hardhearted peasant girl of the opening scenes to the grieving, repentant woman who atones before the church door – had been epitomized in Gerd Hagman's mimically expressive performance in the Molander production of the play at Dramaten eight years earlier: "There is an untamed animal's glint in her eye – and it gleamed fatefully in the beginning – but afterwards we saw the look change to horror, in preparation for reaching the great atonement at the end," critic Nils Beyer had declared on that occasion.[12] By contrast, Kavli presented – both physically and temperamentally – a much rougher and blacker Kersti, in a performance that led this same critic to observe (in *Morgon–Tidningen*) that the audience felt itself "considerably nearer to the sulfurous lakes of hell than to the shining waters of Lake Siljan" (the quintessentially idyllic body of water in the heart of the Dalarna district). This unrelenting Kersti seemed driven to her actions more by an innate compulsion for evil than by any misguided sense of social pressure. As such, she seemed scarcely to require the assistance of Naima Wifstrand's sinister Madame Larsson, the Mephistophelian midwife who is obviously a witch when "seen from behind," to accomplish her dark deed. In this atmosphere of heady diabolism, the figure of the Child in White was completely eliminated and replaced by a demonic figure that sprang from the orchestra pit to disrupt and scatter the bridal dance. Needless to say, neither the uncomplicated Mats nor any of the other characters in the play was any real match for this passionate demon-bride–with the result that, as Henrik Sjögren observed, "even the basic concept of the production was for a long time overshadowed by this robust leading performance, which in the beginning stood far too close to hell and toward the end never really did succeed in coming nearer to heaven."[13] Only in the closing sequence on the ice of Krummedikke Lake, when the sunken church rises (like a Flowering Castle!) to signify peace in Dalecarlia and on earth, did the director finally resolve and reaffirm the major tonic chord of redemption in Strindberg's work.

Unquestionably the main source of critical interest and excitement in conjunction with Bergman's *Crown-Bride* was, and in retrospect still is, the imaginatively simplified mise-en-scène with which he conclusively established his undisputed mastery of the formidable stage dimensions of the Malmö City Theatre.[14] Strindberg's stage directions for this play are often very detailed and specific, and, even as late as 1942, Vagn Børge's influential dissertation would maintain that, in staging it, "there must be the aura of pine forests, of resin and wild roses, over everything, with the great lake in the background and the blue mountains on the opposite side, and then the church in the distance."[15] Without a sense of this realistic pastoral environment, runs such an argument, the basic tensions in the play–between dream and reality, nature and society–will not become clear in performance. Bergman has given his answer often enough: "The theater calls for nothing. TV includes everything, film includes everything, there everything is shown. Theater ought to be the encounter of human beings with human beings and nothing more. All else is distracting." His unadorned, conceptual approach to *The Crown-Bride* dispensed with traditional pictorialism and local color almost completely–with the result that, in many ways, the inner essence of the work revealed itself more clearly than ever before. "Bergman has by and large eliminated the realistic elements," Per Erik Wahlund observed in *Svenska Dagbladet*. "In his hands, the latent dreamplay technique is laid bare and accentuated by the shadowy half-light and a radically stylized décor."

In the first two scenes before the single intermission, Per Falk's stage settings still incorporated realistic elements that evoked that sense of specific–and extremely ominous–places. The craggy, darkly forbidding mountain pasture where Kersti first appears was already set up on the forestage when the audience took their seats, and she made her entrance through their midst. "An enormous romantic spruce of supernatural dimensions lay, felled by the wind, across the proscenium, threatening to crush the performers to dust," Linde remarked. The subsequent and fairly detailed setting for the family council in the millhouse, placed back on the large revolving stage, was dominated by a gigantic open fireplace that perhaps most of all suggested a gaping hellmouth – though none of Strindberg's suggested emanations from the spirit world were allowed by Bergman to make an appearance.

Following the intermission, however, the depth of the stage was increased, and it was gradually and deliberately stripped of all objects and details as the action progressed toward Kersti's humiliation, penance, and death. The fateful bridal procession, during which she is forced to confess her perfidy and forfeit her crown, was choreographed (to music from Ture Rangström's opera on the subject) on a virtually bare and somber stage illuminated only by what Wahlund thought of as "the moon's gigantic, flame-colored stratospheric balloon in the background." Surpassing all else in terms of effectively suggestive simplicity was the climactic scene – very often cut because of its presumed technical difficulty – in which Kersti attempts to cross the treacherous ice on her way to church to perform public penance. The rival factions of the millfolk and the outsiders, for whose sake the girl becomes a divine sacrifice for reconciliation, clashed and fought with oars on a storm-lashed stretch of lake ice that was neither more nor less than the bare floor of the stage itself, which had been opened up to its full, spectacular width of thirty-six meters (117 feet). Using only this immense space and the chiaroscuro effects that are obtained when darkness is penetrated by scattered shafts of light, Bergman literally conjured forth what Wahlund called "the gloomy, perilous emptiness of a darkness-enshrouded, frozen expanse of sea." By no other means than lighting and screening, the empty stage floor was transformed, in the minds of the audience, to what Linde described in *Dagens Nyheter* as "a limitless ice field with a swirling snowstorm coming toward us."

The lesson learned was a profound one that has had far-reaching effects on everything that Bergman has since directed. In an interview many years afterwards, he reflected on the implications of the sweeping dematerialization and elimination of scenery to which he began to turn in this pivotal production:

One of the reasons why I have dispensed more and more with scenery is in fact because I believe that every stagehand on the stage, every use of the curtain, every raising and lowering of settings is a disruptive occurrence.

Because the actors have that wonderful ability to suggest directly. I thought about this very intensively while I was rehearsing the closing scenes of *The Crown-Bride*. Everyone went around in rehearsal clothes and we had only rehearsal lights. It struck me that absolutely no more was needed, no lighting was needed, nothing was needed – nothing more than the performer [*artiste*]. It is that simple.[16]

To be sure, there were reviewers of this production of *The Crown-Bride* who complained that its innovations were mere borrowed finery, and who drew parallels – rather vague and unspecific in character – between Bergman's style and the "German expressionist theater" of the 1920s. *Aftonbladet*, for instance, described the staging as "a gigantic apparatus suffused with mass scenes, ballets, and stage groupings that would have been greeted with genuflections by theatergoers at Am Grössten Schauspielkomplex in Berlin at the beginning of the 1920s. The spectator was taken on Gulliver's travels to the land of the giants, with Ingmar Bergman in the coachman's seat." It is hardly surprising to find that Bergman himself reacts with undisguised impatience to the implied comparison to the more spectacular aspects of Max Reinhardt's style. "I had seen no German theater before 1952. If there was any expressionism in me, it was home-grown." And indeed, if by "German expressionism" we mean such specific traits as the maintenance of a subjective, single-character perspective, the distortion of settings and fracturing of reality that reflect this perspective, and an attendant implicit criticism of the prevailing social order, then it is difficult to feel persuaded of any significant link between this (so decidedly outmoded) mode and the increasingly uncluttered and simplified style of Bergman. The latter's primary aim as a director is the intensification of the audience's involvement with the living actor, placed for the purpose in an ever more direct, more emphatic, and hence more hypnotic position in relationship to it. In a word, Bergman's method in the 1950s does not seem to look backward to Reinhardt, but ahead toward a revolution in the way we perceive the theatrical experience.

Bergman's radio productions of Strindberg during these years add an interesting dimension to this preoccupation with an elimination of external detail and a consequent tightening of focus on the personality of the actor. During the year of *The Crown-Bride*, his radio production of *Crimes and Crimes*, which eliminated the factors of time and the play's Parisian milieu altogether, created an intense concentration – virtually the equivalent of a closeup technique in film – on the individual vocal nuances of Anders Ek's hesitant and inquisitive Maurice and the seductive, glass-hard Henriette of Gertrud Fridh. In *Easter*, also broadcast in 1952 with Maj-Britt Nilsson (*To Joy, Smiles of a Summer Night*) as a completely down-to-earth, even mundane Eleonora and Gunnar Olsson as an overpowering Lindkvist in dialect, the director "tried to cut away all sentimentality, eliminate all sound effects, and bring forth a nakedly oneiric tone."[17] The following year, he succeeded even more conclusively in translating to the radio medium the dreamlike transitions and word music of *The Dutchman*, Strindberg's long lyrical fragment about a latterday Flying Dutchman and his search for love in a loveless world.

Yet it would be totally misleading to leave the impression that Bergman's splendidly eclectic seasons in Malmö were somehow characterized by a tediously single-minded quest for the grail of a more restrained and more austere theatrical syntax. If he shares anything in common with Reinhardt (apart from great theatrical genius), it is the crucial conviction that no one method is sufficient for staging all plays, that "there is no one form of theater that is the only true artistic form," that each play presents a new and distinct problem. Therefore, Reinhardt continues, "do not write out prescriptions, but give to the actor and his work the atmosphere in which they can breathe more freely and more deeply. Do not spare stage properties and machinery where they are needed, but do not impose them on a play that does not need them."[18] Precisely in this spirit, Bergman's directional approach has at all times been conditioned by the particular work at hand. In Malmö, moreover, he was able to adopt and maintain a satisfying alternation – akin in a sense to Reinhardt's tandem operation of the Deutsches Theater and the Kammerspiele in Berlin at the beginning of the century – between the large main stage and Intiman, the theater's small studio stage. On this intimate chamber stage in 1955, for example, he could present *Leah and Rachel*, the Vilhelm Moberg dramatization of the biblical story of the fertile and barren daughters of Laban (Gen. 29–30), with effective simplicity – on a sculpturally lighted circular platform accented only by a suggestive runic block of stone. Yet, earlier that same year, he was as fully prepared to offer his audiences a gracefully oriental *Teahouse of the August Moon* that was as commercially "authentic" (down to the real jeep on stage) as it was entertaining. While working on the Max Brod dramatization of Kafka's *The Castle* (Intiman 1953) he reached a last-moment decision to dispense with the intended stage design completely, and this production was eventually acted on an essentially bare stage furnished only with the barest of necessities – a table, a bench, a pair of chairs, a bed. But, on the main stage a year later, he then treated his public to a spectacularly decorated and festively choreographed rendering of Franz Lehár's

The Merry Widow that called forth delighted critical comparisons with Reinhardt's legendary staging of *Die Fledermaus.* Examples of this flexibility of approach could easily be multiplied. (It might be misleading, however, to overlook Bergman's own staunch preference for a more broadly based popular theater, illustrated by a remark made just before he began rehearsals for *Cat on a Hot Tin Roof* in 1956: "It is more fun to work on the big stage, where one program can draw 100,000 spectators. Of course there are plays that demand a chamber format, but I find it very difficult to feel much satisfaction in putting forty or fifty intensive rehearsals into a production that will play for only a couple of weeks to 200 people. And Intiman does not accommodate more than that."[19])

The principal point to bear in mind, however, is that no single method or sameness of style rules Bergman's work as a stage director. Nowhere is the adaptability of his creative method more evident than in the productions of his Strindberg cycle, in which approaches to different plays – or even different productions of the same play – display such abundant variety. Hence when *Erik XIV,* Strindberg's study of the "characterless character" of that moody and indecisive Vasa monarch, reached the Malmö stage in 1956 as the third major Strindberg revival of Bergman's career, the result was once again boldly different in concept and technique from either *The Pelican* or *The Crown-Bride.* In this production, praised by many critics for its remarkable union of poetic power and formal restraint, the director took full advantage of the theater's imposing spatial potential from start to finish. Although Ebbe Linde commented in *Dagens Nyheter* that "what must have fascinated Ingmar Bergman were the possibilities of making something spectacular out of a text that has so often been regarded as virtually unplayable," it is essential to understand what constitutes "spectacularity" in this regard. A single massive vault spanned the full width of the stage in Per Falk's setting, and this fixed arch, combined with etchinglike projections on the cyclorama, communicated succinctly the drama's predominant mood of impending doom. No solid, ponderous physical apparatus was allowed to divert attention from the human character study that Bergman perceived as the true focus of this parable of destiny. Accordingly, the succession of seven specific, representational interiors and exteriors that the playwright describes in his stage directions were eliminated, and hence no revolving stage was needed to facilitate disruptively complicated changes of scene. Instead, large portions of the play were acted on the projecting forestage, where the magnificently costumed historical characters appeared against the simple background as "a multicolored gallery of Breughel-like figures" (*Sydsvenska Dag-bladet Snällposten*).

At the core, then, of Bergman's highly stylized and physically simplified mise-en-scène was his emphasis on dynamic, swiftly changing compositions of colorful human figures. The focal point of these compositions was the intricately shaded and incisively analytical closeup of Erik created by Toivo Pawlo. The sharpness of the focus was accented and locked in place by the mute presence of a club-footed, hunchbacked court fool, whom Bergman introduced into the play to accompany the king as his ever-present mirror image, observing him and the world around him with silent but suggestive contempt. Pawlo's portrayal of Erik emphasized, with constantly accelerating force, the dangerous capriciousness of the king's moods, the ominous tension between humanity and inhumanity in his personality. His intense characterization built steadily toward the climactic moment of his abject humiliation, when his boycotted wedding banquet turns into a nightmarish orgy of rabble. In Bergman's hands this scene – which provided an interesting foretaste of the wildly grotesque surrealism of the goldmaker's banquet in his much later production of *To Damascus* – became a veritable danse macabre, led by a ghostlike band of black and plaster-white human marionettes whose ghastly figures supplied a mocking contrast to the splendid attire of the bewildered royal couple. Spectacular the production surely was at moments such as this – but it was, at the same time, forcefully simple and direct in its quest for an uncluttered illumination of the inner spirit of the work.

In this sense there is a steady gravitation in these early Strindberg productions, noticeable from *The Pelican* on, toward that strictly controlled, tightly focused form to which both Bergman and Strindberg have given the name "chamber play." Bergman the film maker has, as we know, applied this term to a number of his best-known works for the screen:

Through a Glass Darkly and *Winter Light, The Silence* and *Persona* I have called chamber plays. They are chamber music. That is, the pure cultivation of a certain number of themes for a strictly limited number of voices and figures. Backgrounds are abstracted. They are veiled in a kind of mist. One makes a distillation.[20]

This definition in turn calls to mind Strindberg's own explanation of a chamber play, in his *Open Letters to the Intimate Theatre:*

in this kind of drama we single out the significant and overriding theme, but treat it with moderation. In handling it we avoid all ostentation – all the calculated effects, the bravura roles, the solo numbers for the stars, and the cues for applause. The author rejects all predetermined forms because the theme determines the form.[21]

The broad features that align these two definitions – the distillation of a single unifying theme, its muted, unhistrionic expression in a compressed and fluid form, and the suppression of all distracting effects and disturbingly ostentatious backgrounds – are the very same preoccupations that tend to define the basic contours of most of Bergman's subsequent experiments with Strindberg.

THE GHOST SONATA: THREE PRODUCTIONS

In themselves, Bergman's three separate productions of *The Ghost Sonata*, the third and most demanding of the Chamber Plays, might be said to epitomize the changing nature of his continuous effort to encompass the fearful symmetry and to "seize the fire" of the brightly burning Strindbergian Tyger. His first *Sonata*, significant mainly for its historical rather than its artistic interest, was staged in Stockholm, in the tiny ninety-nine seat playhouse in Medborgarhuset that he had organized as a children's theater, in 1941. His intimately conceived and meticulously orchestrated production of the play at the Malmö City Theatre in 1954 was of a markedly different professional quality, and represents a notable milestone in his artistic development. Nearly two decades later, at the Royal Dramatic Theatre in Stockholm in 1973, Bergman presented his favorite Strindberg play ("the most remarkable drama ever to be written in Swedish," he likes to call it) for a third time, in a memorable and controversial stage interpretation that has even enjoyed the distinction of having had an entire book written about it.[22] Each of these three productions of *The Ghost Sonata* has been dependent on a very different set of human and physical circumstances, and each has reflected changes in the director's attitude toward his subject. At the core of that attitude, however, is a wonderfully lucid, antimelodramatic sensitivity to Strindberg in general and to this play in particular, perhaps best articulated in the remarks made by Bergman to his cast at the beginning of rehearsals for the Dramaten production in 1973:

Everything in this production must be close to us, naked, simple. Simple costumes, hardly any makeup. The characters in the play are not monsters. They are human beings. And if some of them – the Cook, for instance – appear to be evil, it does not follow that they must look evil. The point is that they behave in an evil way toward the figures on the stage, and we must perceive the evil through the reactions of these figures. If we underrate the audience's ability to take note of reactions, we corrupt the theater.[23]

Scene from *The Ghost Sonata*, the ghost supper, with *right*, Benkt-Åke
Benktsson as Hummel. Malmö, 1954.

Clearly, the long shadow that had been cast by the terrifying *Gespen-stersonate* of Max Reinhardt and the magnificently grotesque perform-ance of Paul Wegener as Hummel had vanished conclusively from the face of Strindberg's theater.

Extraordinarily enough, Bergman's intelligent amateur production of *The Ghost Sonata* in Medborgarhuset (September 21, 1941) evi-dently marked the first real revival of the play in Sweden since Reinhardt's touring performance of it startled Stockholm twenty-four years before. (Photographs of the event convey no hint what-ever of Reinhardt, meanwhile, but bear instead a strong family re-semblance to the old pictures of the simple, rather cramped produc-tions of Strindberg's own Intima teatern, where the play had had its inauspicious premiere in 1908.) In a long program note written for the revival in Malmö (March 5, 1954), Bergman describes with infec-tious enthusiasm his earliest experiences with this key work. By the time he was twelve he had seized upon it avidly, with an eye to realizing its strange, hallucinatory images of "childhood terror" – "these suggestions that strike us, powerfully and disturbingly, far deeper than reason and analysis, this scenic music that has imparted to our theatrical feeling its basic features" – in his puppet theater. The inspiration to use the tiny stage of his children's theater in Medborgarhuset for an adult performance of the play was a bold one ("we were in fact a first harbinger of the later so popular cellar and attic theaters") but it met with only limited success and closed after four performances:

However, I recall how the fragile ensemble was lifted as though on a wave by the immensity of the drama, we found ourselves part of the theater as magic: to be cast beyond our own limitations, to be supported in our inade-quacy and not dashed to pieces by it.

Then, continues Bergman in his program article, "came the great, totally shattering experience" – the first of Olof Molander's five ma-jor productions of the play, seen at Dramaten in October of 1942:

Probably never has a fledgling rooster choked on his own cock-crow as emphatically as I did that night, and during a dark and rainy walk in Djurgård Park I resolved to abandon the player's road and heed the wishes of my good parents – to continue my studies. What I experienced that night in the theater seemed to me absolute and unattainable. And it seems so still.

The eloquent tribute to the acknowledged master should not ob-scure the fact that Bergman was, by then, very much his own man, and that his Malmö production of *The Ghost Sonata* was far from a deliberate repetition of the Molander method – though most re-

viewers were more inclined to stress parallels than to discover differences. One exception was the Danish critic Svend Kragh-Jacobsen,
whose review drew upon firsthand comparisons to the Molander
production of the play at the Royal Theatre in Copenhagen in 1948:

Ingmar Bergman acknowledges his debt to Molander, but this new mise-en-
scène possesses his own personal strength, his intensity, and a discipline
that is impressive. The first and last acts are perhaps lacking just a bit in
atmosphere, but the middle act – the core scene – has shattering power in the
Malmö performance and is done with an imagination that at the same time

A comparable scene from the Stockholm production of *The Ghost
Sonata* in 1973. *Right,* Toivo Pawlo is Hummel, with Gertrud Fridh as
the Mummy and Anders Ek as the Colonel. The figure of the Student
can be glimpsed in the background. Dramaten.

subjugates the stage space and fills it, inspires the actors and drives them to their uttermost limits (*Berlingske Tidende*).

The point is well taken, for the ghastly, festering confines of the "ghost supper" – where (as Bengtsson, the valet explains) the living dead "sound like a pack of rats in an attic" as they munch their biscuits and crackers in unison – provided an ideal field of play for Bergman's unique personal ability to stimulate his actors to the most intense and physically emphatic expression of scenic emotion.

In this scene of exhumation and psychic murder, all that is purely verbal in Strindberg found fiercely concrete physical articulation in Bergman's interpretation. Benkt-Åke Benktsson's voluminous Hummel was a "Big Daddy" of a vampire – "a colossus on light feet, a perverted Prospero, an evil God the Father," Ivar Harrie called him in *Expressen* – whose character was delineated in terms of sharply etched emotional peripeties. His muted, scheming tone in the first scene, as he sits in his wheelchair in front of the house, gave way to the overpowering cynical force with which he laid bare the hypocrisy and mendacity of the Colonel and his household – to be displaced in turn by tragic helplessness and terror as he is himself unmasked and destroyed by the Mummy, once his young love Amelia. "His powers were first unleashed in the second act," observed Kragh-Jacobsen: "the frightening, almost magical gleam that is suggested in his glance catches fire; his voice turns to thunder." Once he has systematically and conclusively drained the Colonel – Georg Årlin's "marionette on wooden parade" – of his property, his rank, and even the dignity of his title as father, the vampire himself falls victim to the vengeful fury of Naima Wifstrand's Mummy. No grotesque parrot-woman now, Wifstrand became the avenging dead who remorselessly settles accounts with Hummel, tears the mask from the face of this "stealer of souls," and sends him to die in the closet where she has sat for twenty years to atone for the past. "Her expression as he went, and his tottering along on crutches toward the background were shocking and fascinating – this was great acting, a brilliant dramatist's powerful scene executed so that every strand of meaning and dramatic action stood out," Kragh-Jacobsen declared – and most other reviewers concurred.

Yet, as Henrik Sjögren points out, even this unremittingly bleak climax was relieved, in Bergman's interpretation, by the lighter, conciliatory tone of the Mummy's thematically crucial speech about human compassion and atonement:

I can wipe out the past, and undo what is done. Not with bribes, not with hatred – but through suffering and repentance. We are poor miserable creatures, we know that. We have erred, we have transgressed, like all the rest.

"But I can stop Time." Naima Wifstrand as the Mummy. Malmö, 1954.

We are not what we seem to be. At bottom we are better than ourselves, since we abhor and detest our misdeeds.

This speech – accented in the Malmö performance "as a breathing space that pointed ahead toward the third act"[24] – provided a touchstone for the director's structural image of the play as a progression toward purification and redemption. In his subsequent revival at Dramaten, which in so many other respects differed radically from its predecessor, the Mummy's second-act speech continued to hold the key to his thinking about the work – to the extent that it even prompted him to assign the play's closing words of benediction and peace to the Mummy as well. During rehearsals for the Dramaten production, he commented: "In the end, I have stressed the fact that the only thing that can give man any kind of salvation – a secular one – is the grace and compassion that come out of himself."[25]

In technical terms, Bergman's approach to a key speech such as this is fascinating. His direction, Egil Törnqvist remarks in his rehearsal diary of the Dramaten performance, "suggests parallels with the work of both a conductor and a choreographer. Frequently he demonstrates how a speech can be broken up into shorter movements, each one with its own particular tone, so that the speech as a whole is molded into a word-melody, rich in psychological nuances. And on the stage he demonstrates, usually by applying his hands in various ways, the positions, gestures, and movement patterns of the actors."[26] A glance at the production script itself (in Törnqvist's scrupulous transcription) provides an excellent beat-by-beat illustration of just how the Bergman technique of detailed textual orchestration affects the speech we have been considering:

THE MUMMY *(frankly and seriously):* But *I* can stop time in its course. *I* can wipe out the past, *(looks at the Colonel)* undo what is done.
(The Colonel, the Fiancée, and the Baron raise their eyes to the Mummy. The Mummy crosses to the clock, lays a hand on the dial. The ticking stops.)
THE MUMMY: Not with bribes, not with hatred. But through suffering . . . and repentance.
(The projection of a brickwall [which had appeared earlier on Hummel's sarcastic lines about "this estimable house"] *dims.)*
(The Mummy crosses down behind the Colonel, lays hold of him, looks at Hummel. The Colonel takes her hand.)
THE MUMMY: We *are* poor miserable creatures, we know that. We *have* erred, we *have* transgressed, like all the rest. We *are* not what we seem to be. At bottom we are better than ourselves, since *we* abhor and detest our misdeeds. *(Crosses down behind Hummel. Fighting back tears, spitefully:)* But when you Jacob Hummel with your false name . . .
(The Colonel, the Fiancée, and the Baron begin again to raise their heads.)

THE MUMMY: . . . come here to sit in judgement, *that* proves that you are more contemptible . . .

(The brickwall projection vanishes. The chairs in the round salon [on which the actors in the scene are seated] are lighted very strongly from the back and the front.)

THE MUMMY: . . . than we are. And you . . . you . . . you are not the one you seem to be [. . .][27]

During rehearsals, Bergman provided an additional note that en-larges our sense of Hummel's physical reaction to the Mummy's coming assault in this sequence:

When Hummel, in his long speech, reveals the hidden crimes of everyone present, the audience must be able to feel how he grows and grows, like a frog blowing himself up, while the others keep shrinking. Then comes the counter-attack from the Mummy. She gives Hummel three pricks ["you . . . you . . . you"]. Now it is his turn to shrink. When he has just received the third prick, he thinks: all right, I can stand all this, just as long as you don't

The assault of the Mummy on Hummel. Dramaten, 1973.

start talking about the Milkmaid I've murdered. At this point the Milkmaid appears. Produced by Hummel's anguish.[28]

The lattice of dynamic human relationships into which Bergman translated Strindberg's text in this scene – for example, the obvious bond of tenderness and loyalty between the Mummy and the Colonel, the continuous, oscillating struggle between Hummel and his victims, the role of the Mummy as both prosecutor and executioner – is conceived, here as always in his work, primarily as a concrete, physical pattern of movements and gestures. Inevitably, Elia Kazan's observation that directing "finally consists of turning Psychology into Behavior" comes to mind. One fundamental difference here, however, lies in the nature of the material itself: "Remember, we are not playing psychological theater, but something higher," Bergman told the cast at Dramaten. "The rhythm of the play is tremendously important. Here there are no connecting links, as in Ibsen's plays, which are much easier to act. Here you have to turn on a dime."[29] Nevertheless, the aggressiveness and sheer emotional vehemence that he injected into the ghost supper scene in the 1973 revival of the play might equally well have found a place in a performance of Williams or Albee – as indeed they did, in his own lacerating productions of these two playwrights at Dramaten during the 1960s.

The intense, Shylock-like Hummel of Toivo Pawlo was not the tottering, shattered giant that Benkt-Åke Benktsson had created twenty years before in Malmö. Strindberg's stage directions describe the old man in the black frock coat as basically passive, shriveled up "like a dying insect," once his past is brought to light. By contrast, Pawlo's image of Hummel was a poisonous pistachio-green spider who fought actively and desperately to the last, and who had literally to be dragged to his extermination by Johansson, the servant whom he had enslaved by blackmail. When the Mummy ordered him into the closet to hang himself, he attempted several steps without his crutches, fell, and then rolled sprawling on the floor in an effort to escape, uttering unintelligible noises all the while. Johansson, sensing his slavery at an end, leaped brutally on his struggling master, dragged him bodily into the closet, and shut it. As the Mummy ordered Bengtsson – portrayed in this production as an old enemy of Hummel's – to place the death screen before the closet door and he then stepped ominously behind it, cold light filled the stage and the "normal" projection of a heavy, cluttered drawing room interior reappeared. A snapping sound was heard from the closet, followed by a death rattle; the Mummy, who opened the closet door and looked inside to be certain, spoke her lines to the others with quiet satisfaction: "It is finished. May God have mercy on his soul." Their "Amen" was not spoken in unison as the text prescribes, but was repeated in turn by the Colonel, the Fiancée, Bengtsson, and "very brightly" by the Baron: "It must not become too ritualistic," Bergman explained. When the final Amen was uttered, the sound of harp tones broke in as the Young Lady, seated in the background with Arkenholz, began to accompany the first of the Student's two recitations of the so-called Song of the Sun.[30]

What might seem like harsh usage of Hummel in this production was fully prepared for, however, by the excruciating sequence that Bergman composed to illustrate, in concrete terms, Hummel's brutal "unmasking" of the Colonel–played by Anders Ek in an almost caricatured parade-dress uniform of scarlet and gold braid–earlier in the scene. What is in the text a short, rather inert speech about stripping the pretentious Colonel naked became a starkly physical torture scene–"and the old man greatly enjoys prolonging the torture." Once again, the Törnqvist transcription of the production book affords a very illuminating illustration of Bergman's method of translating text into action:

HUMMEL *(leaps up, pushes the Colonel down on a chair which overturns, landing the Colonel on the floor):*   Take off that hair of yours!
COLONEL *(on his knees, groans, and obeys).*
HUMMEL *(points):*   Have a look at yourself in the mirror! Take out your false teeth while you're at it! Tear off that moustache! *(The Colonel obeys. Hummel thrusts him over to the left.)*
HUMMEL: Let Bengtsson *(slits up the Colonel's uniform so that a corset is exposed)* unlace your metal corset . . .
COLONEL *(closes his eyes).*
HUMMEL: . . . and then we shall see if a certain valet, Mr. XYZ, won't recognize himself! A valet who used to flirt with the maid in order to scrounge in a certain kitchen.
COLONEL *(takes hold of the bell on the table and rings).*
HUMMEL *(grasps the Colonel by the neck and pushes him so that he falls forward on the floor):*   Don't touch that bell! If you call Bengtsson, I'll have him arrested! *(The clock strikes six.)*
HUMMEL *(standing over the Colonel with his crutch):*   Here come the guests!
[. . .][31]

At that point the terrorized and decimated officer crawled on his knees to the table, and began to replace his social mask–his wig, his glued-on moustache, his false teeth–before the eyes of the audi-

Hummel's destruction of the Colonel (Georg Årlin), who holds the
paper disproving his right to his name. Malmö, 1954.

Ek and Pawlo in the same situation in 1973. The Colonel is stripped not only of his name, but also of his hair piece, his false moustache, and finally even his uniform.

ence. Seldom has the critical commonplace "spiritual striptease" acquired such tangible reality in a theater. "When this overstuffed peacock with his center-parted wig, stupidly slack jaw, and a waxed moustache that resembles a question mark is stripped bare before our very eyes by Hummel, he is transformed into miserable, quivering human wreckage," declared Leif Zern in *Dagens Nyheter*.

It is not, of course, the macabre universe of the ghost supper in itself that constitutes the severest challenge to a director undertaking Strindberg's *Sonata*, but rather the requirement that the mood of this dark middle movement must be convincingly integrated into the overall melodic pattern of the composition. Allan Bergstrand observed, in conjunction with Bergman's Malmö production, that any director who attempts this play is in a sense faced with a basic choice: "whether to stage it, as Molander has done with all his Strindberg productions, in terms of naturalistic scenes into which mysticism and unreality are blended as completely natural elements – as they seem to be for all believers in spirits – or, instead, to opt for an undecorated expressionism in which characters appear out of or disappear into the darkness." Gunnar Ollén, who uses the observation in his well-known study of Strindberg, adds that Bergman chose "by and large a middle road" in his 1954 production[32] – a kind of conflation of Reinhardt's unadorned expressionism and the "fantastic realism" of Molander that moved in three deliberate tempi, from the dream-sharp everyday details of the first-act setting to a much more stylized milieu of heavy drapes in the second act and, finally, to a starky simplified, symbolic hyacinth room in the last movement. By the time of the 1973 revival, however, the "middle road" had led Bergman far beyond the confines of either conventional expressionism or the traditions of the Molander style, to the adoption of his own highly expressive, interpretative mode of staging.

In none of Strindberg's later plays is there any hard and fast distinction between what is real and what is not – life, for Strindberg, *is* a dream, and hence the dream (the play) is life itself – not a conceptual comment on "the dreamlike nature" of reality but a projected image of a psychic dynamism, an exteriorization of *what it feels like* to experience existence in this way. As a result, Molander's most strenuous objection to Reinhardt's style was its failure to perceive and come to grips with Strindberg's view of life, and hence his own productions strove to reincorporate the razor-sharp fragments of observed (autobiographical) reality that are embedded in this playwright's vision. Thus, the "facade of a new house on a city square" that is described in such close detail at the beginning of *The Ghost Sonata* was identified by Molander as Karlaplan 10, the stately mahogany-and-marble entrance to the building in the Östermalm district of Stockholm in which Strindberg had resided (with an entrance at the much less patrician address of Karlavägen 40 "around the corner") following his marriage to Harriet Bosse in May of 1901.[33] His first production at Dramaten, which had impressed Bergman so profoundly in 1942, incorporated all the essential details and the characteristic sounds (church bells, horse-drawn carriages, steamship bells from the Nybrovik docks) of this turn-of-the-century Östermalm milieu. The impressionistic projection of the red building on Karlaplan might, remarked Herbert Grevenius in *Stockholms–Tidningen* (October 17, 1942), "at first seem like a color photograph, but there is a slight overexposure that quickly emerges with dreamlike clarity in the colors and contours."

It was with this potent visual treatment of the opening scene that Molander ultimately left his clearest "fingerprint" on his disciple's revival of *The Ghost Sonata* in Malmö. Bergman had once again reshaped the huge stage of the Malmö City Theatre to his own purpose – this time, by narrowing the proscenium opening to forty-six feet (from its usual seventy-two), reducing the seating capacity to a "mere" 1,100 (from the customary 1,700), and raising the stage and extending it out into the auditorium. He thereby succeeded in creating an unexpectedly intimate atmosphere in the vast theater. Behind the proscenium masking on either side of the stage, special light towers were erected to provide for sculptural backlighting of the actors and to facilitate the use of the projections on which Martin Ahlbom's scene design for the play depended. The first of these projections left no doubt about the Molander influence: "Not the walls of Karlaplan 10 – that would have been copying – but in any case a tautly realistic Östermalm prospect with banal doorway statues on guard outside the aristocratic residence, with the advertisement kiosk and drinking fountain, with Oscar's Church projected in the background, and with church chimes and steamship bells as atmospheric sound effects," wrote Per Erik Wahlund in *Svenska Dagbladet*. However, although there was nothing ostensibly abstract or "strange" about the milieu into which the Student innocently wanders, a distinctly hallucinatory, film-gray ambience was created by the lighting and sustained by the eerie, puppetlike movements of the peripheral characters. These individuals, preoccupied with themselves and with life's trivial tasks, seemed to move like ghostly marionettes about the large gray-white house. As Hummel told the

Hummel and the Student (Folke Sundquist) at the advertisement
kiosk. Malmö, 1954.

Student about the unfortunate inhabitants of the Colonel's house "and they appeared in their windows, nodding, laughing, watering flowers," the critic for *Stockholms–Tidningen* felt himself faced with "a perfectly staged marionette number: Hummel sits at the outer edge of the stage as the coldly calculating director."

The focal character in *The Ghost Sonata* is, of course, Arkenholz, the clairvoyant student whose "progress" we follow from his initial meeting with the scheming Hummel outside the house to his final encounter with the Young Lady in the symbolic hyacinth room. But in this dream play is the Student, then, the Dreamer? Bergman's production of it in Malmö was clearly conceived to suggest so, by dissociating Arkenholz from the other characters in terms of tone, makeup, gesture, and general appearance – although the concept caused its share of critical confusion. The idea of the play as a dream was reinforced by a curiously old-fashioned staging device. Behind a neutral front curtain ("smooth and rat-gray like the human consciousness just before sleep comes," thought Wahlund) hung a transparent scrim that actually was kept in place throughout the performance, "as a barely visible veil between the stage reality and the auditorium." Swirling clouds of "mind-mist" were projected on this curtain at the beginning and between the acts, as a pedagogical reminder of the dream – in emulation, it might almost seem, of the film maker's custom-honored semiotic indicators for flashback and dissolve.

The basic concept of the play as the Student's dream did not, however, fully succeed in welding the potentially anticlimactic third act – the traditional stumbling block in most interpretations – to the rest of the play. "Life is terrible and we must toil through it. But since it is at bottom only a nightmare, dreamed in this case by the young student, the last human being in a dying world, then there is redemption to be found beyond time and space," contended Nils Beyer in *Morgon–Tidningen.* Many of the critics took a different view of the conclusion, however. "The lyricism, the Buddhistic doctrine, and the beautiful words about a heaven that shall grow up from the earth are completely lacking in the dramatic bite that the damnation of the ghost supper in the Colonel's salon possesses," declared Kragh-Jacobsen in *Berlingske Tidende.* "It is finely conceived but it is dramatically pale – besides which it follows the bitterest of Strindberg's denunciations of life's most banal vexations." Deliberate paleness seemed in fact to dominate the setting – a severe white interior in elegant *Jugendstil,* furnished chiefly with strongly denotative object–symbols: a white harp (frozen music), a marble statue (petrified beauty), a slender white chair (loneliness), and the obligatory image of Buddha.[34] The complacent vision of Arnold Böcklin's Island of the Dead, which Strindberg's stage directions suggest as the final image following the death of the Young Lady, was banished by Bergman, who considers the painting "a hideous work of art" – perhaps not unexpectedly so, since a reproduction of it hung conspicuously in his childhood home in Uppsala! In his Malmö production, he chose instead to punctuate the play's progression toward purification and atonement with a more human – although perhaps no more dramatically logical – visual effect. In this final tableau, Folke Sundquist's Arkenholz drew aside the death screen once more, in order to take the Young Lady's head in his hands: "The light went down on the Student holding Gaby Stenberg's magnificent face in his lap," Ebbe Linde observed in *Dagens Nyheter* – and one of his colleagues even thought he caught a glimpse of a single ray of golden sunlight playing on the young man's face.

It was clearly his own sense of dissatisfaction with this approach to the final act of *The Ghost Sonata* that animated the radically revised interpretation that Bergman presented at Dramaten almost twenty years later (January 13, 1973). The accomplishment of three basic objectives seemed to underlie this new approach: the forging of an organic relationship between the last act and the rest of the play; the articulation of a less artificially "symbolic" and hence more meaningful resolution to the last act, in line with the concept of "secular salvation"; finally, the adoption of a far more simplified, actor-oriented approach to the production as a whole. The first two of these objectives are related to the specific play. The third point, however, is more general and is related to the radical change in Bergman's directorial outlook that first became evident in his famous open-stage production of Büchner's *Woyzeck* in 1969. A published rehearsal diary of that production makes it abundantly clear that Bergman himself saw it as a turning point. "We in the theater have always sought the best possible circumstances: in terms of staging, acoustics, audience," he told the *Woyzeck* cast at their first meeting:

That is precisely what we have contributed to year in and year out: a theater of circumstances. The time has come for us to skip all that, to be strong enough to compel the audience. We can do that if we are sufficiently convinced, if we perform with sufficient awareness.

All true actors . . . have magnetic power built in. They need only to reveal themselves on the stage for tension to be created. They themselves create the magic.

A busy director can destroy that magic in an instant with too much scenery, lighting, and so on. He can detheatricalize the actors.

Sundquist's Student and Gaby Stenberg's Young Lady in the final moment of the Malmö production.

The fantastic thing about theater is the communication between the audience's longing and the actors' urge to meet it.

I have myself previously preached theater of circumstances. But during the two years I have been away [following a critical failure with Molière's *The School for Wives* in November 1966] I have come to realize that this is a mistake. We must abandon that sort of thing if the theater is to survive.[35]

These principles had an immediate and startling practical effect on the style of Bergman's Strindberg productions at Dramaten during the 1970s – an effect that became apparent at once in the radically simplified, chamber-play adaptation of *A Dream Play* that he presented in 1970, and that was, if possible, even more pronounced in his revival of *The Ghost Sonata* three years later. In the latter case, the play was performed on a virtually bare stage that had to be stripped of every object and every item of scenery that might, in the director's opinion, "block the action or make it heavy." His designer, Marik Vos, devised a remarkable response to this challenge – a permanent, open acting-area enclosed in a semicircle by two towering, almost Craig-like screens, and flanked by low risers at the sides and a sloping platform at the back between the screens (see Figs. 1–3). Two significant objects were positioned at either side of the proscenium, as suggestive physical reminders (not symbols) of key psychological impulses in Bergman's interpretation: an antique standing clock (Time, the passage of which the Mummy is able to halt in the second act), and the marble statue of a young and attractive woman (the Mummy as she once was in the past, just as she is in the present what the Young Lady, her daughter and alter ego, will eventually become). Other objects were used with extreme economy, and their rigorously symmetrical placement underlined the basic thematic relationship of one act to another.

Hence, in the first movement only Hummel's wheelchair and the street fountain at which the ghostly Milkmaid offers the Student a drink of water stood on the empty stage; in the last movement these were replaced, in precisely the same relative positions, by a chair in which the Student sits and the white harp and chair of the Young Lady. In turn, the arrangement of the hyacinth room in this act, with the slender white chairs and the harp occupying the foreground, presented a precise mirror image of the Colonel's salon, where heavy black chairs stood in a somber semicircle for the ghost supper. There, the audience had been able to see Arkenholz and the Young Lady seated on the raised platform at the rear of the stage. When the young couple's turn then came in the final movement, these positions were simply reversed and the room was shown, as it

Figure 1 Floor plan, *The Ghost Sonata*, act 1.

were, from the opposite angle: The audience could now see the funereal chairs of the Mummy and the Colonel on the platform in the background – and could draw its own conclusions about the interchangeability of roles in Strindberg's dream universe.

In general, human figure composition rather than inert scenery was the raw material of Bergman's directorial concept for this production of *The Ghost Sonata*: "The important thing is what happens to the bodies. No furnishings that overshadow the action, nothing that stands around anywhere unless [it contributes to] a choreographic pattern that must be able to move with complete freedom in relation to space and scenery. Nothing must get in the way."[36] The ultimate success of this strategy is illustrated in the very observant description offered by the critic for *Göteborgs–Posten*, Åke Perlström: "The characters are at all times forcefully liberated from the setting. They stand close together on the forestage, and we perceive them in

Figure 2 Floor plan, *The Ghost Sonata*, act 2.

closeups. Stronger than this concentration can hardly become: Bergman has created a pressure from the stage toward the auditorium,
eliminating all distance."

"Scenery," as such, was suggested entirely by means of lighting
and projections on the two concave screens and on the cyclorama
visible beyond them in the background. (Originally, even the marble
statue and the standing clock were conceived of by Bergman as
projections only; ultimately, the tangible reality of these two properties was attenuated in a more unusual way, by means of projected
shadows of palm fronds that played over them.) In the first act, the
projections of an actual turn-of-the-century Stockholm house and
church facade might at first glance have seemed yet another repetition of that familiar Molander trademark, Karlaplan 10. But Bergman's distinctively stylized, antinaturalistic approach to the play
soon adjusted this impression. The *same* film-gray house

Figure 3 Floor plan, *The Ghost Sonata*, act 3.

facade projected on each of the mammoth thirty-foot screens evoked the half-real feeling of a dream. Moreover, during Hummel's descriptions of the blighted fates of the residents, both he and Arkenholz faced the audience continuously and located the imaginary house *in the auditorium* (where, at the same time, the audience continued to look at a distorted mirror image of the house behind the actors). Typically, Bergman explained this Pirandellian maneuver in purely practical terms – as a device to enable the spectator to see the faces and reactions of the actors, rather than just their backs. Just as typically, a number of critics were inclined to attach deeper significance to it as well: "We, the audience, are like the bogus colonel and the other inhabitants of the house – counterfeits with ugly secrets and a guilt-ridden past," proposed the reviewer for *Sydsvenska Dagbladet Snällposten.*

In general, the use of light and of projection techniques in this production reflected, perhaps more strikingly than many previous

Stage setting for the first scene of *The Ghost Sonata*, designed by Marik Vos. Dramaten, 1973.

Setting for the third scene in the 1973 production of *The Ghost Sonata*, with the brickwall projection seen on the high screens in the background.

stage productions by him, the director's extraordinary sensitivity to the atmospheric properties and nuances of the photographic medium. Like the house and church in the first act, both the heavy, picture-cluttered salon interior projected for the ghost supper and the high, drapery-festooned windows that signified the hyacinth room in the last act displayed the same soft, dreamlike diffuseness of focus. One is reminded of Bergman's remark that "there is no art form – painting and poetry included – that can communicate the specifically oneiric quality of the dream the way the art of the film can."[37] Cinematic, too, were the fades and dissolves that were interpolated at intervals. At a crucial point in each of the three acts – when the Milkmaid whom Hummel has presumably drowned emerges (out of a trap in the stage floor) before him; when Hummel begins his denunciation of the household at the ghost supper; and when the Student in turn lashes out at the decay of the house and the Young Lady – the projection denoting place (street, round salon, hyacinth room) faded and was replaced by a purely connotative projection of a high, bare brickwall. The Student's remark about "this penal colony, madhouse and morgue of a world" acquired, in these moments, graphic substantiation. The implications of this recurrent and evocative image are fascinating, however, precisely because they are multiple and unattached to a simple, singular meaning. (At one stage, Bergman had evidently intended to project gradually withering hyacinths as an "illustration" of the hyacinth room; his excision of illustrative projection is characteristic of his resistance to overt, directly attached symbolism. Ultimately, only the bluish white lighting of the scene and the hyacinth blue of the Young Lady's costume were used to convey what Bergman perceived as "a sense that she has surrounded herself with a barrier of color and warmth and fragrance."[38])

As had been the case in the earlier Malmö production, projections were again used to sustain a hallucinatory, dreamlike atmosphere in the auditorium during the brief intervals that were needed for changes of scene and costume. In this instance, however, a much more abstract "snowfall" comprised of rising and falling dots of light projected on an opaque scene curtain took the place of the swirling "mind-mists" of the previous version. With regard to the identity of the dreamer of this dream play, however, a more fundamental change had occurred in Bergman's thinking. Although it is perfectly possible to identify the figure of the Poet in A Dream Play as Strindberg's alter ego and then proceed, as Bergman had done with success in his 1970 production, to present him as a connecting and controlling consciousness in the play, the character of the Student in *The Ghost Sonata* is not – as Bergman himself had now come to realize – particularly adaptable to this role of omniscient observer. "No, it is Strindberg himself who is the dreamer," he told his cast at Dramaten. "Notice the inward movement of the play, from the street to the round salon and finally to the hyacinth room. Strindberg takes us by the hand and leads us ever deeper into the dream."[39] A fleeting visual sign of this idea was the out-of-focus image of the elder Strindberg that materialized on the scene curtain between the second and third acts – almost a reminiscence of the crepe-hung portrait of Strindberg that had decorated the setting for *The Pelican* over thirty years before!

In itself, of course, a visual effect such as this would do little to accomplish what one takes to be the primary objective of this reinterpretation – namely, the forging of an organic relationship between the first two acts of the play and its potentially anticlimactic conclusion. The theatrical solution that Bergman offered to this dramaturgical problem was audacious and, to some minds, even extreme. As always in his work, however, his "solution" was designed to clarify emotional responses rather than to address abstract symbolic considerations; as such, it found expression first and foremost in a realignment of internal character relationships rather than in external visual or aural effects. "The fact that the Young Lady is slowly turning into another Mummy is a fundamental idea in my production," he is quoted as saying. "This is what is so horrifying in the whole situation."[40] To project this idea on the stage, he at first had intended to let the actors who played the Mummy and Hummel also take the parts of the Young Lady and the Student in the last act. Ultimately, only the female half of this astonishing twinning operation was put into practice, and the brilliant and versatile Gertrud Fridh (helped by a nonspeaking stand-in as needed) assumed the exceedingly demanding double role of mother and daughter – the Mummy of the middle act thus became the Young Lady of the first and last movements. Mathias Henrikson's Arkenholz was also provided with enough facial resemblance to the Hummel of Toivo Pawlo (beard, moustache, even a glass eye in common) to suggest the director's view that the Student was in reality a Hummel in embryo: "He is no longer the pure-hearted young man who dashes on the stage in the beginning. In that he has taken Hummel's hand, he is initiated."[41]

These role realignments brought about in turn a full-scale reassessment of the basic tone and the emotional configurations of the difficult final movement of the sonata. "In the third act, Bergman believes, we are led into the deepest part of the dream, the infantile, where all normal proportions have ceased to operate," declared the reviewer for *Svenska Dagbladet*. "The intense aspirations and the everyday torments of human life are here compressed into a single scene of exorcism, supplication, damnation, lamentation, and lyricism." Perlström's fine analysis in *Göteborgs–Posten* came straight to the emotional point of the Mummy's transmutation: "She returns again in the third act, the same person trapped in the daughter's destiny, to become a new sacrificial victim. The Student, the young hero of the first acts, cannot help her, on the contrary he drives her to her death with his absolute demands. He has in fact taken on the role of Hummel, and the Colonel reaches out toward his dead daughter as someone might stretch out a hand to a drowning man."

At the very core of Bergman's remarkable paraphrase is a statement that he made to his cast at an early rehearsal:

And this we must bear in mind continually, that the Student kills the Young Lady. And this is an unpleasant and terrifying scene of unmasking and murder. It corresponds to the unmasking of Hummel by the Mummy in the second act, but here it is enormously much more freed of every shred of reality. . . . Here it is only with ugly words that he touches her, he makes violent gestures toward her, doesn't he, he seizes hold of her, he tears off her clothing. And this kills her.[42]

"That 'doesn't he' is truly disarming," the eminent Strindberg scholar Gunnar Brandell later declared. "Not many would in reality go along with the validity of this interpretation, yet no one in Bergman's ensemble seems to have registered a divergent opinion." Brandell goes on to make a lucid intellectual case for the "traditional" interpretation of the Young Lady's death: in additon to the Hummels of this world, there are in Strindberg also "human beings of a more delicate fibre, who never have been able to harden themselves to live, to withstand the truth of life. This is the Young Lady's situation, and her death in the third part is intended as a liberation, a wandering into the Böcklin picture toward a nothingness that is worth far more than blood, dirt, and tears." The Student, the Sunday child, is "the wanderer, perhaps the poet, standing halfway outside as so many figures in Strindberg do, with traces of the Good Samaritan and perhaps even of Christ." He does not join the living dead nor does he die at all, because "he is essentially just a student on a field trip to 'this penal colony, madhouse and morgue of a world.' "[43]

Bergman's radically divergent and very much harsher stage interpretation of these characters and this scene should not, however, be
misconstrued as deliberate critical "revision" of some established
view of literary scholars – indeed, the fundamental irrelevancy of
such a view to the purely practical concerns of the director is the
essence of his adamant objection that "absolute word fidelity is
trumpery in the theater. The text is not a prescription but raw material, a frequently hidden path into the writer's consciousness."[44]
Rather, he must make choices that can help to articulate, in theatrical terms, the basic thematic transitions in this scene, from the
tenderness of the hyacinth poetry to the bitterness of the household
concerns introduced by the Cook and back to the tenderness of the
final benediction. The path that he charted for the actors was sign-
posted by the simple active verbs (touches her, gestures toward her,
seizes her, strips her, kills her) that are the most striking feature of
the particular directorial comment cited previously and of his in-
structional method in general.

An intricate rhythmic pattern of movement, gesture, intonation,
and tempo changes – supported by suggestive changes in the lighting
and the projections – rendered transparent the moment-by-moment
process of gradual "mummification" in Gertrud Fridh's performance.
"She develops backwards," observed Zern in *Dagens Nyheter:* "the
role of the mother is taken over by her step by step in a process that
the actress reproduces with alarming precision." A vocabulary of
expressively repetitive gestures was devised to reinforce the growing
resemblance of the Young Lady to her grotesque parrot-parent.
When she had to answer a question, for example, Fridh thrust her
head out in front of her shoulders, while her hands fluttered helplessly up under her chin. At other times, her fingertips were seen pressed
against her forehead as her hands covered her face – a movement, one
critic thought, "in which the full impression of a sleepwalker on the
verge of the fatal awakening is concentrated" (*Göteborgs Handels – och
Sjöfartstidning*).

The appearance of the monstrous Cook, who "belongs to the
Hummel family of vampires" and cannot be dismissed, touched off
the final disintegration:

YOUNG LADY *(grabs hold of the Student):* Don't be angry. . . . Practice pa-
    tience. She's part of the trials we have to endure in this house. *(with slight
    "mummy intonation" and parrot gestures)* But we have a housemaid, too.
    Whom we have to clean up after.
THE STUDENT: I can feel myself sinking. *Cor in aethere. (sits)* Music!
YOUNG LADY *(covers her face with her hands):* Wait!

THE STUDENT (*passionately, desperately*):   Music!

YOUNG LADY (*takes her hands down*):   Patience. . . . (*matter-of-factly*) This room is called the testing room. It's beautiful to look at, but it's full of imperfections.[45]

As the desperation of the Student and the defensive "mummy" reactions of the Young Lady grew more emphatic, a cold, harsh light began to dominate the forestage. The long monologue with which Arkenholz "murders" Adele began as a purely verbal threat, made menacing by his alternating moves of approach and withdrawal. The image of the naked brickwall that replaced the hyacinth room interior on the screens was a direct visual response to the Student's bitter description of the madhouse where his father died for truth – but it also carried broader connotations in Bergman's concept: "The Student and the Young Lady," he explained, "are now in the same prison in which the others have lived all their lives, those who have deformed them. They are locked together in a kind of hell, and it is not until she dies that the air and light return."[46]

The brickwall projection, silently proclaiming the prisonhouse in which the young couple found themselves, signaled an emotional change in the Student's monologue, which now acquired a new tone of increased aggressiveness: "If you keep silent too long, stagnant water accumulates and things begin to rot. That's what's happening in this house." His struggle to regain the air and the light became more physical and more overtly violent – while, on the platform in the background, the Colonel and the Mummy (i.e., Fridh's stand-in) began, for the first time, to take notice of the events occurring in front of them in the hyacinth room. The Student's implied sexual challenge to the Young Lady – "speaking of which, where can one find virginity?" – marked another important transition, given graphic and savage physical expression by this Arkenholz, who brutally spread her thighs and thrust his hand between her legs. In Bergman's dynamic orchestration, the monologue reached an explosive climax on the key line that follows the Student's futile attempt to coax music from the Lady's mute, deaf harp: "To think that the most beautiful flowers are so poisonous. They are the most poisonous." At this juncture, in a paroxysm of anger and frustration, he dragged his adversary forcibly to the front of the stage; as she sank to her knees in anguish, her hyacinth blue dress tore loose and fell from her in tatters. Beneath it, she wore a ragged and soiled undergarment of grayish white – virtually a mummy's winding sheet! – streaked with red down the sides and in the outlines of the crotch.

Unmasked and literally put to death by the lacerating truth that the Student has compelled her to face ("There are poisons that seal the eyes and poisons that open them"), the Young Lady calls for the death screen – and at this moment in Bergman's version the wall projection vanished, leaving an empty background bathed in the soft, mild light of liberation (the equivalent of Strindberg's problematic direction that "the room vanishes"). In view of the conception of the Student as the Young Lady's "murderer," he was poorly suited to be the speaker of the closing lines of consolation to her – and one of the director's most interesting moves in this production was to divide these concluding lines between the Colonel and the Mummy. The Colonel, who had undergone a startling change from the stylish, red-uniformed martinet of the second act to a Beckettian old man in a worn gray bathrobe and slippers, delivered the first portion of the Student's speech, "Your liberator is coming – welcome, pale and gentle one," as he gently and affectionately covered Adele with the screen. All religious references were now excised from this moment of purely secular salvation, however, and the only Buddhistic intimation was created by such suggestions as the old man's humble sitting position on the stage floor and by his mild tone of resignation. The Song of the Sun was again spoken by the Student, but the poem's tone of optimistic affirmation was now deliberately undercut by Mathias Henrikson's reading of it, reflecting Bergman's own conviction that the poem is ultimately "nonsense" for a modern audience: "If the Student reads the poem with a skeptical tone the second time he recites it and recognizes that it turns to dust, then it seems to me meaningful. . . . Every second comment in that verse seems dubious. And especially after Strindberg himself gives a brilliant demonstration of man's gruesomeness and madness, I think it is quite right that the Student reaches this conclusion."[47] Unlike the production in Malmö, no touching tableau was struck and no ray of sunlight played on Arkenholz's face. After finishing his recital, he repeated the last word of the poem, "innocent," with utter disbelief in his voice – and then simply walked away into the darkness.

In this version, Strindberg's final words of consolation were spoken instead by the Mummy, and the effect thus created became one of the most arresting moments in this remarkable production. Concealed by the death screen, from behind which an outstretched female arm protruded (shades of the famous "glowing cigar" trick in William Gillette's old play, *Sherlock Holmes!*), Gertrud Fridh exchanged places with her stand-in and was able to resume her Mummy costume during the delivery of the Song of the Sun (certainly one good reason for retaining the troublesome speech). As Arkenholz concluded the poem, the Mummy entered. Slowly, she removed the death screen to reveal the prostrate form of the "Young Lady," and – as harp music sounded from an unseen Toten Insel – she spoke the closing lines of benediction over "this child of the world of disappointments, guilt, suffering, and death" – in essence, a benediction over the corpse of her former self.

"The third act no longer appears as a romantic appendage to the first two acts," Zern declared in his review. "What happens in the hyacinth room is well prepared for during the ghost supper, where the phases of bourgeois family life are depicted and laid bare by a Strindberg more furious than ever. The bourgeois society reproduces itself according to the eternal law of repetition, the main theme and the secondary theme fit together like Chinese boxes." If we overlook the unnecessarily narrow "social" bias that this critic wants invariably to attach to Bergman's approach, his perception of the director's ultimate purpose is clear and helpful: "The truly fascinating thing about this solution is that it reshapes the play into a whole in which everything is accomplished with remorseless dramatic logic."

This "reshaping" process – which we have followed in close detail in the Bergman versions of *The Ghost Sonata* – has been an unmistakable hallmark of all of his Strindberg revivals at Dramaten during the 1970s. That it has encountered its share of opposition from literary critics is perhaps predictable enough. *The Ghost Sonata*, argued Brandell in the article cited earlier, "is not constructed according to the principle three steps to hell. It seems to be a triptych in which each section has its own mood and its own theme, regardless of the fact that Strindberg lets many threads run on through the entire weave." Therefore, by attempting to introduce a dramatic progression and logical continuity ("an almost unbroken crescendo") into his production, Bergman "goes his own way and uses Strindberg's text [to create] a dramatic structure of a fundamentally different character." By subordinating either the vacillating, desultory movement of this play or the deliberately repetitive circularity of *To Damascus* to "a straight line, a steadily increasing intensity, ever stronger and more unsettling dream effects," the director thereby makes a sacrifice: "something of the atmosphere, the heaviness, the wearisome *taedium vitae* also disappears."

Such a line of reasoning may be both informed and intellectually stimulating, at least in theory, but it simply does not address the practical task and responsibilities of the director. There is neither space nor occasion here to belabor that much-debated distinction between the written drama and the acted drama – but the distinction *is* a fundamental one in Bergman's artistic charter. He is not a very voluble theorist and he is unlikely to surprise the world by issuing his personal theater poetics. His unconcealed impatience with what he calls the "trumpery" of pedantic "word fidelity," however, is counterbalanced by a very simple but telling statement that is infused with a fierce fidelity of another sort – a fidelity to the intrinsic spirit of the written work he has before him: "I cannot and will not direct a play contrary to the author's intentions. And I have never done so. Consciously. I have always considered myself an interpreter, a re-creator."[48] The last word in this remark is, of course, the operative one. If the text is, as Bergman insists, a "hidden path into the writer's consciousness," the director ultimately must translate the explicit or implicit choices and values he discovers there into his own theater language – which is, in the last analysis, the only language in which a playwright *can* be heard by a living, contemporary audience. The act of producing a play on the stage creates a new organism, an integral work of art responsive, by definition, to a whole new set of circumstances. "In my case it has always been a matter of reading closely. And interpreting in the same way a conductor interprets a score," Bergman tells us. "My intention is not to be an innovator. I want only to present the play and make it live in the hearts of the audience." For, as he reminded spectators who attended the first open rehearsal of *The Ghost Sonata* at Dramaten, "it is in your hearts, in your imagination that the performance must take place."

DREAM PLAYS

Although Bergman's approaches to *The Ghost Sonata* have all tended to emphasize the hallucinatory, dream-play texture of that work, his first stage production of *A Dream Play* itself (March 14, 1970) displayed the coherence and compact clarity of a chamber play. Nearly all of the philosophical and mystical elements in the drama were either omitted or transposed in this imaginative, poetically faithful reinterpretation of Strindberg's difficult masterpiece. Instead, Bergman established a swiftly paced rhythm of contrasts and juxtapositions that revealed the hand of the gifted film maker at work. Stage settings as such were eliminated entirely, and the fifteen compact scenes in this version occupied a playing time of barely an hour and forty-five minutes, uninterrupted by the distraction of an intermission. "There are remarkably few extraneous elements in it, no convulsions, no exertion – all that seems to have been left behind," Zern declared in *Dagens Nyheter* following the premiere at Lilla scenen, Dramaten's 350-seat studio theater. "In itself this represents an essential part of Bergman's method. He has produced an adaptation of the play that is in part quite radical, in part extremely cautious. But in both cases it is a matter of changes that find their basis in the text."

In its style and method *The Dreamplay* (as Bergman chose to retitle his new stage version) represented an astonishing departure from virtually everything that had gone before – including his own television production of the play in 1963, which he now considers a comparative failure. The traditional identification of the Dreamer, in all three of his voices (Officer, Lawyer, and Poet), with Strindberg himself was abandoned, as were all the elaborate visual effects and atmospheric back projections that had by now become fixed conventions of the Molander school. "No castle burns on the stage, no rhetoric flames in the dialogue," Bo Strömstedt wrote in *Expressen*. "Nor is it a biographical Strindberg Show in Molander fashion. Some wear masks in this production – but no one wears a Strindberg mask." Within the stark and utterly simple physical framework devised for the production, no attempt whatsoever was made to reproduce, in literal terms, the many different localities and spectacular stage effects called for in Strindberg's complicated stage directions. Instead, observed Åke Perlström in *Göteborgs–Posten*, "the only thing we see – and hear – are the actors, who create the illusion that all these places are there on the stage. It is a brilliantly executed activation of the audience that we experience." The end result of this dematerialized, actor-oriented approach was, as Per Erik Wahlund remarked in *Kvällsposten*, to give the text a primacy "it seldom can acquire in more monumental productions; anyone who truly wants to listen to what is being said in the play has a unique opportunity here."

A closely knit ensemble of twenty-four performers, who had been in rehearsal – as is often Bergman's custom – for more than three months,[49] played the forty-three different characters identified in this version. All but nine principal actors took on two or, in a few cases, even three roles apiece. As the performance began, the entire acting company – including five extras and even the prompter for the production – were summoned to the gray-black, curtainless stage, which stood furnished with only a scattering of plain wooden chairs, a few screens, and a single table (see Figs. 4, 5). One by one,

LILLA SCEN   ETT DRÖMSPEL

Figure 4 Plan of the stage (Lilla scenen), *A Dream Play*.

Figure 5 Floor plan, *A Dream Play*.

the actors emerged in twin streams from the circular (under normal circumstances backstage) staircases located at either side of the playing area, and, moving to lively waltz music from a barrel organ, they flooded the stage in a carefully choreographed but apparently random pattern (Fig. 6). A few busied themselves rearranging bits of scenery; meanwhile, the Poet (the fourth figure to emerge from the staircase stage right, numbered 20 in the diagram) moved to the table at the center of the stage, where he drew up a chair and seated himself with his back to the audience. Then, once the prompter and the black-masked Quarantine Master (numbered 10 and 11) had reached their positions, the company joined to form a ring. Slowly the characters circled before the gaze (in the consciousness?) of the meditating Poet seated at his desk. "A metaphysical picture of mankind's shadowy wandering in the wilderness" was the description that *Svenska Dagbladet* applied to this evocative image.

After fifteen seconds, in the midst of a step, the rotating circle of dream figures suddenly froze in position. Quietly, the Poet read to them the six simple lines of verse that were to set the tone for all that followed in Bergman's *Dreamplay* – familiar lines that belong in the original to Indra's Daughter in the second of the scenes in Fingal's Cave:

Figure 6 The entrance of the actors in *A Dream Play*.

The earth is not clean.
Life is not good.
Men are not evil.
Nor are they good.
They live as they can,
One day at a time.[50]

The reading of the verse dissolved the magical circle. Some of the figures disappeared once more down the circular staircases, but the majority simply took seats all around the periphery of the action (Fig. 7) – where they became both characters waiting to be called into being by their creator and actors awaiting their entrances. Agnes, the earthly counterpart of Indra's Daughter, and the Glazier sat silently in a corner, eating. In a whisper, like a prompter feeding an actor his cue, the Poet spoke again – "Agnes, the castle is still rising from the earth" – and only then did the characters in the opening scene achieve speech and dramatic life, as Agnes, looking about her,

Figure 7 Taking positions for the first scene of *A Dream Play*.

began to discuss the Growing Castle and the prisoner who waited there for his release.

In a graphic but unpretentious manner, this opening sequence established the metaphor of deliberate theatricality that governed Bergman's production from its beginning to its end. His *Dreamplay* was anchored firmly in a world of theater that became, in turn, a *theatrum mundi*, a poetic and deeply ironic image of the world we live in. The austere and eminently flexible stage setting designed by Lennart Mörk was, in effect, hardly a stage setting at all. The playing area was opened to the full width of the building, and the bare fire walls and rows of projectors were as fully exposed to view as the players themselves. Any separation between actor and spectator was obliterated completely by eliminating the dividing line of the proscenium and extending the floor of the stage out over the first rows of seats. The single, fixed point of focus in the setting – that indispensable "magnetic point of energy" around which Bergman customarily plans all his moves in a particular mise-en-scène – was in this instance obviously the simple table placed at the front of the stage, squarely in the middle of the proscenium opening. Around the Poet's table – beneath which he occasionally crept to eavesdrop on "his" characters – most of the scenes in the play were arranged. "Time and place do not exist," writes Strindberg in his foreword. In this production the places themselves – the theater corridor, the cathedral where the degree ceremony is held, the Lawyer's suffocating chamber, even the enigmatic cloverleaf door itself – were always represented in the simplest possible manner, by means of rudimentary, rehearsal-type screens that could be easily put in place and as easily removed. A small platform at the rear of the stage was its only elevation, and behind this one glimpsed a large red, nonfigurative design that contributed the one patch of color in an otherwise gray-black void. (Mörk's tantalizing optical rebus led to a desperate guessing game among the critics, who professed to discover in it a picture of everything from "the burning castle of the dream" or "the human circulatory system" to "flickering flames from the earth's interior" or, in the case of one especially lively imagination, even "the inside of the eyelid as we see it when we doze off, when we dream.")

"All this with a curtain, blackouts, illusion – this is a profound depravity in the theater," Bergman had declared during the rehearsals for *Woyzeck*,[51] and that production, with its circus-ring staging, its commitment to intense audience contact, and its use of boldly anti-illusionistic scene changes, clearly foreshadowed the theatricalist approach adopted by him in *The Dreamplay* only one year later. Most observers agreed, however, that his newest Strindberg production represented a significant turning point and achieved a completely new level of emotional communication, less stridently expressionistic and hallucinatory than in *Woyzeck* and far more firmly and concretely human. "There is a proximity here to the characters and to their world, an unmitigated sensitivity to them that Bergman never abandons, even when he depicts their darkest aspects, their torments and their pitfalls," remarked Leif Zern.

In this lucid, down-to-earth interpretation of the play as an unadorned depiction of the human condition – of human beings like ourselves "who live as they can, one day at a time" – the divine presence of an omniscient Indra and his Daughter inevitably became a sublimely absurd poetic irrelevancy. The metaphysical apparatus of Eastern mysticism in the play – itself an afterthought on Strindberg's part – was largely abandoned, but what remained of it became a deeply ironic comment on the spectacle of human sorrow and

The redefinition of the theatrical space in Bergman's production of *Woyzeck*. The body of Marie is seen sprawled on a portion of the forestage that jutted out into the auditorium. The empty wooden chairs at the sides were used in the action. Dramaten, 1969.

Figure 8 The entrance of Indra's Daughter in the third scene of *A Dream Play*.

suffering, rather than merely a convenient "explanation" of it. Taking up the playwright's own reminder that "the characters split, double, and multiply" in this drama, Bergman elected to divide the composite character of Indra's Daughter into two distinct and independent roles. The utterly vulnerable Agnes, played by the young Malin Ek with poignant openness and clarity, was wholly and defenselessly human, stripped of the divine power to reascend from earth that renders the Daughter's suffering so much more equivocal in the original. By contrast, the stately and dignified portrayal of the Daughter – the divine half of the equation – created by Kristina Adolphson emphasized the aloofness of that shadowy deity. She and Indra (renamed the Scald here) remained, throughout the play, remote presences from a rhapsodic, scaldic world of fantasy that existed, perhaps, only in the Poet's vivid imagination.

Ironically, Bergman chose not to eliminate the expository prologue in heaven – as Molander, for example, had done in his final production of the work five years before. Instead, his purpose was perfectly served by abruptly interjecting this scene (slightly cut and rearranged) into the midst of the ongoing action, just before the episode in the Theater Corridor, as a bit of theater-in-the-theater. "Yes, life is hard, but love conquers all. Come and see!" the bewildered Agnes is told by the Poet (who borrowed these lines from the dialogue of Indra's Daughter). Then, as these two sat to one side, Indra and his Daughter rose from their chairs in the background and, in full view, mounted the raised platform-stage at the rear, accompanied by the sound of polite applause from the other characters (Fig. 8). Mörk's enigmatic red pattern glowed obediently. A gushy romantic adagio was played on an old piano.[52] At the end of the prologue scene, when Indra had completed his imperious brief of instructions to his Daughter ("Have courage, child, 'tis but a trial"), she sank to her knees ("I'm falling!"). A moment later, as the divinities left their platform and retired to other seats in the background, a swirl of players again filled the stage (see Fig. 9) and the action continued without interruption. The appearance of the Bill-Poster with his placards and his green fishing net, the Prompter carrying a piece of scenery, and the Stage-Door Keeper with her unfinished star cover-let and her heavy shawl of sorrows[53] proclaimed the beginning of the Theater Corridor scene. And here, the tragicomic spectacle of the Officer (Holger Löwenadler), waiting patiently for Victoria with his bouquet of withered roses, became a hieroglyph of human dis-appointment and self-deception that gave the lie to all the spurious metaphysical consolation of Indra's divine design. "The entire Indra phenomenon is transformed by Ingmar Bergman into the supreme theatrical gesture," declared *Svenska Dagbladet*. "But perhaps Berg-man feels that Indra's Daughter is no more than the dream of some-

Figure 9 Taking positions for the Theater Corridor episode in the fourth scene of *A Dream Play*.

one who knew that Indra never had a daughter, and that Agnes is in reality something quite different: the mortal woman, imperturbable in her endurance and her humanity."

Specifically, Indra's Daughter seemed the Poet's dream in this production. Her later appearances at the close of the play were likewise removed from the reality of the situation and remained expressions of the Poet's creative imagination. Seated at his table, he began to read aloud the strophes on poetry, dream, and reality in the Fingal's Cave scene, and alone his reading called forth the Daughter's responses and her presence – although no "soft music" accompanied their recitation, no rolling billows were seen or heard, and no leisurely discussion of "life's unsolved riddle" was allowed to interrupt the insistent flow of the drama toward its conclusion.

In this respect and in others, the greatly expanded role of the Poet – played with effectively restrained intensity by Georg Årlin – replaced the figure of Indra's Daughter as the controlling consciousness in the work. His was the only character to be given a function more important than that in the Strindberg text. He was present throughout but seemed more often to be a detached observer wandering though the proceedings than a participant deeply engaged in them. At times, he appeared to listen to the conversation of the characters as if to a play that he himself might have written. And he, rather than the Officer, became Agnes's guide for the brief, dazzling white glimpse of the "paradise" of Fairhaven that was, in this production, instantly shattered by a bombardment of harsh, visually concrete realities: the palpable dirt and poverty of the Coal-Carriers, the misery of ugly Edith, the pathetic plight of the Blind Man (acted by Hans Stråät, who also played Indra) who possesses everything except his sight, and finally the relentless drudgery of domestic life, which Agnes – deprived here of the comforting ability to "return to the place from which [she] came" – is condemned to resume.

Perhaps the best single illustration of the ironic tone and highly theatricalized style of Bergman's conception is his treatment of the Degree Ceremony in the Cathedral. This remarkable pantomimic tour de force was singled out by virtually every reviewer of the production as one of its most expressive moments. All traces of the grandiose formal trappings that had traditionally encumbered this scene were systematically eliminated, so that only a stark, forceful dream image of the sensation of human humiliation remained. Chopin's Funeral March – the favorite musical choice of Molander for this episode – was turned into a rowdy academic fanfare for the

The appearance of Indra and his Daughter in Bergman's reinterpretation of *A Dream Play*. Dramaten, 1970.

The Officer, Agnes, and the Stage-Door Keeper in the Theater Corridor scene from *A Dream Play*. The cloverleaf door, represented by a free-standing screen, is visible behind the Officer.

occasion. The "cathedral" itself was indicated by the simplest of devices – a contorted tableau of human figures was composed on the Poet's table to suggest an altar painting of the crucified Christ, arms outstretched and head bowed beneath a crown of thorns. Behind this Crucifixion tableau, shadowy figures crept forward with long black screens – the pews of the church – from behind which they watched. The academic procession, too, had the distorted proportions of a dream. The standardbearers of the four faculties were tiny minischolars, played by children, wearing formal attire and student caps, while a dignified gnome assisted the Chancellor in his duty of conferring laurel wreaths on the doctoral candidates. Entering this bizarre scene, the Lawyer (Allan Edwall and, later in the run, Max von Sydow) found himself literally trapped in a nightmarishly logical Chaplinade from which he could not extricate himself. This "terribly ugly, unsuccessful, embittered character in an old tailcoat, shiny with use, that hangs around his shoulders" (Zern) stumbled onto the stage, bowed to the assembly – and then discovered that he was still wearing his galoshes. Desperately, he tried to unbuckle and remove them – only to be assaulted by the foul smell of his wretched old coat, heavy as all his clothes are with "the stink of

A comparable scene from the Munich production of *A Dream Play* at the Residenztheater in 1977.

other men's crimes." Quickly the sniffing spread; soon everyone present was holding his nose. In his mortification the Lawyer then tried to remove the offending coat – with the result that his trousers fell down, and he was reduced to the ultimate indignity of hopping about, unable to pull them up again. All the other candidates were crowned with laurel; the Schoolmaster even did an ecstatic war dance of joy. Only the humiliated advocate was turned away and obliged to rest content with a more "appropriate" crown – the crown of thorns, which Agnes took from the crucified Christ in the tableau and placed upon his head. One final ironic pirouette punctuated the scene. After the crown of thorns had been cast aside, the Poet strolled forward from the background, picked it up and tried it on for size before a mirror (the audience!), cocked it at a rakish angle, like a *chapeau claque*, and strolled away.

The play concluded – in a scene Bergman entitled "Many Persons become Visible" – as it had begun, with the assembling of the characters around the Poet's table. Each one brought forward his or her emblem of suffering to be burnt – the Stage-Door Keeper's shawl, the Officer's roses, the Glazier's diamond, the black mask that made the Quarantine Master "a blackamoor against his will" (but beneath which his face turned out to be just as black as ever). "Instead of casting their masks or their symbols into the fire," observed Wahlund in *Kvällsposten*, "the figures stepped forward one by one to the poet's desk and laid them there. The play has ended, the vision has vanished, and the characters who searched for their author can wander back into the darkness." Once again, the Poet's concluding lines – spoken by Årlin "with moving restraint, as a confidential message directed straight to the audience" – were "borrowed" from the dialogue of Indra's Daughter:

> In the moment of goodbye,
> When one must be parted from a friend, a place,
> How suddenly great the loss of what one loved,
> Regret for what one shattered. . . .

"He steps forward to the edge of the stage, all the others gather around him, as he contemplatively and quietly speaks of parting and of the process of living," wrote the Norwegian reviewer for *Dagbladet* (Oslo). "Because all ornamentation has been eliminated, the words, the actor's voice, and the faces – so far forward on the stage that they appear as closeups – succeed in engraving the Poet's visions upon each spectator's imagination."

Silently, the actors left the stage. The spotlight on the Poet's table

Agnes in the Lawyer's suffocating chamber. Kristin ("I'm pasting")
peers over the top of the screen.

was extinguished. The final image was certainly no Strindbergian
picture of a flowering castle of redemption and deliverance, but
simply a glimpse of Agnes, the woman who has taken upon herself
all of mankind's suffering in her heavy gray shawl, still seated alone
on the empty stage, her hand pressed convulsively to her face in
speechless anxiety.

Although this remarkable contemporary paraphrase of *A Dream
Play* stands as one of the great milestones in Bergman's career as a
stage director, it has by no means become a stopping place for him
in his thinking about this cherished work. Seven years afterwards,
he turned to the play again for his first production in the German-
speaking theater, although here the desired effect of dematerialized
simplicity was largely overshadowed by the Wagnerian dimensions
and solidity of Walter Dörfler's immense setting. ("I wanted a wall,
and he built me a ruin," Bergman remarks wryly.) A new production of *A Dream Play* is definitely included in his plans for the future.
In the interview with which this volume concludes, he describes a
fresh and distinctively different alternative to what he now regards

The Degree Ceremony in the Cathedral: Max von Sydow in the role of
the Lawyer at Dramaten.

as the excessively "pure" and "dogmatic" style of the Stockholm version. Underlying his changing approaches to this play, however, is an unchanged and abiding attraction to the fundamental doubleness of its poetic vision – the perception of the dreamlike quality of reality that is at the same time always conjoined with the insistent reality of the dream. We recognize this perception as a touchstone to which Bergman has returned very often in his more recent work, both in film and theater. His virtuoso "theater film" of Mozart's *The Magic Flute*, which was first presented as a television broadcast on New Year's Day 1975, offers an unexpected but particularly choice example of a production animated by this essentially Strindbergian perception of a reality that is "more than reality – not dreams, but waking dreams." In Mozart's opera, Bergman told a newspaper interviewer, "we experience the strange reality of the dream and the fairy tale":

I see someone, and I am in love with her for all time, in all eternity. The tenderness of the charm, but also the dream's pain and longing. In *The Magic Flute* these things are all present: poetry, fairy tale, and dream. . . .

The final scene of *A Dream Play* as it appeared in the much more elaborate Munich production in 1977.

Tamino outside the temple of wisdom, Pamina with her mother's dagger in her hand, Papageno's search for a Papagena who has suddenly materialized and just as quickly disappeared. These small individuals chase and are chased through a dream and a reality that might just as well have been created by their own imagination.[54]

One important condition invariably qualifies Bergman's strong affinity for the oneiric properties of art, however, and it is a point upon which he insists. "I am extremely suspicious of dreams, apparitions, and visions, both in literature and in films and plays. Perhaps it's because mental excesses of this sort smack too much of being 'arranged,' " he writes in a letter to the cast and crew of *Face to Face*, the four-part film for television that followed soon after *The Magic Flute*. "So when, despite my reluctance and suspicion, I go to depict a series of dreams, which moreover are not my own, I like to think of these dreams as an extension of reality. This is therefore a series of *real* events which strike the leading character during an important moment of her life. . . . The 'dreams' [in the second part of the film] are more real than reality."[55] His major Strindberg productions of the 1970s all afford abundant evidence of this determination to anchor vision and dream in a firm, tangible bedrock of heightened reality.

TOWARD A NEW DAMASCUS

For Bergman, the one true basis of all reality is to be found in the direct confrontation between the audience and the living actor. The spurious realism of a physical setting that purports to be a "facsimile" of life holds no interest for him. "Once you agree that the only important things are the words, the actors, and the audience, then it isn't the setting that matters," he reminds us. Hence, even in the face of severe technical challenges, he has remained steadfastly committed to a style cleansed of everything that would dissipate or detheatricalize the hypnotic presence and power of the living actor. An informal memorandum included at the beginning of the director's own script for his epoch-making production of Strindberg's *To Damascus* – certainly one of the severest challenges he has ever faced in his theatrical career – sheds some revealing light on his method in this respect. This memorandum, entitled simply "Technical Solution," reads in part as follows:

It is always best if one uses for the setting nothing other than lighting, which always indicates the distribution [of scenes]. But I cannot do that here, where all sorts of things have to be shown and must appear and disappear. Therefore I see that we must avail ourselves of our stage platform and a few precise elements and pictures and *four young men who will sit on the stage throughout* and will carry things in and out. . . . Then, the problems are eliminated. All the things are there, standing right there from the beginning.[56]

Bergman's production of the first two parts of the *Damascus* trilogy, which opened at Dramaten on February 1, 1974 to a tumultuous reception, represents in many ways a new and spectacular synthesis of the aims and techniques we have observed at work in the previous productions of his Strindberg cycle. The scheme of visual presentation that his technical memorandum describes is, as always in his work, intimately related to his overall directorial image of the play. In practice, this scheme proved to be in perfect harmony with the mutational dream rhythm that Strindberg's mystical drama of pilgrimage establishes – a drama regarded by the playwright himself as the beginning of "a new genre, fantastic and shining as *Lucky Per*, but playing in a contemporary setting and with a full reality behind it."[57] The scenography, Alf Thoor declared in his review in *Expressen*, "consists of some few, easily portable things that are carried in and out swiftly and noiselessly – here a screen, there a sofa – together with projections on a black wall. In the nightmare scenes, the background is suddenly and silently drawn aloft to reveal a ghostly banquet or a wretched barroom on the outskirts of hell. And then, gone again. Completely without effort, one scene glides into the next in a matter of two or three seconds." Marik Vos, also Bergman's designer in *The Ghost Sonata*, created in this instance a far more complex collage of giant back-projections, consisting for the most part of stylized white-on-black drawings projected on the cyclorama or on a high screen in the center of the stage. (Strindberg, too, had hoped that his backgrounds "could be produced by a shadow picture painted on glass and projected onto a white sheet," but the bold attempt by Emil Grandinson to use sciopticon projections in the first production of *To Damascus I* [1900] had been too far ahead of its time to be technically feasible.) Small movable screens and other portable elements had, of course, earlier been used by Bergman to great advantage in *A Dream Play*. In his *Damascus*, however, the neutral and rather colorless quality of the setting was offset – particularly in such vividly phantasmagoric episodes as the Goldmaker's Banquet – by strong color accents created by the costumes, masks, and figure compositions of the characters. The one other significant detail to which Bergman's technical memorandum makes reference is the low "stage platform" that is clearly visible in several of the production photos reproduced here. This raised, rectangular platform – specified in Figure 10 as measuring 6.4 m in width and 3.6 m in depth, placed 3.0 m from the background but only a bare 20 cm from the forward edge of the stage – deftly established the requisite "magic" point of focus and concentrated energy in Bergman's stage space. Its use has been a hallmark of many of his classical productions in recent years – but in this particular case its presence also seems a direct response to Strindberg's own vigorous plea for a simple, neutral platform stage ("something in the style of Shakespeare's time") that would help to eliminate "all this theatrical tinsel that now engulfs the stage and makes a play heavy without increasing its believability."[58] Indeed, this playwright's ceaseless campaign for the dematerialization of the theater has had no more ardent or intelligent champion than Bergman. Thoor's remark in his review of *Damascus* is characteristic: "This is theater that interests itself almost exclusively in human beings and hardly at all in the things that surround them."

The "full reality" that, Strindberg insists, underlies the anguished pilgrimage of his protagonist toward a distant and elusive salvation is an inner reality – a spiritual, magic realism of the soul that Bergman's interpretation delineated with laser-sharp clarity and with a powerful undertone of black humor and irony. "Strictly speaking only one character in the play is real, and he is called the Unknown," observed the critic for *GT* (Göteborg). "Whatever else happens on the stage may appear more or less real, but in the last analysis it is all a projection of the fantasies, memories, dreams, and imagination of the Unknown." The painful journey of this figure through a private, subjective Inferno was amplified, in Bergman's evocative production, into "a thrilling voyage of discovery into a spiritual landscape . . . where no values are constant, and where reality changes shape with all the remorseless, unpredictable logic of a nightmare. Figures, thoughts, situations recur, lines of dialogue rebound among the characters like symphonic leitmotifs. It is a drama that embraces wisdom and madness, werewolves and beggars, hell and heaven."[59] As this comment suggests and as we might also expect of Bergman, the director appeared relatively uninterested in a conventional religious approach to *To Damascus*, as a drama of conversion and atonement, and was far more concerned with the emotional, lyrical, and even social aspects of the central character's spiritual torment. "He demystifies the drama," wrote Bengt Jahnsson in *Dagens Nyheter*. "At times the projection screen in the background is filled by a searching eye. But this is not God's eye

Figure 10 Blueprint plan of the stage (Dramaten) for *To Damascus*.

watching the Unknown and us. The memory of the past watches over the actions of the Unknown, intensifying his terror and anxiety. Our victims watch over us." Accordingly, Jan-Olof Strandberg's virtuoso performance as the Unknown carved out an intensely human and existentially divided protagonist, vacillating in an instant from tenderness to savage sarcasm, hopelessly trapped between rebellious arrogance and a gnawing self-torment. "Not infrequently he is so naive and comical that we laugh at him," commented *Expressen*. "But then suddenly the poetry in his words blossoms forth, the magic is there, and it falls silent around him." The end result became, in the opinion of many observers, "a drama of atonement in which the central character never repents." Both in Bergman's direction and in Strandberg's acerbic performance, the closing moments of Part Two, as the Unknown passionately embraces the Lady before leaving her to follow the mysterious Confessor ("Come, priest, before I change my mind!"), provided no clear or firm assurance that this ferocious struggle with the riddle of existence had been resolved. More than one critic called the ending "only the beginning of a new round." And yet the experience of the struggle itself – the sense of having gone through a trial that may turn out to be a blessing in disguise – inevitably does suggest its own kind of purification and reconciliation, in Bergman's world as in Strindberg's.

This three-and-a-half-hour stage adaptation of *To Damascus I–II* was, in strictly technical terms, an astonishing feat of dramaturgical compression that rivaled Per Lindberg's legendary one-evening production of the entire trilogy, seen in Oslo more than forty years before. The arrangement of Bergman's nineteen compact and tightly focused scenes is given in outline in the following table:

To Damascus

Bergman	Sequence of scenes	Strindberg
1	At the street corner	act 1, scene i
1A	At the cafe	
2	The veranda (At the Physician's)	act 1, scene ii
3	By the sea	act 2, scene ii
4	On the highway	act 2, scene iii
5	The kitchen	act 2, scene v
6	The Rose Chamber	act 3, scene i
7	The asylum	act 3, scene ii
8	The Rose Chamber	act 3, scene iii

9	The kitchen	act 3, scene iv
10	On the highway	act 4, scene ii
11	By the sea	act 4, scene iii
		[Part 2]
12	Outside the house	act 1
13	The laboratory	act 2, scene i
14	The kitchen	act 2, scene ii
		[Rose Chamber]
15	The Goldmaker's Banquet	act 3, scenes i, ii
16	The kitchen	act 3, scene iii
		[Rose Chamber]
17	The cafe	act 4, scene i
18	The highway: a void	act 4, scene ii
		[The mountain pass]
19	The Rose Chamber	act 4, scene iii

While faithfully mirroring the sequential logic and flow of Strindberg's original creation, this skillful reorchestration infused the two parts of it with a remarkable new sense of coherence and organic interrelatedness. Those critics who objected to the disruption of Strindberg's satisfyingly symmetrical design in part 1 – eight scenes leading up to the pivotal episode in the asylum, followed by exactly the same number and sequence of scenes in reverse order – were evidently overlooking the fact that an analogous and no less deliberate formal design governs Bergman's repatterning. Although four short and relatively inconsequential scenes (in the hotel room [2.i and 4.iv] and in the mountain pass [2.iv and 4.i]) have been eliminated in his scheme, the centrality of the Unknown's unnerving experience in the asylum is still manifestly emphasized by the arrangement of the incidents. Following this episode, the Unknown retraces his steps exactly. Four scenes later, he is reunited with the Lady at the very spot – by the sea – where they first began their wearisome journey as man and wife, after leaving the home of the Lady's former husband, the Physician.

Part 2 thus emerged as the direct, infernal consequence of this reunion. "I have at all times seen the second part as [a vision of] the depths of hell. Just as in a spiral, one sinks ever deeper, at last giving up the struggle and going over to religion, to the church," reads part of a note in the director's script. With this clue before us, it is not difficult to discern the logic of Bergman's decision to eliminate the final three scenes of Part 1 (4.iv, 5.i and 5.ii) and proceed, with the master film maker's uncanny sense of an effective cut,

directly to the much more harrowing domestic and emotional con-
flicts that culminate in the appalling ritual of humiliation known as
the Goldmaker's Banquet. "The effect is so strong and the decision
so obvious that we only ask ourselves why it had never been done
before," *Expressen* was brought to conclude. "For here we have a
pattern that is eternal, a structure that will never weaken. It begins
with their meeting. It ends with their parting. 'Scenes from a marriage' would not have been a bad subtitle for *To Damascus* in this
interpretation." One might add, though, that it was after all Strindberg himself who first recommended the sort of dramaturgical conflation that Bergman so successfully accomplished.[60]

Each individual scene in this production stood out with a sculptural
clarity, like a figure cluster on an ancient frieze or vase. One distinct
group of scenes were "close-ups" very tightly focused within the
defined limits of the small raised platform, utilizing only a back projection or a screen or two (often to facilitate entrances or exits) and the
barest minimum of furniture. Four of the most striking of these moments are captured in the accompanying production photographs.

The initial, hypnotic encounter between the Unknown and the

At the street corner. The first meeting of the Unknown and the Lady
in *To Damascus*. Dramaten, 1974.

Lady ("At the street corner") was played against a projected background that evoked a dreamlike, spiderweb image of a Gothic
church portal and a house facade. The sole piece of furniture on the
stage was a simple wooden bench, around which the rhythm of the
moves of approach and withdrawal, union and separation, was choreographed with all the precision of a pas de deux. Helena Brodin,
dressed in cool green as the Lady, created an intense but restrained
impression in this scene as a listener holding back her passion, "a
well-dressed woman of the world who watches this strange and
singular man with interest. Later, love and hatred alike obliterate
this restrained facade, and the strife between the man the pregnant
woman takes on that frenzy that we usually call "Strindbergian."[61]
As their first meeting drew to a close with the Lady's impulsive kiss
and passionate declaration ("Come, my liberator!"), an inquisitive
human eye gazed down ironically from the projection screen. The
reason was a very practical one: "It is essential to finish on the
Unknown," the director noted, for in this version the Unknown
remained throughout the play the controlling consciousness through
which all its events are perceived and recorded.

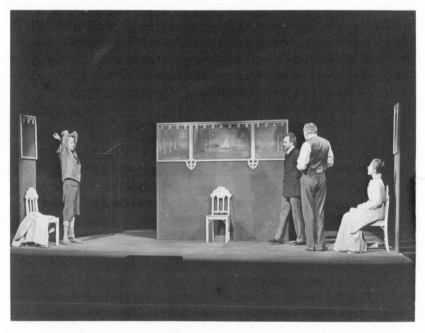

At the Physician's. The Unknown's first encounter with Caesar, the
madman, in *To Damascus*.

The first station on the couple's journey is the home of the Physician – the "werewolf" husband from whom the Unknown has rashly vowed to free his fairy princess. The "veranda" setting for this scene consisted of no more than a trio of low screens and three simple chairs, arranged to enclose and confine the action. A naive triptych depicting Swedish country scenes adorned the rear screen, as the merest hint of the elaborate milieu that Strindberg describes in his stage directions. Here in this haunted house of ticking death clocks, the demonic, vengeful doctor ("bizarre at first, later terrifying in his threats and hatred" in Ulf Johansson's performance[62]) confronted the Unknown with the most sinister of his exhibits – Caesar, the laurel-crowned madman who dwells in the cellar and in whom the Unknown is horrified to recognize a grotesque mirror image of himself. "Why does it all come back again – corpses and beggars and human destinies and childhood memories," he cries as he falls to his knees in desperate supplication.

Unlike the localities of these first two incidents, the "kitchen" of the Lady's childhood home becomes a recurrent station on the Unknown's journey, reserved in particular for his humiliating confrontations with the Lady's taunting and remorseless Mother. Bergman

The suggestive, semiabstract setting for the Kitchen in *To Damascus*.

returned to this setting four times in his production, for it was also here that, in part 2, the vindicative mother-in-law robbed the Unknown of all joy in his newborn daughter. Each time the kitchen reappeared, the sparse furnishings of the scene were slightly rearranged but one strongly connotative element remained constant – a plain white screen upon which, as its sole adornment, a large crucifix was prominently displayed. (When turned around the screen had a rose-colored reverse side, for use in the Rose Chamber scenes!) The illustration in which the Mother and the Maid are seen joined with the old Grandfather in prayer depicts the opening moment of the fifth scene in Bergman's version (Strindberg's 2.v). In his use of a suggestive, semiabstract setting such as this, the aim of the director is obviously in no sense to provide a picture of a recognizable place – that is, Strindberg's "roomy kitchen with white calcimine walls" in all its details. Instead, the spectator is faced with an evocative and disturbing image of a state of mind – a recurrent visual image of the harsh, hell-fire religious orthodoxy that the Unknown encounters in this place. What this particular illustration omits to show is, incidentally, the highly theatricalized use that Bergman invariably makes of his total stage space. Although "offstage" while their predicament is being so unfeelingly discussed by the others, the Unknown and the Lady were, in fact, already standing in full view to the right of the platform at this very moment, waiting silently to make their "entrance" and place themselves at the mercy of the family's grudging charity.

Often, the most effective of these "close-up" moments in the *Damascus* production made use of no scenery at all. Such an instance was the moving scene in which the Unknown is reunited with the Lady ("By the sea") – "a scene of great tenderness, closeness, desperation, and love," Bergman describes it, with which he concluded Part 1 in his adaptation. The stage was completely open and empty. The overall visual impression was, at the outset, one of winter whiteness and extreme cold. The only scenographic accent was provided by projections of shifting cloud formations in the background. Among these was perhaps the most striking of all of Marik Vos's projection effects in this production – the haunting impressionistic image of shipmast crosses that loomed up on the horizon during the closing moments of the episode:

THE UNKNOWN: Put your hand in mine, and let us leave this place together. (*He reaches out his hand. She takes it. He lowers his head, she kisses him on the mouth, and he rests his head against her shoulder.*) Are you tired?
THE LADY: Not any longer! (*Music*)

THE UNKNOWN *(facing the sea):* It's growing dark and the clouds are gathering . . .

THE LADY *(quietly consoling him):* Don't look at the clouds . . .

THE UNKNOWN: And over there? What is that?

THE LADY *(consoling):* Only a sunken ship!

THE UNKNOWN *(in a whisper):* Three crosses! – What new Golgotha awaits us now?

THE LADY *(consoling):* But they're white: that's a good sign!

THE UNKNOWN *(looking at her):* Can anything good happen to us ever again?

THE LADY *(consoling smile):* Yes, but not right away.

THE UNKNOWN *(laying his arm on her shoulder):* Let us go![63]

The illustration that captures the final moment of this exchange may inevitably cause some to recall its famous counterpart – the old rehearsal photograph of August Palme and Harriet Bosse, at the same moment, in the world premiere of *To Damascus I*, in which Carl Grabow's heavily pictorial backcloth now seems so much at odds with the fleeting, visionary character of Strindberg's first dreamplay.

A dynamic rhythm of contrasts was established in the *Damascus*

By the sea. The reunion of the Unknown (Jan-Olof Strandberg) and the Lady (Helena Brodin) on an empty stage, accented only by Marik Vos's evocative background projection.

The Confessor (Anders Ek) and the Unknown in the Asylum scene
from *To Damascus*.

production between the intimate, close-up scenes and another kind
of stage composition entirely. In these latter *changements à vue* (so
Bergman himself calls them), nightmare penetrated reality in an
instant, and the Unknown suddenly found his private demons and
innermost fears transmogrified into hideous scenes of public con-
demnation and disgrace. The background opened, the small platform stage was absorbed into the new figure composition, and the

The Asylum scene from *To Damascus,* with the soup-eating participants in the ghostly supper.

Unknown found himself at the focus of a mass spectacle that was always different and yet always the same. Each new public mortification became an amplification of the previous one. And, in one form or another, the Unknown's constant companion in these ordeals was the shadowy dual character of the Beggar-Confessor created by Anders Ek. "Visible or invisible he is always present, prodding or provoking the Unknown," remarked one observer. "Ek holds the stage with a combination of the clown's jesting – the trait that seems to run through to the very core of his personality – and a massive, almost annihilating authority" *(Nerikes Allehanda).* It is he who guided the Unknown on the road to Damascus, he who commented on every station along the way. In the role of the Latin-quoting Beggar who bears the mark of Cain upon his forehead (and hence is the Unknown's grotesque double), his presence first brought down public ridicule on the Unknown in the crowded cafe filled with brown-clad pallbearers that suddenly materialized and just as abruptly disappeared during the opening scene on the street corner. As the Dominican confessor in the asylum scene, his attack became fiercer and more harrowing as he intoned the litany of curses from Deuteronomy over the Unknown, who sat virtually like a condemned prisoner. (His chair, Bergman noted, "must have a high backrest and high armrests so he sits cramped.") At a long table in the background sat the ten spectral, soup-eating participants in the ghostly supper – Caesar, the Beggar, the Physician, the grieving parents, the cruelly treated sister, the abandoned wife and her two children, and, farthest to the right, the Lady, who sat knitting rather than eating. "Decide whether they are the same [i.e., identical to the actual characters from the Unknown's past]! No, they should wear masks and [different] costumes," reads an interesting memorandum in the director's script.

The most crucial scene in Bergman's theatrical paraphrase of *To Damascus* was, however, not the Unknown's confrontation with his past sins during his ordeal in the asylum, but rather the garish, trenchantly satirical episode of the Goldmaker's Banquet, which occurs toward the end of part 2. Previously in the laboratory scene—condensed by Bergman into a brief, somnambulistic dream sequence that began *allegro furioso* and concluded with the tempo indicator *retard.* ("the dream that you cannot stand up and cannot speak")—the Unknown had revealed to the Lady his true motive for attempting to make gold:

> . . . so as to destroy the world order, to bring chaos, you see! (*more heavily*) I am the destroyer, the annihilator, the arsonist of the universe, and when everything lies in ashes, (*more heavily*) I shall run *hungering* through the ruins and rejoice in this thought: (*more heavily*) that *I have done* this, I who have written the final page of the world's history – which can now be regarded as finished.
> (*The face of the Dominican appears in the open window, unnoticed by them. They fall silent.*) Who's there? Who is that terrible being who follows me and paralyzes my thoughts? – Did you see anyone? (*She only looks at him.*)[64]

Absorbed in his own rebellious vision, the Unknown readily permits himself to be acclaimed and decorated at what he conceives of as a glittering testimonial banquet held in his honor. It was composed, in

Bergman's production, of a smirking, bugeyed troll court of absurdly uniformed gentlemen and enormous barebreasted society
ladies–a fantastic vision that seems more reminiscent of earlier productions like *Peer Gynt* or *Caligula* than of anything he had attempted before in staging Strindberg. No sooner had the unsuspecting Unknown been crowned with laurel and hailed by the tawdry
multitude as the Great Goldmaker than this bizarre assembly began
to undergo a metamorphosis. Swiftly, in accordance with a carefully
choreographed four-stage pattern of visible transformations, the be-
ribboned officers and gentlemen were turned into beggars, vagabonds, and *clochards*, while the fine ladies became whores and other
more disreputable (unfortunately unprintable) types. By the time
Caesar, the Physician's madman, had launched his terrifyingly irra-

The Unknown is crowned with laurel and hailed as the Great
Goldmaker in *To Damascus.*

tional, virtually Hitlerian tirade against the Unknown, the change was complete. What the latter had perceived as a "royal celebration" and a "sincere tribute" that had restored "[his] faith in himself" was now an ugly, shabby, and distinctly hostile collection of ruffians gathered in a dingy cafe.

Virtually every reviewer had words of praise for the startling visual effect created by this scene ("altar painting" is perhaps the term that crops up must frequently). One or two critics were even prepared to congratulate the director on having made, for once, an acceptable anticapitalistic comment on the hollowness of the ruling classes: "As far as one can remember, this is the first time that Ingmar Bergman has uttered a word in the sociopolitical debate – the scene is a comment on the representative establishment and its relationship to those it represents," ventured Åke Perlström in Göteborgs–Posten. However, these generalizations are of little help in understanding the thematic relevance of this episode to Bergman's directorial image of To Damascus and, indeed, to his conception of Strindberg's drama as a whole. One might well argue that, above all, the Goldmaker's Banquet became in this production the ultimate nightmare of humiliation – in this sense it bears a direct relationship to the scene of the Degree Ceremony in Bergman's Dreamplay. In it, the ridicule and scorn heaped upon the dreamer are exacerbated and confirmed by his own innermost sense that they are justified and represent the truth about himself. Transformation was the governing theatrical technique in the production, and this served to establish irony as its predominant mode of communication.[65] With the swiftness and logic of a dream the Unknown found himself cast, without a transition, from the happy illusion of the banquet into the inferno of degradation. As such, this scene represented the culmination of a perpetual ironic process in which every potential happiness in the Unknown's existence – love, family ties, children, success, even royalty statements – had been suddenly transformed into dust and ashes in his hands.

A projection of dissolving, disintegrating house façades in the background provided a concise visual image of the aftermath of the grotesque banquet. In the final "public" scene, the Unknown returned to the wretched cafe, hopeful that "a mud bath" might "harden [his] skin against the stings of life." Instead, in a macabre atmosphere filled with the sprawling, writhing shapes of beggars, cripples, and whores, his spirit was poisoned and his life virtually sucked out of him by the savage, hypnotic power of the "werewolf" Physician. The ceremonial entrance of the hooded

Confessor, carrying the monstrance to "a dying man inside," co-incided with the Unknown's horrified realization that he, too, was perhaps dead without even knowing it. "The dead claim that no one knows the difference," agreed the venomous Physician "with ghastly emphasis."

In Bergman's radical abridgment of the remaining episodes in the drama, the last stages of the Unknown's journey were swiftly covered, and they led toward a distinctly and deliberately arbitrary resolution of his plight. Several intermediate, explanatory steps in the process – his anguished dream-encounter with his abandoned children, the destruction of Caesar and the Physician, the consulta-tion between the Lady and the Confessor about his salvation – were omitted. Instead, the closing moments in this version were tightly concentrated on the last of the "scenes from a marriage." Our final

"The dead claim that no one knows the difference." In the wretched cafe filled with beggars and cripples, the Physician (Ulf Johansson) destroys the Unknown with his psychic power.

glimpse into the connubial Rose Chamber revealed a deadlock from which there could be no escape – a timeless, airless domestic hell of hatred and guilty conscience, from which the Unknown was powerless to extricate himself. ("The Unknown is locked into his position. He cannot move an inch. He is in catatonic paralysis," reads a characteristic note in the director's script.) Hence, the Confessor's mystical option represented at least a kind of exit visa – in Bergman's distillation a very simple, open alternative to the ironies and torments of this life's Inferno. This concluding scene, which condenses some two pages of discussion in the original into six emotionally expressive speeches, provides a forceful example of this director's determination to forge a living theater text that "listens" to the inner emotional consciousness – "the poet's anxiety-driven fever pulse," as he called it back in 1945 – that is the authentic core of the Strindbergian dramatic vision:

(The Confessor enters, carrying a small, open prayerbook.)
THE UNKNOWN: Why, it's the beggar, isn't it?
CONFESSOR: Yes. Once, you foreswore your soul to me when you lay sick and sensed madness approaching. You promised then to serve the powers of good. But when you became well again, you broke your promise.
THE UNKNOWN: Come, then, before darkness falls!
CONFESSOR *(When he begins to read, he goes forward to the Unknown and shows him the text. Possibly it is he himself who reads the last line):*   "Over all the earth shone a bright, clear light, and men laboured without hindrance, doing their work. Over them, night spread its thick blackness – a foreboding of the darkness that was to set in over them! *But they themselves were harder upon one another than the darkness."*
(When they finish reading, they intend to leave. Before they can take any steps, the Lady speaks.)
THE LADY: Let no harm come to him!
(He goes forward to her and falls to his knees, but not too close. Concerned about the child she places a finger on her lips.)
THE UNKNOWN *(passionately):*   Listen to her: how kindly she can speak, and how evil she *is!* Look at her eyes: weep they cannot, but they can caress and can sting and can lie! And yet: "Let no harm come to him!" – Look, now she's afraid that I will wake her child, the little mischief that took her away from me!
(She goes forward to him, falls to her knees, embraces him and kisses him lingeringly on the mouth. Then she rises. Still kneeling, he lifts a hand to his mouth. Then he rises and goes toward the priest. He reaches out his hand.) Come, priest, before I change my mind!
FINIS MALORUM[66]

One detects no single Bergman "formula" at work in his continuing cycle of Strindberg productions. Each play in the canon has stood for him, and continues to stand, as a new and unique challenge, calling for a fresh perspective and a renewed creative response. The intuitive daring of his stage interpretations of Strindberg's plays has, however, been combined with a conspicuous loyalty that bespeaks the true consanguinity of these two artists. Although probably no other modern director has been less influenced by the idea of text as unalterable literary masterpiece than Bergman, his profound sensitivity to what one reviewer calls "the evocative musicality of the words and the special rhythm of the sentence structure in Strindberg's language" colors every decision he makes. "In his production of *To Damascus* he occasionally introduces a distancing effect solely for the sake of the language. One listens, fascinated by the singular beauty and forcefulness of this poet who, even when all else fails him, always has words in his power."[67] The special and lasting bond between Bergman and the man who once referred to his own talent as "the greatest fire in Sweden" has been forged, in large measure, through this director's ability to grasp the magic of those words and to ignite the creative imaginations of his actors and his audience with them.

4   A theater for Molière

Et c'est une étrange entreprise que celle de faire rire les honnêtes
gens.

Critique de l'École des Femmes

Ingmar Bergman is, in a very basic sense, a classical director. He
has, on repeated occasions over the past three decades, professed
his particular preference for classical plays. "I am fascinated by the
classics because they often express the problems of our own time
better than the drama of our time does," he told a press conference
before the start of rehearsals for his 1973 revival of Molière's *The
Misanthrope* at the Danish Royal Theatre – a production that in retrospect ranks among the high points in his theatrical career. "When
a play becomes a classic, it is because it expresses something that is
timeless."[1] In general, Bergman's most significant achievements as a
stage director have unquestionably been his productions of either
the modern Scandinavian classics – Strindberg, Ibsen, Hjalmar Bergman – or, on the other hand, of the classical comedies of Molière.
His approach to these two broad and distinct categories of "classical" plays has, in virtually every instance, been inspired by that
persistent quest for essentials that constitutes a cornerstone of his
directorial method. Within either category, his determined effort to
eliminate extraneous elements or devices in a production ("superimposed trappings" that "hang loosely and rattle," as he likes to call
them) has been his means of molding a charged and clarified theatrical image capable of projecting the full force and density of a given
text. His interpretations of these two different kinds of classics –
modern Scandinavian and seventeenth-century French – have usually followed very dissimilar approaches. Bergman's highly indi-
vidualistic theatrical paraphrases of the plays of Ibsen and Strindberg have, by and large, been characterized by a conscious search
for new forms – a revolt against established conventions and precon-
ceptions. By contrast, the Bergman approach to Molière has drawn
its strength from the director's deliberate reaffirmation of the relevance of the dual values of tradition and innovation in the theater.
"I don't believe that one flourishes as an artist without roots," he
has often declared in one fashion or another, about film as well as

132

theater. "I feel that I am a small stone in a great building – I am dependant upon what is beside, what is beneath, and what is behind me."[2] In his revivals of the French classics, he has built steadily upon a tradition that is, in turn, continually shaped and interpreted by him.

Bergman's first direct contact with the vigorous French tradition of Molière production occurred at a comparatively late point in his career, during a stay of several months in Paris in the autumn of 1949. The result was a dramatic and complete change of attitude. Previously, as he himself wryly admits, he "despised" French culture, in particular the great classical writers; Corneille was dismissed as "moss-grown," Racine as "dust-covered," Molière as – plainly – "dull."

Then I found myself directly confronted by the French cultural heritage, and I came face to face with Molière in his true, living context. . . . It had been a severe shortcoming in me that I had not discovered the great fundamental source upon which the culture of Europe has continued to build during the course of the centuries.[3]

Since this romantically epiphanic moment of discovery, Bergman's special attraction to Molière (he has until now directed no Corneille or Racine) has, characteristically, been an attraction to him as a man of the theater. Like Louis Jouvet before him, whose epoch-making efforts to reevaluate and retheatricalize Molière were animated by his desire to recover the playwright's theatrical heritage – "everything that charmed the audience and the actors who performed his comedies for the first time"[4] – Bergman, too, perceives Molière as above all an artist "who truly commands the vocabulary of the stage; he is to the very fingertips a man of the theater."[5] This appreciation of the comedies as intrinsically theatrical creations has constituted the real essence of the director's approach in all six of his major productions of them to date.

Otherwise, however, Bergman's various interpretations of Molière's plays – Don Juan (Malmö in 1955, Stockholm in 1965), The Misanthrope (Malmö in 1957, Copenhagen in 1973), The School for Wives and, as a curtain raiser, Criticism of the School for Wives (Stockholm, 1966), and Tartuffe (Munich, 1979) – have differed widely enough in concept and design. The range has extended from his first, broadly comic Don Juan, presented in the intimate studio theater at Malmö on a marketplace-style stage of rough boards as a deliberately primitive recreation of a production by a band of provincial strollers in Molière's own time, to the elegantly stylized for-

Orgon (Walter Schmidinger) as the madcap bourgeois whom no one –
not even the charming Dorine (Gaby Dohm) – can rescue from his folly
in *Tartuffe*. Residenztheater, 1979.

mality of his highly successful productions of *The Misanthrope*. His
recent production of *Tartuffe* at the Residenztheater in Munich – consciously designed, as he himself explained, to emphasize the "ironic
charm" of the play rather than its "blackness," and consequently
featuring an undangerous Tartuffe, whom some German critics
went so far as to call "closer to Nestroy than to Molière" in spirit[6] –
has been his most boldly untraditional (and probably also his funni-
est) Molière interpretation to date. In it he chose to take no notice
whatsoever of the commonplace notion of the play as a moral comedy, a bitter satire of hypocrisy and deceit. His main concern was
not with the oily religious imposter who hoodwinks those around
him and very nearly takes over the world in the process, but rather
with the nature of the absurd society – epitomized by the madcap
Orgon and his topsyturvy household – that allows such a creature as
Tartuffe to flourish. Neither the blandishments of Orgon's wife Elmire nor the straightforward common sense of the charming Dorine

could deflect this folly-fallen bourgeois from the path of his elected destiny. He virtually demanded to be gulled and plundered by the imposter.

In Molière's bitter comedies, theater as motif and metaphor is present everywhere. Throughout the plays we are made to witness the triumph of theater, of make believe, in a world that has little room for seriousness, a world where the concern with appearances and the readiness to assume a mask and play a double game are the only things that really count. Accordingly, Bergman's method in staging Molière has invariably been to underscore this element of theatricality – to remind the spectators that they are in a theater and these are actors performing before them, in order to make them initiated partners in the comic intrigue. In these performances the machinery of the stage stands exposed, the prompter sometimes becomes a visible participant in the action, changes of scene are handled by costumed stagehands or even by the actors themselves. From the very outset, in the opening sequence of his first Molière production in which a yawning, scratching, barelegged, and decid-edly unromantic Don Juan in ludicrously short nightshirt was seen being dressed in his seducer's costume of silk and ruffles by a totally illusionless Sganarelle, Bergman kept no secrets from his audience. "What was it that made us see right through Don Juan's noble exterior into his soul in all its corrupt tawdriness? Answer: those naked thighs," remarked Ebbe Linde in *Dagens Nyheter* (January 5, 1955). The device of this seriocomic pantomine with costume and wig served at once to enlist the audience as an informed witness to the continual process of demasking that formed the core of the di-rector's concept for *Don Juan.*

The German production of *Tartuffe* afforded an exceptionally vivid example of Molière as *theatrum mundi:* the world as a stage, the stage as an image of the world. The characters in the play were viewed not as more or less rationally motivated human beings, but as wildly exaggerated masks of human folly who inhabit a cardboard world of duplicity and painted canvas. From the moment the actors made their entrance onto the raked platform of rough boards that was erected in the middle of the stage and illuminated across the front by the obviously artificial glow of old-fashioned footlights, the audi-ence was continually and wittily reminded by Bergman and his de-signer (Charlotte Flemming) that this was a piece of theater they were watching. After the actors had appeared, a painted canvas backing was carried in and put in place. Whatever changes took place in the stage decor – a primitive pastiche of a baroque theater

The highly theatricalized stage setting, designed by Sven Erik
Skawonius, for Bergman's second production of *Don Juan*. Stockholm,
1965.

Another variant of Bergman's deliberate theatrical artifice is his staging
of *Criticism of the School for Wives*. Dramaten, 1966.

set, composed of canvas-covered screens at the sides and back that were painted with light gray, Watteau-like motifs on a white ground – were integrated into the action as ironic punctuation marks. As the intrigue snowballed and the fabric of the comedy became steadily more entangled, the scenery itself offered a telling visual comment on the reigning confusion. Orgon's bewildered world gradually became one in which pieces of the setting occasionally stood, defiantly, upsidedown, or else were placed with the unpainted side of the canvas (neatly stenciled "Tartuffe" for easy identification!) facing the audience. And when the tumult reached panic proportions – as it did when a thoroughly beguiled Orgon departed with Tartuffe in a whirlwind of ecstatic delight at the end of the third act, or when the imposter later made his hilarious attempt to seduce Elmire, Orgon's wife – the actors gave vent to their high spirits by violently toppling the painted screens.

The broad farcical spirit of the *commedia dell'arte* runs very close to the heart of Molière's comic theater, and the lighthearted *lazzi* and burlesque *coups de théâtre* associated with this performance tradition have occupied a cherished place in nearly all of Bergman's revivals. In his second production of *Don Juan*, for instance, which was

Charlotte Flemming's pastiche of a baroque theater set for *Tartuffe*. Note the exposed footlights and the upsidedown piece of scenery in the far background.

staged for the schoolchildren of Stockholm in a local variety theater, the climactic entrance of the statue that summons Don Juan to eternal reckoning was immediately hailed, as the production script directs, by the appearance of "all the guys" – the four minor roles in the performance – making as much noise as they could with pistols, a rattle, a bass drum, and even the theater's thunder sheet.[7] Small wonder that the terrified Sganarelle dashed out into the auditorium in fright – a trick that generations of Sganarelles before him had been prone to play since Gert Londemann first tried it, at the Danish Royal Theatre, in 1749. Similar strokes of the broadest comedy enlivened the German production of *Tartuffe* – to the manifest displeasure of the more disagreeable of the German critics. Cléante, the weary spokesman for rationality and order in the play, needed first a cane, later a pair of crutches, and finally even a wheelchair to get around in a world in which reason is crippled, sanity paralyzed. To Molière's famous artificial resolution, in which justice is reimposed and the victims of folly are saved from Tartuffe's clutches through their King's gracious intervention, Bergman added a final ironic flourish. The Royal Messenger rattled off his improbable proclamation, *in French*, like a tape recorder on rewind; Cléante, as Reason,

Tartuffe's attempt to seduce Elmire is baffled. The erotic background motifs now stand completely on end.

sprang up from his wheelchair, magically restored to health; and Orgon and his dispossessed household were rescued from their madness – but only barely. In fact, only *The School for Wives* – Bergman's bitterest and least humorous Molière interpretation – remained relatively impervious to the commedia tradition. Even here, however, the flamboyant entrance of Enrique, Oronte, and Chrysalde at the end of the comedy received the terse but telling notation "Marx Brothers" in the stage manager's script – although the moment was but a tame reflection of Enrique's triumphal entry in Louis Jouvet's legendary 1936 production, where this comic deus ex machina, just back from America, arrived in a chaise borne by four stately red Indians in full regalia.

It is also interesting to notice the growing extent to which, especially in recent years, this commedia dell'arte spirit of broad farce has spilled over from the Molière productions to infuse other Bergman performances as well. The most prominent example of this crossfertilization to date has been his highly acclaimed interpretation of Witold Gombrowicz's extremely difficult tragifarce *Yvonne, Princess of Burgundy*, which he staged at the Residenztheater in 1980. In Gombrowicz's theater, as in Molière's, life is conceived of as a perpetual mas-

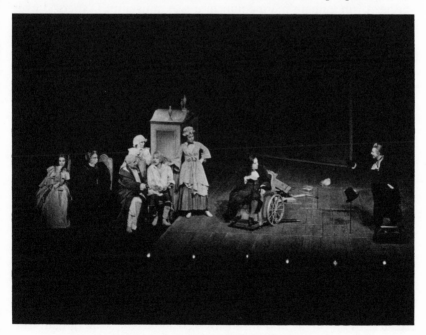

Cléante, the image of Reason crippled, is eventually confined to a wheelchair in the Munich production of *Tartuffe*.

querade, a game of theatrical appearances in which neither those who refuse to play nor those who deviate from the prescribed social minuet have any place. In Bergman's approach to this modern theater fable, a combination of grotesque buffoonery and remorseless irony turned the mock fairytale kingdom of the play into a modish world of cardboard and tinsel. Its inhabitants seemed to be absurd human puppets – "ghostly figures," the critic for *Süddeutsche Zeitung* (May 12, 1980) called them, "who move in the artificial manner of marionettes, giggle mechanically, stir in their teacups like automatons, and react for the most part as a collective."

The irreversible process of dehumanization was the ruling idea that governed every movement and every intonation in this swiftly paced production. To articulate this concept, Bergman perfected a consciously exaggerated, wildly theatrical style of acting that seemed the logical outgrowth of the spirit of slapstick parody that had prevailed in his *Tartuffe* and also in portions of his *Misanthrope* seven years earlier. The gaudily dressed figures of the court – headed by the addlebrained King Ignaz (Klaus Guth), his zany Queen (Gaby Dohm), and their bored, querulous son, Crown Prince Philipp (Robert Atzorn) – were revealed in a satirical opening tableau as a species of inanimate mannequin in a wax museum. Dispersed over the entire playing area with the regularity of chessmen, they faced the audience with blank stares as they declaimed their opening lines in unison, in a strident monotone that was partly spoken and partly chanted. Then, as this grotesque puppet show came abruptly to life, the angular gestures, contorted poses, and sudden feverish dancing of the characters created a precisely orchestrated rhythm of ritualized emptiness and repetitiveness. The result was a vivid demonstration of the progressive deterioration that is inevitable in a world in which everything moves in a circle. The set patterns upon which such a closed system depends can never be broken and are repeated over and over again. Yvonne, the ugly, silent, and utterly passive creature who is drawn into this tinsel world without willing it, is the mute negation of all its accepted standards and expectations, and hence her very presence sets off an epidemic of frantic, wildly confused reactions that lead in the end, with sinister inevitability, to her ritualized murder.

Nearly every other major production of Gombrowicz's challenging play has tended to idealize and sentimentalize the character of Yvonne, turning her into a symbol of mute, suffering humanity crushed by a vulgar and insensitive society. Not so Bergman. The coolly detached, farcical spirit of his interpretation precluded any such simplistic bifurcation of the characters into "positive" and "negative" camps. As the frenzy and madness engulfing the obstinately silent and helplessly impassive Yvonne took on progressively more savage proportions, she acquired a curious sort of stubborn, pathetic dignity. Viewed through the unflinching perspective created by the director's darkly comic vision of the play, however, this limp, hideously deformed marionette—so graphically the outsider, so absurdly out of place—seemed ultimately as much a caricature, as much a reduction of humanity as everyone else on the stage.

Never for an instant in this production was the audience permitted to relinquish its role as an aware and active witness to a disturbing masquerade, in which the masks do not conceal reality but are in themselves the only reality. Strategies to control and adjust the intensity of the communicative relationship between the spectator and the actor are, as we have already seen, common to virtually all of Bergman's theater productions. One such strategy, used by him to great advantage in *Tartuffe* as well, is the device of what might be called the "watching" character—a silent spectator-actor whose presence in itself implies an objective critical comment on the action. In the Molière production, the tiny role of Tartuffe's manservant Laurent had been amplified in this way to become a stern, omnipresent watcher—a mute and expressionless critic of the folly of the Orgon household and the fiendish intrigues of his unscrupulous master. In *Yvonne,* the presence of this kind of observer exerted a much darker and more emphatic effect upon the thematic fabric. Here, a pale, silent, stoney-faced old man (played by ninety-year-old Erwin Faber, one of Bergman's favorite character actors) appeared at regular intervals, observing everyone and everything around him with cold, cynical contempt. Seen in the opening scene as an old beggar carrying a scythe and subsequently as Valentin, a lackey at court, Faber's eerie, unbidden watcher, older than death in his appearance, became virtually a mask of Death—a living memento mori whose implacable attendance assigned this grotesque and meaningless puppet show of life to its proper, ultimate context. This grim presence served both to direct and control the audience's perception of the events taking place and to render transparent, in a startlingly palpable manner, the underlying spirit of chilling irony and disillusionment that shaped Bergman's interpretation. ("Gombrowicz has written it that way—it's not from me," he insists, adding with a twinkle: "but nobody else has, I think, understood it.")

The multiplicity of perspective achieved in this manner had its fullest and most powerful impact in the concluding scene, during the sinister banquet at which Yvonne meets her bizarre end (she is murdered by being induced to eat boney fish, on which she chokes to death). Dramatic continuity and believability alike were consciously shattered, prodding the audience into a renewed awareness of its role as informed witness. Before its eyes the entire stage swung ponderously around, exposing the empty space surrounding it, the creaking machinery, and the skeletal construction of canvas flats. Slowly a ghost supper of Kafkaesque dimensions glided into view, its immobilized and masked participants dressed in identical costumes of black and glittering silver. As these malevolent phantoms, ranged symmetrically along two legs of an imaginary triangle, sat watching their victim from behind their ugly, pitiless masks, the mysterious figure of Valentin, robed in red and seated at the apex of the imaginary triangle, presided over them in silent judgment. In this context, Yvonne's inevitable fate seemed thoroughly desentimentalized – she died by collapsing backwards over her chair, abruptly and without making a sound, like some drab puppet whose strings had suddenly been cut. The fact of her destruction was only a single, limited facet of the complex and evocative theatrical image that Bergman had prepared. The sense of critical distance inherent in his handling of the scene provided for a depth of perspective that reached beyond the murder to encompass the subjects

The sinister banquet at which Yvonne (Andrea-Maria Wildner, center) meets her bizarre end in *Yvonne, Princess of Burgundy*. The shadowy figure of Valentin (Erwin Faber) is seen seated in the background. Residenztheater, 1980.

of Valentin's icy scrutiny – the destructive force of the dark powers that had kindled the madness, the anguished despair of the Prince who now knew himself to be corroded by them.

Engagingly broad slapstick effects on the one hand and strategies for establishing critical distance on the other are both essential components of Bergman's deliberate design upon his audience, from whose point of view every move and every effect in his mise-en-scène is calculated. For him, as for Jouvet and countless other artists and theoreticians whose views have helped to reshape theatrical art in this century, the vocabulary and craft of the theater are inextricably bound up with its audiences – with their presence and spontaneous reactions, with the dynamic interplay that is established between stage and auditorium. In Bergman's case, his repeated insistence on the importance of intense audience involvement is based on the conviction that the drama must always be played in two locations at once, on the stage among the actors and in the consciousness of every spectator. "A performance is not a performance before it encounters its audience. The audience is the most important part of it," he explained again at the press conference held in connection with the 1973 *Misanthrope* revival in Copenhagen.[8]

One of the most interesting practical applications of this theoretical preoccupation with the audience as an active collaborator in the creative process has been Bergman's unusual and occasionally controversial custom – first adopted for the production of Büchner's *Woyzeck* in 1969 – of conducting open, public rehearsals. "It is essential to undramatize the whole system of theatrical distribution, the hysteria surrounding dress rehearsal and opening," he explained when he first announced the idea. "I now believe that all this atmosphere of secrecy that surrounds us, and that I myself have enthusiastically supported, is finished."[9] The underlying purpose of the open-rehearsal experiment, which has since become an established part of Bergman's method in preparing a play for production, is twofold. First, it reflects his determination to eliminate the sense of a barrier that separates the actor from the audience. The latter must, he insists, be made "to see that there is no magic in our work, and that there is nevertheless a magic in it." In short speeches delivered to the audiences at these public rehearsals, he has regularly tried to explain this aspect of his attitude: "Remember that every performance is dependent upon involvement. You come here with a longing to experience something. The actors are trying to meet that longing, and they perceive how you react. Try to experience the play as intensely and directly as you can."[10]

The second and more important part of his intention is to assist the actor by preparing the ground upon which those two vital forces in the creative process, the actor and the spectator, will encounter one another in the finished performance. The open rehearsals are seen by him as a means of helping the actors to maintain a healthy, unneurotic, and disciplined attitude toward their work in this respect. "The audience comes to be influenced, not to influence us. We are the ones who give; we must radiate strength, self-confidence, joy in our activity on stage," he told the cast of *Woyzeck*. "No private neuroses must be allowed to come between us and the audience. It is a terrible mistake to confuse private neuroses with talent. It is significant that the more firmly the details are implanted, the stronger, freer, and happier the actor will feel."[11]

In the Copenhagen production of *The Misanthrope*, the practice of holding free public rehearsals constituted an intrinsic part of the preparatory process. "In accordance with the wishes of the Swedish director, certain rehearsals were made public, so that the audience (who picked up tickets at the box office) might attend a quite ordinary rehearsal of *The Misanthrope*. IB had done something similar in Stockholm," recorded an obviously puzzled stage manager in the Royal Theatre's official daily journal.[12] "During the open rehearsals we perform the entire play, and we then discuss the audience's reaction after they have left," the director himself explained to the Copenhagen press at the outset of the nearly eight-week rehearsal period.[13] The date of the first open rehearsal, to which the stage manager's notation refers, was March 17 – little more than a month after rehearsals had begun and only four days after the company had held its first rehearsal on the stage itself. By the time of the actual opening (April 6), Bergman had conducted a total of seven such open rehearsals – at first, with the cast in rehearsal clothing, for a limited audience of some 150, subsequently, with complete costumes and makeup, for a much larger general public.

The director's stake in such a procedure emerges most clearly from one of the unabashedly hortative little speeches that he delivered to the audience at a public rehearsal for *Woyzeck:* "The actors collaborate with you all the time. I want you to know that everything is done for your sake. You are the sounding board, and they listen to you all the time. They adjust their roles, their voices, their spiritual processes to you. And they see you all the time!"[14] In Bergman's theater, the finished performance itself is thus the product of a highly conscious and calculated process of give and take between the actors and the audience – a process overlooked and facilitated by the figure of the detached director–mediator, whose task

Work photograph of Kerstin Hedeby's stylized baroque setting for *The Misanthrope*. Danish Royal Theatre, Copenhagen, 1973.

it is "to indicate the concept for the production and then to function as eye and ear, security factor, stimulator, coordinator, work fore-man, and, to a certain degree, teacher."[15]

PORTRAIT OF A MISANTHROPE

The three elements that Bergman regards as the only essential ones in the theater – a subject, actors, and audience – confront and interact with one another continuously. The nature of this interaction is, in turn, invariably influenced and conditioned by the physical space that contains a performance, and which thereby becomes, for the actors, "a co-performer in visual and acoustical terms."[16] In his

Figure 11 Plan of the stage (Danish Royal Theatre) for *The Misanthrope*.

Copenhagen production of *The Misanthrope* – which may be said to exemplify his vision and method as a classical director perhaps better than any of his other Molière revivals – the immediacy of the contact between stage and auditorium was strengthened by eliminating the front curtain and constructing a raked platform that reached out over the orchestra pit to form a roughly semicircular forestage. Figure 11 illustrates both the shape of this construction and the disposition of the twenty-nine platforms needed to create the gently sloping stage that Bergman required. To achieve the same purpose in the earlier production of the play at the Malmö City Theatre in 1957, Bergman and his designer had actually moved the backdrop forward almost to the proscenium opening, and had extended the forestage so far into the auditorium that it seemed to include the audience in the same continuous space. ("Everything was faraway and yet close to us, remote and yet very familiar," one critic remarked on that occasion. "It was the kind of aesthetic distance that creates an intensified perception of what remains eternal beneath the changing masks."[17]) In the less adaptable gold-and-stucco precincts of the Danish national theater, so radical a structural fusion of stage and auditorium would hardly be feasible – or appropriate. Here, however, as the audience entered the theater the soft, subdued lighting served to erase the separation between the two spaces and make them one. The observant spectator was introduced at once to the play's visual ambience – an elegant pastiche of a baroque perspective stage, a theater erected within a theater, designed to evoke the period flavor and the sense of graceful formality of the age of the Sun King, Louis the Fourteenth. The balanced recession of parallel flat wings in designer Kerstin Hedeby's stage setting – four on each side, decorated with feather-light motifs of trees and birds seen against a golden ground – created an emphatic, deliberately stylized impression of perspective depth. Hedeby's neutral, symmetrical stage picture – which served to place the vivid cos-

The stage as it appeared in the earlier production of *The Misanthrope*. Malmö, 1957.

Figure 12 Blocking plan for *The Misanthrope* (V.i), indicating positions of actors' chairs in the wings.

tumes and three-dimensional figure compositions of the actors in high relief – was completed by a formal balustrade at the back, beyond which one glimpsed the luminous outlines of painted trees. Only a bare minimum of furnishings – a pair of baroque chairs, a bench, a mirror – occupied the stage proper. The floor of the stage was divided, by means of white lines, into a pronounced pattern of large rectangles, quite different in character from the more representational checkerboard floor employed in the Malmö production. This distinctive grid imparted to the acting area an imposing sense of choreographic regularity and formality – an impression further enhanced by the symmetrical rows of ornate chandeliers (four pairs in all) that cast their festive, subdued illumination over the action.

To the atmosphere of elegant artifice established by the physical setting, Bergman added an unusual and suggestive touch to his Copenhagen revival that had the effect of deepening his comment on the intrinsic theatricality of Molière's conception. Seated on the outskirts of the stage, in the dimly lighted area just beyond the side wings, the performers involved in any given act of the play could be seen nonchalantly awaiting their entrances. When their cue came, the actors simply rose from their chairs in the wings and mounted the three broad steps that led to the elevated platform-stage (cf. Fig. 12) – while at the end of their scene they stepped back into the wings and again resumed their seats (Fig. 13). The actors " 'take on' their roles,

Figure 13 Acaste and Clitandre return to their chairs in the wings, during act 3, scene 3 of *The Misanthrope*.

so to speak, as they enter Célimène's salon, where the audience, too, becomes a guest," noted Henrik Lundgren in *Information*. They seemed, thought Robert Naur (*Politiken*), to be "inanimate properties until the action summons them into its living space." The striking overall impression thus created was likened by this critic to "the toy-theater effect of a magic box." In Bergman's view, the experience of watching the costumed, concentrated actor – or the circus performer – waiting to step into the performance is indeed a special, magical one. The presence of these silent, waiting actor–spectators facilitates the movement from reality into the world of the imaginary event, he feels, thereby preparing and urging the audience to take the step "from the realm of everyday existence into something extraordinary." The effect created on an audience while a large symphony sits tuning its instruments is a favorite analogy of his in this connection.

Like the stage set itself, of course, the visual perspective introduced by the presence of these actor–spectators in *The Misanthrope*
calls to mind certain specific historical antecedents. In the conversation "Talking about Theater," Bergman describes the tradition that
actually inspired his use of this strategy – the old custom at the
Comédie Française that the actors did in fact remain on the stage,
behind the scenes, throughout the entire performance of a play
("like shadows, as a presence") – each one with his own chair, with
his name on it. However, the mere resurrection of an historical
tradition is obviously not the reason for Bergman's adoption of a
technique such as this. Rather, it is his abiding preoccupation with
the bond between audience and actor that would inevitably attract
him to the device of the performer–spectator, as one of those
simple, concrete "suggestions" that, taken together, "create a dimension" in his theatrical method. In *The Misanthrope*, the device

In this scene between Alceste and Philinte, from the Copenhagen
production of *The Misanthrope*, the costumed actors seated in the wings
can be seen to the right of the picture.

was an ingenious means of sharpening the focus, thereby stimulating a climate of expectation and intensifying the communicative rapport between stage and auditorium.

From the moment of his first, fiery entrance, the figure of Alceste remained the undisputed center of dramatic interest in Bergman's production. Every development of the action was orchestrated to accentuate the potential drama around his figure. For Bergman, the key to this role – and hence to the shape of the play as a whole – is to be found in Alceste's relationship to Célimène. "I do not experience this work as a wordy play about an apostle of the truth," he remarked in an interview in *Helsingborgs Dagblad*. "I see it instead as a fascinating love story; about how love becomes one of the most important motivating forces in our lives." By locating the mainspring of the action in a concrete situation of human interaction rather than by defining it in the more static and abstract terms of a character study, the director deftly underscored the comedy's dynamic peripeties and suspense. He made of Molière's play "not merely a painting of manners, set in the superficial, make believe world of the salon," declared the reviewer for *Berlingske Tidende*, but "a drama about the love relationship between two incompatible people." The central character became not simply a man incapable of hypocrisy, singlemindedly upholding his ideal of absolute integrity to the very end, but more important, a man caught in an intensely human predicament. In this production a remarkable bond of sympathy was forged between Alceste and the audience, bringing the character much closer to the spectator. "The Misanthrope, as we encounter him in the black-clad figure of Henning Moritzen, is neither pathetic nor a psychological case study nor pure clown," Robert Naur observed.[18] "He is an impassioned young man intent upon changing the world for the better, intent upon transforming his beloved Célimène after his own image, and, on top of it all, quivering with jealousy." This critic added an interesting visual descriptor to his analysis of the character that Moritzen drew – "he bends a little forward as he moves, as though forever battling an imaginary head wind."

In the Malmö production of the play sixteen years before, Bergman's Alceste had been Max von Sydow, who played the character as a rebellious, restive, rather confused idealist – "a disoriented Don Quixote who is perpetually shocked to discover that people are not as noble as they are in Gothic romances."[19] Henrik Sjögren draws a convincing portrait of von Sydow's Misanthrope as "a relative of the angry young man who had just [1957] begun to make his presence

The passionate, black-clad Alceste of Henning Moritzen, who seemed "as though forever battling an imaginary head-wind," is seen here in an exchange with Eliante (Hanne Borchsenius). Copenhagen, 1973.

felt in English drama. He went around, like another Gregers Werle, with his demand for the ideal; his call for absolute truth, his severe, rational absolutism obscured his vision as much as his uncontrollable love for the coquette did."[20] Harald Engberg (*Politiken*), commenting that Bergman "would not have been who he is if he had not transposed the key of Molière's comedy of manners into the tonality of a drama of passion," also aligned this Alceste with John Osborne's angry antiheroes – "an aggressive and demanding personality with a hopeless love-hatred of the circle in which he moves,

The Alceste of Max von Sydow, in the Malmö production of *The Misanthrope*, 1957.

a pathetic figure among the fools of his time, who wins our sympathy precisely because he does not try to but, on the contrary, does
all he can to fend it off."

In the Copenhagen production, Henning Moritzen's authoritative
interpretation of Alceste traced a far darker, more tragic pattern than
his famous Swedish predecessor had done. Incapable of pretense
and at the same time painfully aware of the compromises upon
which society is based, this Alceste seemed "an awkward and paradoxical but pure soul, in the midst of a world of deceit, superficiality, and altogether too much cold detachment" (*Kristeligt Dagblad*).
In spite of his disillusionment, however, Moritzen's Misanthrope
shared with von Sydow's earlier characterization the quality of poignant youthfulness – "the youngest that one recalls," recorded
Svend Kragh-Jacobsen, the dean of Danish critics, who added: "it is
precisely this youthfulness that explains the character, the hot-
headed vehemence, the intolerance, the demand for all-or-nothing."
The emphatic sensation of alienation and of suffering inflicted by the
searing conflict between a hot heart and clear reason made Moritzen's black-clad Misanthrope seem, to many observers, a Hamlet-
like figure: "Alceste is an *angry* man, not a bad-tempered one,"
wrote Inge Dam in *BT*. "His noble outlook on life clashes decisively
with the mendacity of society. Like a young Hamlet, he is puzzled
by the smiling villains who surround him."

Bergman himself once remarked, in working on *Hedda Gabler*
(1964) and *The School for Wives* (1966), that he was struck by "a
tremendously strong impression that Ibsen and Molière – each with
varying strength – are giving deeply personal and overt expression
to a profound depression. Molière in the guise of a rather brittle
humor – and Ibsen with a shocked despair that he has covered over
with an elaborate superstructure, precisely because he is so desperate."[21] Bergman's second production of *The Misanthrope* conveyed a
forceful impression of this accumulating sense of outrage, bitterness,
and blackness that lie just beneath the comic veneer of the play. A
neatly printed exclamation in his director's script, commenting on
Alceste's speech about his physical revulsion at even the slightest
distortion of the truth, speaks for itself concerning the Ibsen–
Molière affinity that he perceives:

> there's none I'd choose to spare.
> All are corrupt; there's nothing to be seen
> In court or town but aggravates my spleen.
>
> (I.i.87–90)[22]
>
> BRAND! GREGERS!

Figure 14 Blocking plan indicating Alceste's first, diagonal entrance movement in *The Misanthrope.*

Nevertheless, Bergman's interpretation very carefully maintained and emphasized the paradoxical syntax of Molière's play. Hence, though virtually every reviewer summed up his ultimate impression of the performance as tragic, it derived its distinctive, dynamic tone and texture from its preservation of juxtaposed and contrasted moods: pathos and comedy, a seriousness and an exaggerated humor that bordered on the grotesque.

As the house lights dimmed to half and two warning thumps of the stage manager's baton paid homage to the traditions of the Comédie Française, the performance opened on a note of high intensity. A violently agitated Alceste ("already out of balance because of Célimène," notes the director's script) rushed swiftly and purposefully in a diagonal line across the stage to the very front right-hand wing (Fig. 14) – behind which he actually disappeared before speaking his first line ("Leave me alone, I beg of you"). In a production built predominantly on strong, single emotions and emphatically defined juxtapositions of mood and objective, Philinte was similarly supplied by the director with a pointedly contrasting attitude to the explosive situation: "What has caused this crisis? Philinte surprised and pleasant." Reemerging, in high dudgeon, from his hiding place behind the side wing, Alceste again stormed across the full width of the stage in front of his puzzled friend, who remained standing calmly at its center. Abruptly, the perpetually angry Alceste sat down and deliberately turned his back on Philinte as he expressed, with a typically brusque, seriocomic gesture of finality, his firm determination to remain furious and not to listen ("I choose to be rude, Sir, and to be hard of hearing"). Move followed restless move to produce a meticulously coordinated, boldly accentuated pattern of poses, gestures, and sculptural figure compositions – a pattern governed at all times by an unfailing harmony and formal control. This strong sense of design, coupled with the astonishing visual eloquence of Bergman's attack, prompted most reviewers to comment, in one form or another, on the "classical" qualities of simplicity and clarity so evident in a mise-en-scène that "progressed in crystal-clear, almost mathematically structured scenes, amazingly controlled . . . yet saturated with vitality and dramatic tension" (*Kristeligt Dagblad*).

Although the emphatic figure clusters and movement patterns in this performance stood out on the gridlike ground of the stage floor with relieflike definition and firmness, the ultimate impression was never one of static tableaux. On the other hand, Bergman made no attempt, as a naturalistic director might have done, to animate his composition by means of a particularized mosaic of realistic stage business or a multitude of painstakingly detailed, fluctuating objectives geared to the slightest nuances in the text.[23] He deliberately placed the emphasis on the artifice and lively theatricality of the comedy by relying throughout on consciously formalized blocking patterns that underscored the broad tempo variations and vigorous rhythmic flow of Molière's alexandrines. Typical of Bergman's method as well was the fact that he relied to a very large extent on close-up scenes, played at the front of the stage and deepening the direct rapport between actors and audience, rather than on the detached naturalistic technique of locating characters within the context of a "living" environment.

Alceste's misfortunes, as the French scholar Alfred Simon succinctly observes, seem during the course of the play "to multiply to a tempo of burlesque that mocks his seriousness," as the representatives of the fashionable society that surrounds him force him into a succession of hopeless situations. Bergman consciously broadened the comedy of these encounters by depicting the *fâcheux* – the fops who descend on the beleaguered Misanthrope in an apparently

never-ending stream–in a spirit of fierce, scathing parody, as representatives of the "enslaved, dangerous, and terrifying society" that
the director sees reflected in Molière's play. "The worst and most
dangerous thing that can happen," he told his audience at the outset of one of the first public rehearsals,

is to fall into disfavor with the king and to cease to be part of the ruling
class. This can happen by saying the wrong thing, by not having the right
emotions, by having any emotions at all. Certainly one can be very sentimental. And one can cry, provided they're crocodile tears. But one must
never display *genuine* emotion, never admit how things really stand. One
must continually have an intrigue in motion. All watch one another, spy on
one another, but at the same time smile to one another, pay perpetual
compliments to one another.

Accordingly, the vain poet Oronte, the two foolish marquises,
Acaste and Clitandre, and even the Officer of the Marshals of France
all appeared as grimacing caricatures, decked out in colorful, elabo-
rately adorned period costumes, topped by enormous edifices of
makeup and wigs. The sumptuous riot of color produced by their
parodic appearance identified these figures as a species of puffed-
up, basically inhuman creatures–akin to the figures of peacocks and
other birds worked into the stage setting itself–vainly and aimlessly
parading themselves in their finery. "Who could forget the black
figure of Alceste in contrast to the radiant color profusion of the
scoffing fops. Superb," proclaimed *Berlingske Tidende*.

Only the occasional critic was inclined to object, in the name of
"realism," to the broadly stylized exaggeration of the *fâcheux*. "I
cannot understand why these figures and the scenes around them
are made so grotesque in their humor," one reviewer had written of
the Malmö production in 1957. "The comedy is not necessarily lost
in a more cautiously elegant treatment, and that alternative has the
added advantage of providing a better background for Alceste's be-
trayal."[24] Essentially the same kind of literalistic objection was
raised in Henrik Lundgren's review of the Copenhagen revival:
"Why has Bergman depicted Célimène's admirers and friends with
so little understanding of her personality," this critic demanded.
"Would she not have sensed it to be a waste of time to associate
with these ridiculously caricatured marquises?" The question can
have no meaningful answer, however, for it reflects a fundamental
misunderstanding of the director's intent with such a strategy. "One
has to be an enormously unresponsive spectator not to recognize
that here is an example of theater that has nothing to do with naturalistic psychologizing," Jens Kruse declared bluntly in *Jyllands*

Posten. Seen from this angle, then, the confrontation with the would-be poet Oronte (I.ii), the first of the direct clashes between Alceste and the "terrifying society" of fops that surround him, served less to establish a believable psychological relationship than to illuminate the threatening tension that Bergman perceives throughout the play between humanity and inhumanity, seriousness and near-burlesque. In Ebbe Rode's portrayal, Oronte stood out as "a monumental caricature . . . the epitome of imbecile self-confidence" (*Aktuelt*); his physical appearance was that of a fabulous monster, "a mixture between a bull and a turkey" (*Berlingske Tidende*). One purpose alone propelled this fatuous poet–monster: "Oronte's sole objective is to get to read his poem aloud," reads a characteristic note in the director's script. This single objective – the self-styled sonneteer's frantic desire to display his artistic achievement, his sonnet, and to be duly praised and admired for the accomplishment – became the motivation for his every action: the overdone, even oily respect that he pays to a decidedly reluctant and increasingly embarrassed Alceste; the kiss on each cheek with which he seals his declaration of "friendship"; not least, his unyielding determination to occupy center stage.[25] Swelling with pride at the idea of having written a sonnet, Oronte delivered himself of his masterpiece – bound in a small, elegant book – in a deep, declamatory voice, looking to Alceste for approval at every pause. As the latter, seated ("like a block of ice") at the farthest physical remove from the poetaster, tried resolutely to avert an open conflict over the "masterpiece," Oronte's blissful self-satisfaction gradually wilted until, at the end of the scene, he left the stage in a fury, yet nonetheless bowing and smiling as affably as when he first appeared. The high point in this exchange – and one of the brightest moments in the entire production – was Moritzen's sincere, unaffected delivery of the old song with which Alceste pointedly counters Oronte's bombast ("Si le Roi m'avait donné/ Paris, sa grande-ville"). This verse, in whose simple, unassuming rhymes one is meant to sense something of the voice of the true poet, was first sung and then recited simply and directly by Alceste, framed by the totally immobile figures of Philinte and Oronte.

A crucial aspect of Bergman's interpretation of *The Misanthrope* is reflected in the fact that, in this scene, the vivid contrast established between Oronte and Alceste was heightened by the comic rigidity of the poses of *both* characters – a rigidity that, in Alceste's case, continued throughout the performance to be seen as a predominant feature of his character. On the one hand, this Misanthrope possessed

Right, Alceste with the would-be poet Oronte (Ebbe Rode), whose sole objective is to read his poem aloud. Copenhagen, 1973.

"a basic sympathetic normality" that, as the critic for *Politiken* observed, made him "not a caricature but a portrait of a human being with whom everyone could somehow identify." On the other hand, however, Moritzen's Alceste was, from the very outset, so filled with disgust at any trace of hypocrisy, so unbendingly and self-righteously obsessed with honesty, so absolutely charged with his own integrity that the very inflexibility of his attitude inevitably provoked laughter. This sense of rigidity was suggestively expressed in many ways in the physical mise-en-scène as well. At the close of the first act, for example, the moves and gestures that accompanied

Figure 15 Alceste's exit in the first act of *The Misanthrope,* reversing the pattern of his entrance cross.

Alceste's passionate refusal to listen to the ever-patient Philinte ("Je n'entends rien") constituted a virtual replay in reverse of the very same moves and the long diagonal cross that had been used to bring him on the stage at the beginning (see Fig. 15).

Precisely this kind of carefully structured balance and design remained an abiding characteristic of the production as a whole, as it unfolded in a series of almost musically phrased contrasts and parallelisms, some lightheartedly comic, others tinged by a strong note of pathos. Perhaps nowhere was Bergman's concern for formal coherence more in evidence than in his original treatment of the intervals between the acts. These transitions were fashioned into a sequence of pantomimic interludes that not only maintained a satisfying sense of continuity, but also accounted in themselves for some of the most entertaining visual conceits in the performance. During each of the four intervals between the respective acts of the play, Célimène's servant Basque – a virtually nonexistent role in text, transformed by Bergman into a major one – appeared and proceeded, with great ceremony and an elaborate show of superiority and self-importance, to rearrange the few pieces of furniture on the stage, dangling his fan (in imitation of his mistress?) and flirting broadly with the audience all the while. Following each of the acts, the ubiquitous Basque, brimming with a mixture of urgency and supreme *hauteur*, would turn up to repeat his "number," and only his signal to an invisible stage manager permitted the play to proceed. Like so much else in the production, this device has its obvious antecedents in theatrical history. In the theatre of the Baroque period and during the eighteenth century, as we know, the task of clearing unneeded furniture and props from the stage was left, whenever possible, to the servants and other minor figures in a play. In Bergman's hands, however, this venerable convention became far more than merely a useful practical expedient; Basque's *lazzi* provided their own suggestive comment on the motif of theatricality and role playing that is so central to Bergman's interpretation of Molière's comedy.

In another and equally important respect, moreover, Bergman's development of Basque as a dramatic character illustrates this director's scrupulous attention to even the smallest details in the overall fabric of a given work. Every one of Basque's brief appearances – which are included in the text merely as a means of announcing the arrival of a new character – was textured in such a way that the comic momentum was sustained while a new facet of the zany servant's personality was revealed. Basque's three appearances in the second act serve to demonstrate the point briefly. To announce the arrival of Acaste, he came dashing onto the stage and then stopped abruptly, interrupting a tense encounter between Alceste and Célimène with a one-word announcement spoken with an air of regretful anxiety. ("Basque is a little afraid of Acaste," was the clue provided by the director at rehearsals.) Next time, however, his behavior had altered completely, and he came tripping in on the tips of his toes to deliver his message ("Clitandre, Madame") beaming with delight, contentedly inspecting his own image in the mirror. (The reason: "Clitandre has said such fantastically nice things that Basque comes dancing in, in a tiptop mood.") The servant's last appearance in the act revealed yet another side of his temperament. Obliged to announce the arrival of the legal officer who comes to serve a summons on Alceste for allegedly having affronted Oronte, the humorously complex Basque was directed to be "virtually in tears with fear" at the very thought of this awe-inspiring individual.

At the critical core of Bergman's interpretation, imparting perspective and bitter irony to the seriocomic encounters between Alceste and the world of deceit that surrounds him, was the director's ap-

The coquettish Célimène of Gertrud Fridh, seen with von Sydow's
Alceste in the Malmö production of *The Misanthrope* in 1957.

prehension of the play as, above all, "a fascinating love story" about
a relationship between two basically incompatible people. Bergman
views Célimène as "a woman who has chosen to conform, who
wants to 'survive,' " Bibi Andersson (who played Eliante in his
Malmö production of *The Misanthrope*) recalls. "She wants to enjoy
herself and, at the same time, she is an unusual personality, more
intelligent than average. Therefore she is doomed to come into conflict in her love for Alceste. . . . With his striving after righteousness
and his impossibly ideal demands, he is doomed to succumb, no
matter how right he is. He judges and condemns and becomes
trapped in his own excellent intentions."[26] Gertrud Fridh, who
acted Célimène in Malmö, had possessed a quality of playfulness
that lent distance and kept her from appearing overly cruel in her
coquettishness. "One capitulated completely before her; we asked
neither for breadth nor depth, but simply recognized that she was

what she was and could not be different, almost innocently cynical, a woman who forms no attachments but captivates everyone," recorded one observer on that occasion.[27] In the revival at the Danish Royal Theatre, Ghita Nørby presented a warmer and more human Célimène, who took an almost childlike delight in game playing–a woman, Svend Erichsen called her in *Aktuelt*, who "toys with reality, with men . . . and with herself. She establishes a distance between her own life and that of others." To the critic for *Information*, this Célimène seemed "not wicked, but only spoiled by her association with flatterers and rumormongers"–"not an expert but only a novice in the craft of creating scandals. She gradually feels her way forward, mesmerized by her own success." In this performance, Célimène's love for Alceste was real enough in its own way. He represented what was serious in her life, and that seriousness seemed always present behind the games she chose to play.

The first movement in their relationship, their initial encounter at the beginning of the second act in which the impetuous Alceste ultimately proclaims the utter singularity of his overwhelming passion for Célimène ("Morbleu! faut-il que je vous aime!"), established the paradoxical syntax of the conflict–the crackling erotic tension generated by the juxtaposition of Alceste's furious infatuation and Célimène's elegant, composed, invariably lighthearted enjoyment of control. The climax of their first scene was a memorable illustration of Bergman's remarkable ability to "orchestrate" a classical text–that is, to establish a swiftly but precisely oscillating rhythm of speech patterns, eloquent pauses, moves, and gestures. As Alceste's final passionate tirade of devotion soared, Célimène absentmindedly kissed her handkerchief and casually let it fall to the floor–compelling her lover to take to his knees to pick it up. His closing couplet, spoken on his knees, crystallized into a flash of pathos that was immediately counterpointed and undercut by Célimène's brittle comic rejoinder:

ALCESTE *(kneeling before Célimène):*   Words can't describe the nature of my passion,
(He makes a distinct pause, and passionately kisses her handkerchief before continuing): And no man ever loved in such a fashion.
CELIMÈNE *(replies promptly, lightly and brightly):*   Yes, it's a brand-new fashion, I agree;
You show your love by castigating me.   (II.i.523–6)

The gracefully controlled erotic contest played out between Alceste and the reluctant Célimène was, however, anchored firmly by Bergman in the larger context of the "dangerous" courtly society

Figure 16 Blocking plan for the formal, vertical entrance march of
Acaste and Clitandre in *The Misanthrope,* act 2.

that enveloped these mismatched lovers – the world of superficiality
and duplicity to which, as Alceste must learn to his grief, Célimène
ultimately belongs. With the intrusion of this world – in the person
of the two marquises, Acaste and Clintandre – into Célimène's salon
in the second act, the mood of the preceding love scene was swept
away in a gust of broad, boisterous parody. These two sumptuously
costumed gentlemen – living examples in Bergman's production of
folly ripened to the point of bursting – made their pompously ceremonial entrance together, commanding a maximum of attention as
they marched with great delight down the central axis of the stage
(Fig. 16). Met at the halfway point by an equally delighted
Célimène, they greeted her with effusive hand kisses and ecstatic
outbursts of falsetto laughter. "The marquises must feel that they
are a gift to the nation!" Bergman's assistant had noted during rehearsals, and their behavior throughout the performance certainly
radiated precisely this point of view. Bergman, a superb director of
farce (though he himself denies it and one might not guess it from
his films), delineated and differentiated these gross and gorgeous

caricatures of human folly with a loving eye for telling visual and vocal comic details. Peter Steen's Clitandre, propelled by an over-powering self-esteem so intense that it threatened at times to lift him off the floor, maintained a piercing falsetto voice and a laughter "that resembled the cry of a peacock" (*Fyens Stiftstidende*). His smaller, more earthbound, and decidedly more venomous colleague Acaste was acted by Erik Mørk in a contrastingly deeper tone of voice that had a grotesquely birdlike, cackling quality about it. Their exchanges with Célimène – colored by an intoxicating sense of com-radeship as they joined together in the stimulating game of double entendre and murdered reputations – assumed the character of a symphonic composition for three voices and three distinct sorts of laughter. An entire vocabulary of contrasting sounds and gestures – ranging from "little-marquis laughter" and "little-marquis approval" through "great-marquis laughter," "general laughter," and a com-plete battery of assorted "marquis glances" – accompanied Céli-mène's successive attacks on the reputations of their absent "friends." (The pointers offered by Molière himself in *L'Impromptu de Versailles* for playing a foppish marquis – "with that swaggering manner they call the society air" and "with a special way of talking, to distinguish themselves from the common herd" – must surely have exerted an influence on Bergman's conception.) However else they were differentiated, meanwhile, the twin marquises moved, gestured, and reacted in perfect harmony, united, as it were, by their mutual conviction of unmitigated superiority. Their entrances and exists and the general arrangement of their movements on the stage were all organized by Bergman in precise patterns of parallel, geometrically clean lines – a technique that might even remind one of the formality and contrived control of the entrées in a *ballet de cour*. However, in their strictly measured movements, in their deep, elaborate curtsies, and in the wide sweep of their lace-festooned arms as they gestured, these figures suggested grotesque, effemi-nate automatons, parodying the ideals of decorum and grace in *le grand siècle* in a capering crescendo of comic excess.

Although Bergman's broad satire of the *fâcheux* afforded a con-tinuous and carefully balanced comic contrast to the passionately serious tone of Alceste, the overall directorial concept of the comedy dictated a subtle but steady movement toward a black conclusion. Consequently, his treatment of the famous third-act encounter be-tween Célimène and her older rival, Arsinoé – played with dignified composure in this performance by Lise Ringheim – deliberately min-imized the scene's comic potential, emphasizing instead the essential vulgarity of the jealousy that animates their catty confrontation, the hollowness and even the brutality of the respective poses that they strike in their bid to gain control over one another.

Darker still was the tone of humiliation and suffering that pervaded the second major scene between Alceste and Célimène (IV.iii). In Bergman's view, Alceste's appeal here for compassion on the part of an unmoved and increasingly self-confident Célimène ("Good God! Could anything be more inhuman?") became "an almost Strindbergian passage," expressing the insoluble dilemma of a situation in which love and hatred are inextricably bound up together. In this scene, with its harsh and distorted resonances of their earlier encounter in the first act, Célimène seemed to be enjoying Alceste's defenselessness, as though it were a kind of applause for her performance. This time, as he fell to his knees to reiterate the absolute force of his love for her ("I love you more than can be said or thought"), she stood at the opposite end of the stage with her back turned, idly fingering one of the yellow roses in a magnificent bouquet that she had carried in with her at the beginning of the scene. In response to the "étrange manière" of her suitor and to the ideal demands that he seeks to impose upon her, she laughed harshly and then, ceasing to laugh, she threw the rose in his face. The moment anticipated Alceste's final bitter confrontation with the cardboard world of mendacity that surrounded him.

Bergman steadfastly resisted either sentimentalizing the play or distorting its basic tone into a uniformly and oppressively tragic one. Accordingly, his version did not conclude, as countless stage interpretations of *The Misanthrope* have done, with Alceste's angry departure from a world wrenched apart by irreconcilable contraries. It ended instead, as Molière's text of course does, with Philinte's closing lines to the effect that Alceste must be dissuaded from his purpose – a couplet that restored the sense of irony, the emphasis on a universe of paradoxes and unresolvable contradictions, on which the entire production had built. "After the final curtain has fallen," Bergman's production assistant has in fact remarked, "Philinte will bring Alceste back and the same game will begin again."[28] Nevertheless, this implied ironic repetitiveness in no way dispelled the atmosphere of darkness and finality that lies close beneath the brittle surface of Molière's bitter comedy. This mood was brought forcefully and decisively to the fore as the characters in the play confronted one another, for the last time, in a spirit no longer camouflaged by their previous gaiety.

The central character's disillusioned vision of the world as a jungle in which right is systematically overthrown and justice perverted, in which intrigue and self-interest alone govern and human intercourse is mere sham and theatrical make believe, was restated in the final act with the same vehemence and energy that had been dominant traits of his turbulent temperament from the beginning. "He wants to be angry," reads a note in the director's script (an echo, of course, of Alceste's own remark in the first act), and, charged with this overriding wrath, Moritzen's Misanthrope remained as trapped in the passionate intensity of his somber vision as the glittering society around him remained enmeshed in its own hollow masquerade. Locked in their single vision, the *fâcheux*, too, maintained to the

Alceste is rejected by Célimène (Ghita Nørby) in act 4. The rose she has disdainfully flung in his face still lies on the floor, in the far left corner of the picture. Copenhagen, 1973.

very end that fixity of character that they had displayed at their first appearance. The ludicrously overblown Oronte ("the winner of the sonnet-feud," as the production book calls him) seemed, if anything, to have grown in stature when he turned up again – in the scene that Bergman labels "Alceste's humiliation" – to present his proposal of marriage to Célimène, who haughtily declines to drop her mask or indicate her preference. The foppish affectations of the twin marquises were not a fraction diminished as they made their splendid inquisitorial entrance, with Arsinoé and Basque (who came in backwards). Marching straight down the central axis of the stage (see Fig. 17), they triumphantly displayed the incriminating letters that expose the perfidious Célimène for what she really is. Only when their masks momentarily slipped and the superficiality of their

The formal, frontal staging of the letter-reading scene in the Copenhagen production of *The Misanthrope*. Alceste stands in isolation to the right, his back to the audience.

Figure 17 The inquisitorial entrance of Acaste and Clitandre, accompanied by Basque and Arsinoé, in the letter-reading scene of *The Misanthrope*.

own poses stood revealed did these figures acquire a curious kind of unsentimentalized dignity; but they quickly resumed their poses and, trapped in their pretense, they remained to the very end of the performance what Bergman had so pointedly made of them from its start – players acting out their roles, playing their game of make believe.

Once they had departed, with self-possessed and greatly exaggerated salutes to a visibly chastened Célimène, and the two lovers were left face to face for the last time, the undertone of moving pathos that critics found so remarkable in Moritzen's performance reasserted itself. Utterly dejected and at a loss for words, he turned to Célimène. Admitting her guilt, she in turn faced him, head bent, as he reached out in an attempt to take hold of her hands. However, as he replied ("almost with a smile") by expressing his sense of being inescapably trapped in his irrational love ("scornfully and with self-reproach, not sentimentally"), the intensity of his anger began to return. At Célimène's subdued but firm refusal (spoken "like a child – with sincere directness") to follow him in renouncing the world (for, after all, "la solitude effraye une âme de vingt ans"!), his utter contempt for her compromising spirit exploded, and in a final gesture of outrage he knocked away her outstretched hand. Seeking some support for her position and finding none, she left the stage in a hurt, childish pout.

Following Célimène's departure, the play moved swiftly to its conclusion. Burying his face in his hands as she left, Alceste turned (after "a long pause of despair") to Eliante and spoke his last lines to her and Philinte in a restrained but vibrantly emotional tone of regret and resignation. Betrayed on all sides, overwhelmed with injustice, this Misanthrope made of his final exit a striking visual image of bitterness and isolation – an image that bore the stamp of his director's astonishing ability to create an interplay of gestures and words, glances and movements. Describing that "distant place"

The receding figure of Alceste in the closing scene of *The Misanthrope*. Danish Royal Theatre, 1973.

where one might be free to be an honest man, Alceste made his way up the stage, walking slowly backwards and facing the audience directly, his hands outstretched in a final, eloquent gesture of leave-taking—a receding black figure, etched in solitary, three-dimensional relief against the flat, artificial wing-and-border world of the stage setting. And then, having made his exit, he moved swiftly to take his vacant chair in the wings.

"There are two kinds of reality, that which you carry within yourself and which is mirrored in your face, and then the outer reality," Bergman has said in an interview, shortly before beginning work on *The Misanthrope* in Copenhagen. "I work only with that little dot, the human being, that is what I try to dissect and to penetrate more and more deeply, in order to trace his secrets."[29] Perhaps more than anything else, it has been this passionate preoccupation with the inner, spiritual reality of the work, the character, and the actor that has been the guiding impulse behind his finest classical productions.

5   The essence of Ibsen

> A theater which gives the imagination of both dramatist and actor
> greater freedom of movement and greater audacity, a simpler,
> more immediate, and more expressive form.
>
> Pär Lagerkvist

Like Molière, Ibsen has been a dramatist whose work Ingmar Bergman first began to direct in the mid-1950s, at the height of his
Malmö period – and, also like Molière, he has continued to occupy a
central place in the director's oeuvre ever since. Bergman's famous
reinterpretations of *Hedda Gabler* and *The Wild Duck* will surely remain milestones in the stage history of Ibsen's plays in the modern
period; and his 1981 production of *A Doll's House* in Munich seems
destined to become one. Although his first Ibsen venture – the mammoth, five-hour revival of *Peer Gynt* at the Malmö City Theatre
(March 8, 1957) – is perhaps less generally familiar than these later
accomplishments, it was certainly no less startling in its rejection of
older stage traditions. The overall effect, most reviewers agreed, was
"astonishing; it [was] like seeing a painting cleansed of its yellowed
exhibition varnish."[1] Enthusiasts and skeptics alike concurred that
here, at last, was "Ibsen's poem liberated in word and picture from
the lyrical and musical paraphernalia of theatrical tradition."[2]

Musical liberation was indeed no small part of Bergman's innovative approach to *Peer Gynt*. Ever since 1876, when it was first composed for the world premiere of the play, Edvard Grieg's familiar
musical score (Opus 23) has been inextricably linked to a "romantic"
conception of Ibsen's work. The richly melodious and nationalistic
strains of Grieg's music inevitably endow any production of *Peer
Gynt* with a basic tone of lyricism and sentimentality, casting over it
a conciliatory aura of folklore and romance that obscures the deeply
ironic and antisentimental undertones in Ibsen's conception of Peer.
For the poetic dreamer of dreams must *also* be recognized as the liar,
the egoist, the self-deceiver, the man who shirks responsibility and
shuns reality, determined instead to follow the easier course of "going roundabout." A change in attitude came slowly. By 1948, however, the Norwegian actor–director Hans Jacob Nilsen's controver-

sial antiromantic production was ready at last to take the decisive step of replacing Grieg's inappropriate romanticism with the stark, dissonant tones of a muscular new score by Harald Saeverud (Opus 28), whose music attempted to create a coherent pattern of "musical–psychological development" for the play.[3] It remained for Bergman to conceive the bolder and simpler expedient of dispensing with the rival claims of Grieg and Saeverud alike. In his *Peer Gynt,* the orchestral element was finally silenced, and musical accompaniment was restricted to the barest minimum needed in the play. Solveig's song was sung to a simple Norwegian folk tune; Ingrid Thulin's Anitra gyrated grotesquely to the stark accompaniment of a drum solo. "He has placed Ibsen back in the poet's seat and closed the orchestra pit," declared Martin Strömberg in *Stockholms–Tidningen.* "The inner logic of the drama, carried through to the final scene, has never been made as clear on the stage as it is here."

The real thrust of Bergman's conception was to lay bare the inner, deromanticized essense of Ibsen's drama – "Ibsen looked straight in the eye, without extenuating circumstances," as one critic phrased it.[4] To this end, he endeavored to cleanse both the play and its central character of all the sentimental associations, poetic stereotypes, and conciliatory idealizations that had accumulated about them over the years – and, what is more, to do so before the very eyes of the audience. "For us," declared a program note for the ambitious revival, "the essential thing has been to present the work as it is, without expressionistic trappings and topical political pointers but also without wrapping it in a romanticism that it had broken with at its very inception." In itself, the decision to present the play virtually without cuts represented a staggering challenge. The program lists a cast of fifty-six speaking roles, only eight of which were doubled. In all, Bergman required some ninety actors and extras for his production. His motive for undertaking the challenge in the first place is characteristic of his attitude in general: "Only once every ten or twenty years does a theater possess a Peer Gynt. Therefore we must do the play now – while we have Max von Sydow."[5]

Bergman's faith in his brilliant young star, not yet twenty-eight and fresh from his triumph as Antonius Block in *The Seventh Seal,* was not misplaced, and von Sydow's rootless, compromising, inwardly self-doubting Peer provided a solid basis on which the director could plan and execute his strategy. Instead of presenting *Peer Gynt* as a traditional kaleidoscopic series of more or less lifelike scenes, the entire visual framework of the production was subordinated to a single, ruling directorial concept–that of the play as a drama of pilgrimage, of the inward, spiritual journey of Peer, the man who is lost in illusions, toward disillusionment and nothingness. To articulate this idea, Bergman gradually and very deliberately removed the various decorative physical elements from his stage as the action progressed. In the earlier scenes, action was supported by a mixture of solid realistic details and stylized back projections of black-chalk landscape sketches, designed by Härje Ekman. The wedding celebration at Haegstad Farm, for example, took place in a basically realistic setting, framed by a vaguely sinister and threatening vision of mountains in the background–a vision that reemphasized the predominantly antiidyllic, even demonic tone that informed Bergman's interpretation of the wedding scene as a raucous, noisy brawl that culminates in the raw brutality of Peer's abduction of the bride. "It is no idyll, this wedding at Haegstad–there is drunkenness and violence and when the folk dance sounds over the farm, malicious laughter and evil words fill the air," commented Åke Perlström in *Göteborgs–Posten*.

As the play moved on, however, a development toward greater and greater simplification and dematerialization of the stage environment became apparent. Projections alone were now used to establish, in a nonrepresentational manner, the basic mood of a given scene, until, by the end of the play, these too had been eliminated and the stage was left completely stripped and empty. In the last act, all theatrical paraphernalia had vanished; the immense stage at Malmö now became an apparently limitless, black, and empty space that accentuated the old man's spiritual impasse and intensified his isolation and despair as he roamed about near the last crossroads of life, unable now to fantasize himself away from the reality and finality of death. In the darkness of the void, Peer encountered figures of an obviously and entirely symbolic character, who threatened him with doom and final extinction in the Button Moulder's casting ladle. The concluding moments of the play thus resolved themselves on a bleak and extremely subdued note of loneliness and of ultimate reckoning. "The onion had been peeled, Max von Sydow had penetrated to Peer's innermost, naked core, the human being beneath the troll."[6]

The more perceptive critics had by this time begun to notice and to debate with energy Bergman's unique sense of choreography, his "ability to mold a scene with many figures in such a way that the controlling hand of his artistic intent is evident in every aspect" (*Göteborgs Handels– och Sjöfartstidning*). His use of static or animated figure compositions as the most important decorative element on the stage was fast becoming a trademark of his production style. "But in that Ingmar Bergman utilizes far fewer individuals for this purpose and often arranges them within an optically almost vacant space, he places far more severe demands upon his supernumeraries than, for example, Reinhardt did, and he also achieves far more sophisticated effects," Ebbe Linde observed in connection with Bergman's presentation of Goethe's *Ur-Faust*, a kind of companion piece to *Peer Gynt* that he staged at Malmö the following year.[7] In both of these productions, gestures, movements, positions, and groupings were all integrated into an architectonic pattern that yielded a flow of expressive pictorial compositions, each one designed to support and enunciate the inner logic of a particular scene. Some reviewers were troubled by a sense of stiffness and construction in the very tightly stylized *Faust* production, but the freer and more robust scenes in *Peer Gynt* stood out with an almost explosive plastic eloquence.

The intensely colored episode in King Brose's troll court resembled a macabre Hieronymus Bosch vision of hell, with the trolls "grouped like grotesque, animallike creatures carved into the very mountain walls" (*Politiken*). The strongly erotic nature of the encounter between Peer and the Greenclad One ("lust ran like molten metal through her body, on which pouting red nipples had been applied to her skintight tulle") gave the scene the character of an orgastic, trollish amplification of the raucous festivities at Haegstad. The restless, opportunistic Gynt of Max von Sydow seemed in danger of being virtually swallowed up by a troll court that rolled forward in a block "like an infestation of vermin, fluttering and waving in uniform reactions until it breaks up, like an avalanche of lava-colored rocks, and sucks itself firmly around [him], a sticky mass of hair and snouts that already is halfway the Boyg" (*Göteborgs Handels–och Sjöfartstidning*).

The sheer visual force of this scene lent it a nightmarish quality that continued to persist throughout the performance. This sense of nightmare recurred again and again – in Peer's horrified brush with the shapeless, faceless Boyg, whose voice drew him trancelike across the empty stage toward the background; in the writhing contortions of Anitra, who (false rump and all!) bumped and grinded for him in the desert; but above all, in his Kafkaesque encounter with the madmen in the Cairo lunatic asylum.

Retention of the "detachable" fourth act – albeit somewhat shortened – was a cardinal point in Bergman's interpretation of *Peer Gynt*, and the closing scene of this act, in the Cairo madhouse, became the

most harrowing experience of all in Peer's long journey through a
hostile world. Here, in the realm where "Absolute Reason passed
away at eleven o'clock last night," the inhabitants were "staring,
yawning, half-sleeping, aimlessly revolving and grimacing monsters
in the same khaki-colored institutional outfits."[8] Neither the barred
windows nor the iron cages mentioned in Ibsen's stage directions
were to be seen in Bergman's production. Nor were they necessary,
for the lunatics themselves comprised the "scenery." In the darkness of the vast empty stage, bare except for a few simple benches,
these figures were isolated in pools of light to form a grotesque
tableau around Peer and Begriffenfeldt, his guide to this chamber of
horrors. A few of them demonstrated their personal specialities:
"Someone hanged himself, and his neighbor, who could no longer
be bothered to carry his own head, leaned it against the corpse,"
wrote Allan Fagerström in *Aftonbladet*. "Another lunatic in an effective Einstein mask cut his throat, while the remainder of this contorted company marched in a stately polonaise that would be un-
thinkable on any other stage but this one." The topical satire with
which Ibsen was concerned in this part of the play was subordinated
to the more coherently dramatic purpose that the scene was made to
serve here – a concrete and frightening nightmare vision of an inferno of madness, absurdity, and despair that marked the outermost
station on Peer's weary pilgrimage in search of his true self.

Bergman's production of *Peer Gynt* is especially noteworthy because it presented a coherent and completely unified interpretative
image of the entire play – one that reached beyond the folklore and
pictorialism of the first three acts into the dark and threatening
dimension of the work's final movement. "Forward and back is
equally far," Peer is fond of repeating – but his journey home was far
bleaker and more lonely and it took him through an endlessly dark
and empty universe of a stage, where menacing presences awaited
him everywhere. In the depths of the darkness, Toivo Pawlo's Button Moulder crouched over his bellows, his ladle, and his doomsday
book – and out of the same darkness stepped the light and redemptive figure of Solveig (played by Gunnel Lindblom). Every trace of
sentimentality was expunged from Peer's reunion with her. The
final picture that confronted the audience was that of "only two
human beings on an immense stage, and in the background the
mute, bent figure of the Button Moulder, his casting ladle in his
hand and his box of tools upon his back."[9] (Always reluctant to
waste a good effect, Bergman managed to give this striking tableau
an effective "reprise" in his subsequent production of *Ur-Faust*. In

The writhing contortions of Anitra (Ingrid Thulin) are watched with
obvious relish by Peer Gynt (Max von Sydow). Malmö City Theatre,
1957.

the final dungeon scene, played by the same constellation of actors, Faust [von Sydow] tried desperately to penetrate the madness of Margarete [Lindblom] while the brooding silhouette of Mephistopheles [Pawlo] loomed ominously in the background.)

"The theater calls for nothing," Bergman has said. "TV includes everything, film includes everything, there everything is shown. Theater ought to be the encounter of human beings with human beings and nothing more. All else is distracting."[10] This expressed determination to strip away all inessential representational details in order to focus on the face-to-face encounter between actor and spectator has been a singularly persistent feature of all his Ibsen productions through the years. With *Peer Gynt*, it removed the play decisively from the realm of amiable but confused pantomime to which it is so often confined in the theater. But there is another side to Bergman's work with Ibsen that must also be emphasized, namely this director's exceptional critical sensitivity to those details in the plays that *are* essential, but that are often overlooked by less incisive minds. When asked to give an explanation for the unusual power and effectiveness of the scene in which Mother Aase (Naima Wifstrand) dies in *Peer Gynt*, he apparently had a ready reply:

Quite simply because we followed Ibsen. It is all there in the stage directions, you see – that he must sit at the foot of her bed. He cannot watch Aase die – he dares not do so – and therefore she summons the last of her strength to help him. It isn't he who comforts her, quite the other way round. It pays to show solidarity with the playwright, especially when his name is Henrik Ibsen.[11]

It can be argued that this remark points to a more general truth about Bergman's artistic attitude, not only toward Ibsen's plays but toward any work he undertakes to present on the stage. In his drive toward simplification and intensification, certain extraneous or overtly symbolic things (vine leaves, portentous portraits, white horses, visiting cards marked with black crosses) may well risk being eliminated – but nothing is added that does not find its ultimate basis and justification in the text.

THE AIRLESS WORLD OF HEDDA GABLER

Hedda Gabler, Bergman's second Ibsen production, burst like a bomb on the European theater scene when it first appeared at Dramaten in 1964, and in retrospect it has remained one of the truly revolutionary and influential Ibsen productions of this century. As he had done in *Peer Gynt,* Bergman resolutely swept aside the dusty impedimenta of accumulated tradition–in this case the assumptions acquired through three-quarters of a century of naturalistic performances. In his hands *Hedda Gabler* emerged, with almost hypnotic intensity, as a work whose vision extends far beyond the realistic or the social plane. His starkly simplified and stylized interpretation created a tightly controlled distillation in which nothing was permitted to distract from the ruling image of the play as a drama of destiny, a cold fable of characters buried alive in a deadly vacuum. "His inspiration transformed the mathematical reality of the play into the workings of a dream, over whose outcome one has no control. He illuminated the drama in a light that was not of this world," wrote Siegfried Melchinger in *Theater heute.* [12] In no other Bergman production has his instinct for clarity and purity, his extraordinary ability to comprehend and transmit the inner shape of the drama found more pregnant expression than in this boldly untraditional *Hedda.*

Bergman, who says he envies the musical conductor his unlimited opportunity to return again and again to a favorite score, has tried to adopt something of the same approach with those plays that "pursue" him – and *Hedda Gabler* has decidedly been one of these. Until now he has restaged this particular work twice since his Stockholm premiere, both times outside Sweden, and in each instance a different set of artistic and personal circumstances has prevailed. In 1970 he was invited to direct members of the National Theatre company in a London production that featured Maggie Smith in the title role. On the surface in terms of the physical setting and the details of the external mise-en-scène, little seemed to have changed since the Stockholm production (which had been seen on tour in London in 1968). In fact, however, having no control whatsoever over the selection of the cast and confronted with extremely exacerbating rehearsal conditions, Bergman found it impossible to direct the English revival in a satisfactory manner. The sense of a disturbing discrepancy between his concept and the execution of the English actors–*Punch* maintained that "this is a director's idea undermining an intelligent performance," while *The Observer* was inclined to suggest that "a naturalistic production would fit most of Maggie Smith's performance better"[13]–was the inevitable result of the working conditions that Bergman himself describes in the conversation entitled "Talking about Tomorrow," found at the end of this volume. These circumstances have caused him to since disown this unrepresentative production.

A very different result was achieved in his subsequent production of the play at the Residenztheater in Munich (April 11, 1979), where the difficulties that had so obviously beset the English cast of the National Theatre revival had vanished completely. In Munich the play emerged once again with the full force and intensity that had made Bergman's first *Hedda Gabler* so memorable – which is not to say that this third revival was merely a replica of the Dramaten performance. In the Residenztheater production, Ibsen's four-act drama became a chamber play, an even more precise formulation than it had been before, played now as one fluid and unbroken action, without an intermission. There were also differences between the Munich and the Stockholm productions both in terms of certain features of the setting and in terms of the choreography of particular moments in the play. Unlike the distinct conceptual differences that separate Bergman's versions of *The Ghost Sonata*, however, the changes made in this case concerned matters of detail rather than matters of substance. In essence, all three of these productions of *Hedda Gabler* projected a fundamentally identical vision of the play as a drama of entrapment and isolation, of ghostlike figures – "dead souls in the ashes," as *Süddeutsche Zeitung* called them – caught in a world in which there are no second chances.

To articulate this vision, Bergman relentlessly stripped away the heavy mosaic of realistic details present in Ibsen's "handsomely and tastefully furnished drawing room" – the thick carpets, the dark porcelain stove, the curtained French windows, and, not least, the portentous portrait of Hedda's father, General Gabler, were all eliminated, for much the same reason that the symbolic allusions to the Dionysian vine leaves in Løvborg's hair (pointers so dear to the hearts of literary scholars) were ruthlessly expunged by him. "No fascination with museumlike interior decorating is permitted to divert the audience's concentration away from the human drama," declared Per Erik Wahlund (*Svenska Dagbladet*) following the Stockholm premiere (October 17, 1964). The entire stage space was transformed by Bergman and his designer (Mago, in all three cases) into an immense, nonrepresentational box that reflected and contributed to the prevailing atmosphere of claustrophobia, rather than illustrating it in a photographic manner. Uniformly lined with a dark red, velvetlike fabric, this mausoleum–stage radiated an oppressive sense of enclosure and lifelessness. "One looks into this strange locale and wonders how human beings can breathe there. It is as though there is no air in this red chamber of horrors," wrote Nils Beyer (*Stockholms–Tidningen*) of this "ghostly vision." There were neither actual windows nor walls, only a succession of simple screens, all covered in the same dark-red velvet, which demarcated a shallow playing area within the empty space.

A smaller, movable screen–sometimes a door, sometimes a barrier in the central character's mind–bisected the stage vertically into two separate spheres of simultaneous action. "A red screen divides life into two compartments," remarked *Dagens Nyheter*. "In one of them the dull routine of living drags on, in the other Hedda Gabler writhes in desperation and frustration." This was the "inner room" of Ibsen's stage directions, the physical and psychic retreat where Hedda keeps her piano and the General's pistols, which Bergman now laid bare to view. Only the strictest minimum of stylized period furniture–a dark-red sofa, a pair of red chairs, a black bookcase, a black piano on which stood a bouquet of dark-red roses, a large mirror–dotted the monotonous landscape of Hedda's prison-world. In this all-consuming red vacuum, the exits at the back and to the side seemed veiled in obscurity. Now and then during the performance, the wall screen in the background opened, as if moved by a ghostly hand, to reveal a dark void in which offstage characters were seen to move. Of the world outside, the world of reality, there was no trace anywhere. "It exists only as a quotation," observed Hans Schwab-Felisch in *Frankfurter Allgemeine*. "It impinges on what happens, and it even has the power to affect actual events, but it has no real meaning."

Perceived in the eerie unreality of this airless, timeless red inferno, illuminated by a uniformly cold light that tampered with contours and erased any secure sense of spatial dimensionality, the characters in the drama appeared like figures suspended in a void. Each was dressed in a muted, unrelieved monotone–Hedda in dark green, the others in yet more subdued color values that ranged from pale gray and olive to black. A hint of period flavor in the costumes– pointedly simplified and stylized–completed the impression of characters that existed, independent of any material surroundings, in an atmosphere in which reality had no place. ("We had no intention of making the costumes symbolic," Mago has stated specifically. "We wanted them to be simple, uniform, and suggestive of another time, only vaguely dated, vaguely period."[14]) Inevitably, perhaps, the impact created by these isolated human figures, seen against a ground of strangely menacing vacancy, evoked allusions to Bergman's own austere vision as a film maker and, in particular, to Edvard Munch's brooding studies of a mood of spiritual desolation and paralysis. "The memory of Munch's great canvas of humanity

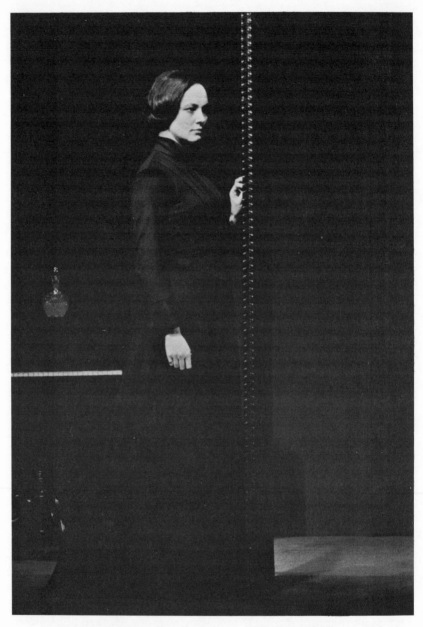

Hedda Gabler (Christine Buchegger) watches from behind the screen that bisected the stage vertically in Bergman's *Hedda Gabler*. Residenztheater, 1979.

haunts one's inner eye: those swaying figures of women in monochrome, suffused in the color of blood. . . . It is oppressive, subdued, and enclosed," remarked one critic.[15]

In Bergman's theater poetics, as we know, the various external components of a production – the setting, the costumes, the lighting design – have importance only in so far as they conspire to stimulate the imagination of the audience. This process of spectator activation – the need to make the performance "live in his heart, in his mind" – is, to Bergman, the essential requirement, the basic and immutable law of the theater. Every decision and every spatial arrangement in his mise-en-scène is calculated to contribute to a spectrum of suggestions, a visual and aural rhythm that will accomplish this end as forcefully and directly as possible. Accordingly, his conception of *Hedda Gabler* endeavored to establish, from the very outset, the strongest possible sense of an imaginative bond between stage and auditorium. In the Stockholm production at Dramaten, the theater's ornate front curtain rose – but only halfway – several minutes before the play began, allowing the audience to breathe in the atmosphere beforehand.[16] Deprived by the director of the comfortable naturalistic fiction of an invisible fourth wall, the spectator felt himself to be in the Tesman "home," virtually face to face with its inhabitants. "Everything is quiet. We experience the theatrical space as a unity. We are made to understand that actors and not real people from the nineties are about to make their entrance. The screens are not walls in a house, but rather the kind of screen that the Chinese put up to force evil spirits to alter their course," commented the reviewer for *Arbetarbladet*. In the Munich production, which was played entirely without a curtain, Bergman accomplished his purpose of establishing a sense of rapport between actors and audience by extending the stage of the cavernous Residenztheater so far forward into the auditorium that virtually all the scenes were acted in front of the line of the fire curtain. (Notice the extreme frontal placement of the sofa and Hedda's chair in the ground plan seen in Fig. 18). In both productions the houselights were dimmed only after the play had begun, and later a glaring projection of light from the rear of the house, sweeping directly above the heads of the audience, further obliterated the separation between stage and auditorium.

Ultimately, however, the real impact of Bergman's interpretation of Hedda Gabler derived not so much from his revolutionary dematerialization of the physical setting as from his analytical, almost surgical dissection of the enigma of Hedda herself. In Bergman's version Hedda was never allowed to disappear from sight. She

Figure 18. Plan of the stage (Residenztheater) for *Hedda Gabler*.

stood trapped before us on the stage, caught in a Pirandellian situation of having to watch her innermost spiritual agony dragged into the spotlight of public scrutiny. Even when she was not directly involved in the action, she remained a visible, restless, solitary presence isolated on her own side of the stylized dividing screen. "She is the secret director of the events, but there remains always a glass wall between her, the defeated human being, and the others," wrote *Frankfurter Allgemeine* of the Munich production. Here, Christine Buchegger established an unhysterical Hedda characterized not by frantic desperation, but rather by a strangely detached sense of composure, of authority and control blended with an almost cynical disdain for the destiny she knows she has chosen for herself. At Dramaten, Gertrud Fridh drew a more mature and more strikingly aristocratic portrait of General Gabler's daughter, possessed of an even greater degree of self-control and displaying an ironic remoteness from everything and everyone about her. Her isolation seemed predestined, grandiose. The common denominator of both these performances was the accumulating sensation of isolation, alienation, and entrapment that they created.

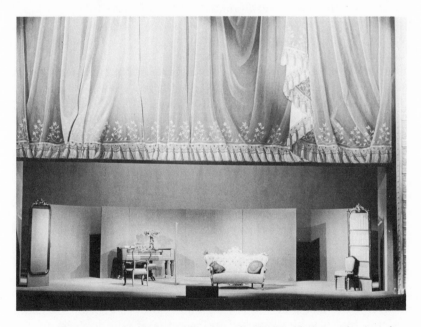

The stage setting, designed by Mago, for the Stockholm production of *Hedda Gabler*, 1964. The vertical dividing screen is visible to the left of the prompter's box.

From the outset, in the dreamlike opening pantomine with which Bergman prefaced and defined the play proper, Hedda's entrapment was boldly underscored. Silently, like a sleepwalker, she came on to the empty stage, her features locked in a death mask of despair and frustration. "We do not experience her as a human being of flesh and blood," wrote Nils Beyer of Fridh's extraordinary appearance: "It is a damned soul who is stirring in this strange abode, before Ibsen himself starts to speak and the intricate clockwork mechanism begins to operate." As the light focused on Hedda and the auditorium gradually darkened, she moved noiselessly towards the audience. At the very front of the stage she stopped and, for a frozen moment, she stood, utterly immobile and expressionless, staring with wide open eyes into vacant space. Melchinger provides an unusually vivid description of this moment: "For a long time to come, I will see Hedda Gabler before me: standing at the front of the stage, aristocratic, with her chin tilted slightly upwards, the Titian-red hair outlined against the dull red of the stage space, with her sarcastic, tense mouth and those eyes that stared into the darkness, where we sat." Turning away, she walked over to the (empty) mirror and began a critical examination of her person—first of her face, then her figure, letting her hands run slowly down her body to her stomach. Then, in a violent reaction of revulsion and despair, she suddenly bent double and pressed her hands to her abdomen, pounding it several times with the full force of her clenched fists. At last, in an effort to regain control over herself, she walked to the piano, lit a cigarette, stubbed it out at once, and then settled herself in an armchair. Meanwhile, the intrusion of the outside world, in the persons of Aunt Julle and the maid, began, as their expository small talk broke the silence for the first time.

Hence, the outcome was inevitable from the start. This preliminary, oneiric movement in Bergman's production proclaimed a relentlessly closed framework of doom from which there was clearly no escape. "She is forced into a corner because she is a woman who, when she is pregnant, is left with no choice. She is in a blind alley. Whether she likes it or doesn't like it, there it is. It says so in the score," Bergman himself has declared. Nor, he is quick to add, should the opening pantomime be viewed as an interpolated embellishment upon that score: "It is there in the play. Not the scene itself, but the fact that she is pregnant and doesn't want the child. It's only that it is so disguised in Ibsen that if you don't listen very carefully, it will elude you. It is precisely the same in a musical

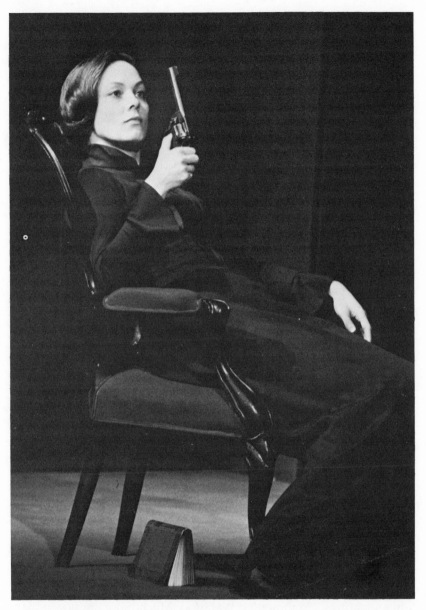

Buchegger's Hedda dispassionately planning her suicide. The book she
previously had dropped in boredom still lies at her feet.

composition. If something is more weakly scored but needs to be brought out, then you lift it up. That is precisely what I have done in *Hedda Gabler*."[17] The director's point communicated itself forcefully both in the Stockholm and in the Munich productions (neither of which exhibited the risible morning sickness antics that eventually crept into the English performance). "She appears in a wordless scene that is not in the play, as a woman whose despair manifests itself only as a last and, as she knows, a vain protest against circumstances," remarked *Frankfurter Allgemeine* of the 1979 revival. "She is defeated from the very beginning."

Once established, the pattern of Hedda's alienation and spiritual nausea proceeded to grow and develop through a continuous sequence of peripheral actions, performed as she listened – or pointedly refused to listen – to the conversation taking place on the other side of the dividing screen. The spasmodic movements of Hedda in her cage – lighting and extinguishing cigarettes, biting her own hand in a sudden neurotic gesture of self-contempt, or ironically perusing a book in a parody of the manners of the well-educated nineteenth-century woman, only to let it fall to the floor a moment afterwards – were signposts marking her inexorable progress towards destruction. "One might have thought that Hedda was spying; but the impression produced was rather than the stage spied on Hedda, that she was being dissected by it against her will," observed Melchinger. The point is an essential one. Attention was fixed not on the act of Hedda's suicide – for that was a foregone conclusion from the outset – but on the existential *process* of the act, as analyzed by the character who commits it. Out of self-reflection arose Hedda's consuming soul sickness. Humiliated by the superimposed identity that Tesman's world has prepared for her, she searched in vain for some reliable evidence of her elusive self. Tormented by the thought of this incarceration in a role, she found herself drawn to the mirror – that most central of all props in Bergman's art – in which she could watch herself live and watch herself prepare to die. She was "continually shown before the imaginary mirror, striking poses, testing attitudes, examining her fading complexion, trying as it were to convince herself that she is truly real; now and then she stands so close to the mirror that it seems as if she wants to breathe away her human features," commented Wahlund. Much more important than as a device for reassuring Hedda of her reality, however, was the mirror's function as a glass in which *the actress* observes her own performance. Standing before the mirror at the end of the first act, staring at a reality that is already fixed forever, she coolly and dispassionately rehearsed the aesthetically pleasing suicide she has planned for herself. She removed her high-heeled pumps carefully, both as a gesture of fastidiousness and as a practical measure that allowed her to stand more steadily when she fired. And she again stood before the mirror when, with the utmost composure, she actually pointed the pistol to her temple and squeezed the trigger at the end.

From her first entrance into the world of the others, Bergman's Hedda stood demonstrably alone, cut off from everyone else about her. Whether reacting with disdain or thinly disguised disgust to the insinuating conversation between her husband and his precious Aunt Julle or coldly contemplating the bleak autumn landscape outside ("so golden–and withered"), her entire behavior emphasized that she was the outsider, the alien who acted and reacted on a different level and with far greater intensity than these ordinary– and in this case actually paler–figures around her did. Tesman, her husband, was in Bergman's interpretation an affable, middle-aged pedant whom she treated with bored, impatient politeness, and whose ceaseless pursuit of data from a dead and meaningless historical past epitomized the futility of her own situation. Both in Ingvar Kjellson's discretely comic performance in Stockholm and in Kurt Meisel's very sympathetic portrayal of the character in Munich, Tesman's contentedly self-centered preoccupation with his own small world lent him a certain childlike innocence that, in itself, deepened the impression of the gulf between him and Hedda. His reactions invariably reflected the egoistic simplicity of a child. "He became utterly distraught when the anticipated professorship seemed to be slipping away from him and, when Løvborg refrained from competing with him, he glowed with overflowing, naive, and grateful happiness," remarked one reviewer of Kjellson's performance.[18] Perhaps even more strikingly in the Munich revival, as Meisel's Tesman ran excitedly towards a totally disinterested Hedda with the news of Løvborg's decision, the unbridgeable distance between them materialized with graphic clarity.

There are two other men in Hedda's life–neither one of whom represents a viable means of escape from her predicament. In Bergman's productions Judge Brack was a smiling, insolent blackguard who offered an alternative she had certainly considered and had long since rejected. This coldly detached and ruthless libertine–who like a spy or a villain in a melodrama made all his entrances and exits through a concealed door in the proscenium–was the only one

Hedda Gabler (Gertrud Fridh) with Tesman (Ingvar Kjellson), the husband she treats with bored politeness. Dramaten, 1964.

to whom she could actually communicate her boredom, her excruciating sense of life as one unending and tedious railroad journey
that one spends locked in a compartment with a single traveling
companion. But, as she well knew, the cynical Brack was also the
only one who saw straight through her at all times. As a kind of
male counterpart of Hedda, he recognized the potential danger
when she threatened him with her revolver–yet he was at the same
time maddeningly unwilling to treat her threat as more than an
empty theatrical gesture ("People don't do such things").

Eilert Løvborg, the third man in Hedda's life and, in Bergman's
interpretation, so obviously her former lover, was from the beginning a man who had reached the end of his rope. This deromanticized Løvborg–played with particularly moving and passionate
desperation by Martin Benrath at the Residenztheater–was no free-
spirited Dionysian visionary. He possessed neither vine leaves nor
a future any longer, and the "masterpiece" containing his prescription for the future of human civilization was nothing more than a
pitifully few sheets of paper. (Questioned about this very suggestive detail of the strikingly thin manuscript, Bergman finds a characteristically concrete explanation, pointing out that had it been
any thicker Løvborg would certainly have noticed his fatal loss of it
at once.)

The fact that no one else but Hedda seemed aware of the stifling,
hermetically sealed atmosphere ("the odor of death" she tries to
describe to Brack) in which they moved and in which she was imprisoned heightened the sense of her alienation from the other characters in the drama. "They behave as though they came here
through gardens, from animated soirees, and from the forests of the
North; and they depart in due time, as a matter of course, to go out
into their life again, to drink, to work, to socialize. And nobody
realizes that they . . . have been drawn into a somber classical
drama in which it is impossible to be lighthearted or to maintain an
everyday attitude," remarked *Süddeutsche Zeitung.* The deep irony of
this tonal discrepancy (which this critic in fact failed to comprehend)
was clearly a deliberate strategy on Bergman's part. This suggestion
of a perceptional gulf was continually amplified by him in terms of
the spatial and compositional patterns he developed. Taking the
fullest advantage of the width of his stage–reinforced by a strong
impression of shallowness created by the barricade of low screens
encircling the playing area (and by the half-lowered curtain at
Dramaten)–he stressed widely separated groups, conversations
conducted from opposite sides of the stage, and vivid images of

Hedda seated apart or faced away from other characters during even the tensest of confrontations (e.g., in the second-act scene in which she so ruthlessly destroys the relationship between Thea and Løvborg). Each choreographic nuance of this kind was in turn blended into a broad, firmly conceived sculptural plan, in which the creation of an illusion of reality played no part at all.

Instead, the graphic bas-relief effects that Bergman favored in his *Hedda Gabler* were at the same time both powerfully abstract and eloquently expressive of the unspoken subtext and inner rhythm of the drama. A sinuous interplay of colors, lighting changes, and figure compositions produced at times a distorted, impressionistic, even dreamlike quality in the many scenes in which silhouette or bas-relief effects predominated. In both the Stockholm and the Munich productions, for example, a chilling physical sensation of stale-

A visual image of Hedda's isolation from Løvborg and Thea in act 2 of *Hedda Gabler*. Residenztheater, 1979.

ness and futility was conjured up for the moment at the beginning of the third act when Thea and Hedda awaken from their anxious all-night vigil. Here, low-angle projectors (so-called Bergman lamps) that hung at the back of the auditorium illuminated the forestage so glaringly and piercingly that the plastic contours of the characters' faces were momentarily obliterated. "There they sat, facing the front of the stage, opening their mouths, carefully choosing their gestures, now and then looking at each other in profile," wrote Melchinger. Bergman's antinaturalistic emphasis on unmitigated frontal playing and severely linear, flattened picture compositions was even compared by this critic to Cézanne's revolutionary redistribution of the elements of pictorial space.

Time, like space, is a dimension with which Bergman often experiments freely in his stage productions. As a film maker, of course, such an idea is very close to him: "I found out at a very early stage that time doesn't exist in films. That is: logical time ceases to exist for the spectator. In fact one can play about with time more or less as one likes . . . it's part of the magic of film, that one's awareness of time vanishes completely."[19] The translation of this line of thinking into theatrical terms has yielded some fascinating results in Bergman's work – not least in *Hedda Gabler*, where his manipulation of temporal perception played a sometimes crucial role in creating a precise atmosphere or directing audience response towards a specific emotional stimulus. The compression of hours or even days of real time into only a few moments of stage time is among the fairly routine conventions of drama and theater. Far less common, however, is Bergman's (characteristically cinematographic) attraction to the obverse process – the expansion of perhaps only a moment of real time into a much more prolonged slow motion replay of that moment on the stage. "One second of reality can be two minutes on the stage," he persuaded the cast of the Munich production of the play, and his consequent application of a kind of theatrical slow motion at times added a striking extra dimension of suspended animation to the finished performance.

Perhaps nowhere was this dimension more forcefully projected than in the first face-to-face encounter between Hedda and Løvborg (in Ibsen's second act), in which a sense of time and motion in suspension governed the expressive vocabulary of signs and gestures in the sequence.[20] As Løvborg's arrival was announced, Hedda's forcible attempt to conceal her apprehension and to remain, as always, in control of the situation found its expression in languid, automatonlike movements. She tried first to sit down dispassionately, but, unable to remain seated, she rose again "in slow motion" – watched closely by the cynical Brack who, as usual, lost no time in signifying that he, too, had taken note of her unrest. When Løvborg did appear, he stopped at once to search out Hedda; looking fixedly at her – and completely ignoring Tesman, who stood directly beside him – he walked slowly toward her and took her hand, which he held "a little bit too long." The virtually mesmeric influence that the mere physical presence of Løvborg exerted on Hedda overshadowed his subsequent conversation with Tesman about his new work ("This is my real book. The one in which I have spoken with my own voice"). As he sat down to show Tesman his manuscript, Hedda, who had been restlessly prowling in the area behind the sofa, abruptly went around it and sat down as well – clearly unaware that she was in fact copying Løvborg's movements, and narrowly observed all the while by the ever-vigilant Brack. But to this Hedda, her former lover's vision of the future obviously held as little meaning for her as her husband's empty pursuit of a dead past.

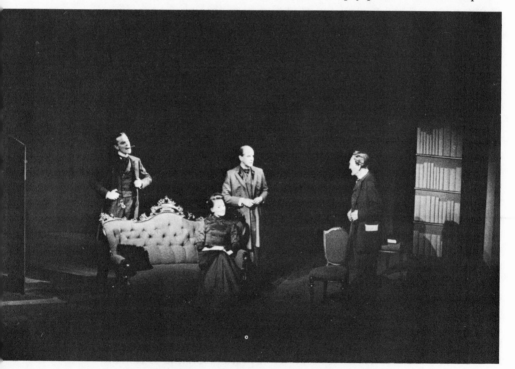

"This is my real book." Løvborg, manuscript in his pocket, is received by Hedda, Tesman, and Brack. Dramaten, 1964.

Accordingly, she drifted nervously into her private sanctuary as the two men continued to talk – only to reemerge moments later, curt and determined to remain collected for the encounter that was to come.

With steadily accelerating force, Bergman's staging of this focal scene between Hedda and Løvborg articulated the essence of the total impasse between them – not as a "breakdown of communication" in conventional terms, but rather as a situation in which the unspoken communication that passed between these two was all too audible and clear. The passionate emotionality of Løvborg's first impulsive outburst ("Hedda. Hedda – Gabler!") was coupled with a conviction of his own strength in this encounter ("he knows he is dangerous for Hedda"). She, in turn, met this from the outset with her own determination to avoid an emotional scene altogether and, above all, to regain her dominance over him. In the initial phase of this power struggle, a variety of strategies – her calculated formality, her avoidance at first of any eye-contact, the ferocious insistence with which she concentrated her attention on the photographs from her honeymoon that she stiffly displayed for him, and the exaggerated amiability with which she greeted Tesman's interruption of their tête-à-tête – contributed to her campaign for perfect aloofness. Gradually, however, the mood of the scene began to change. As Løvborg insistently demanded to know whether there had not been a trace of love between them, Hedda's stinging retort – that their relationship had been that of "two good friends who could tell each other everything" – was spoken "to herself, full of sadism," and this marked the beginning of an emotional transition in her behavior. From this point on, as the conversation drifted to remembrance of things past, she became both more responsive and also increasingly more aggressive. Her realization that "you think I had some power over you" even prompted her to smile.

As the scene between Hedda and Løvborg took on the character of a virtual reenactment of similar scenes between them in the past, Bergman's choreography and lighting established an eerie visual adumbration of unreality and déjà vu. Much as the presence of General Gabler had hovered over their meetings in the past, so too the figures of Tesman and Brack could now be seen through the open screens, as menacing presences that loomed in the background. By the time the scene had reached the point at which Ibsen's stage directions indicate that it had begun to grow dark, Bergman's lighting scheme – which was, of course, completely independent of Ibsen's naturalistic considerations, as there were neither windows nor obvious sources of light in his setting – had undergone a subtle but marked change. The penetrating light that fixed the two characters on the forestage had dimmed, and long, oversized shadows began to be cast upon the wall screen behind them. The contours of the figures themselves were erased, and for a moment the distinction between the living human characters and their own ghostly silhouettes seemed actually to be obliterated.

Immersed in this dreamlike atmosphere of brooding shadows, Hedda and Løvborg pursued their futile journey into the past with a bitterness and an increasingly overt aggressiveness that drew the scene several degrees closer to Strindberg's vision – or to the more harrowing sexual confrontations in Bergman's own films. "But tell me, Hedda – the root of the bond between us – was that not love?" cries Løvborg – and that outcry became the explosive juncture at which he decidedly lost his serenity and the balance of power reverted inexorably to Hedda. Their discussion of Løvborg's new relationship with Thea was suffused with a savage, menacing belligerency on his part that communicated itself directly to Hedda and conditioned her own response. Her defiant "I am a coward" erupted into a sudden outburst of hatred, expressed both in her harsh tone of voice and in her abrupt movement as she sprang up from her chair. The struggle reached its climax when Løvborg, in a final and erotically charged gesture, impulsively embraced Hedda from his seated position, passionately pressing his face against her. For a single instant she seemed about to relax her steely self-control. Then, brutally reasserting her dominance, she thrust him away with both hands. Immediately afterwards Thea entered – "as in a dream," Bergman had observed during rehearsals, "because when you want something to happen in a dream, it does. And Hedda wants a showdown with Thea."

Hedda's ruthless determination to reassert control over Løvborg ("For once in my life I want to have power over a human destiny") stood remorselessly exposed in Bergman's interpretation, as a critical step in the progression that led with relentless dramatic logic to her own destruction. The scene, near the end of the second act, in which she goads the reformed alcoholic to drink again was more than merely an act of deliberate, malicious irresponsibility. It was also a violent metastatic eruption of the deadly cancer – the perception of entrapment and internment – that fed on her inner being. The emphatic slow motion effects that Bergman introduced again in this scene gave it both an hallucinatory intensity and also a virtually mythological signification that several critics associated in their re-

views with the somber fatality of the gesture with which Isolde seals
her own and her lover's destiny in the first act of Richard Wagner's
Tristan und Isolde. "In the terrifying scene in which she sits with the
glass of punch in her hand and tempts her former lover to drink it, it
is her own destiny that she is preparing and not merely her lover's,"
Jahnsson remarked in his review of the Stockholm production in
Dagens Nyheter. "Great catastrophes always begin very quietly,"
Bergman himself had explained to his cast at the Residenztheater
when setting the tone of suppressed tension in this crucial incident.
In the rhythm of feeling that he established for the play, this scene
directly prefigured and prepared for the powerful emotional climax
in which Hedda destroys both Løvborg and his manuscript.

This final, destructive encounter between the two gained emotional intensity through some shrewd editing of the text on Bergman's part. In general, although *Hedda Gabler* was presented by him
substantially uncut, he was resolute in pruning away the punctilious
exposition and naturalistic "small talk" that link the play to the
theatrical conventions of an older period – but that, in his terms,
only serve to dissipate the potential emotional impact on a modern
audience. Bergman's commitment to the view that cinematic or theatrical art must speak directly to the subconscious mind rather than
to the conscious intellect has provoked its share of critical quarrels,
to be sure. It is a view that necessarily resists the imposition of any
closed framework of "meaning" – be it symbolic, Freudian, feminist,
political, or whatever – that will point the spectator in a single predetermined direction and deny him imaginative alternatives, thereby
voiding his truly creative participation in the dramatic event. If Bergman has any reservations about Ibsen as a theater poet, it is, he
says, because Ibsen "points the audience in the direction he wants it
to go, closing doors, leaving no other alternatives." Kenneth Burke,
in an essay called "Psychology and Form," has distinguished two
kinds of literary composition, "syllogistic progression," in which the
reader is led from one point of the composition to another by means
of logical relationships, and "qualitative progression," in which the
reader is led, according to a "logic of feeling," by means of association and contrast. Francis Fergusson, from whom these remarks are
freely borrowed, relates Burke's qualitative progression to the compositional principles of Wagnerian music-drama – but the analogy
might be extended with equal validity to Bergman's art as well.[21]
"How tired I am of hearing that imagination must always be respon-
sible to the intellect! Inspiration should be well behaved in the face
of reality's accusations," he protests in *Cries and Whispers.*[22] But art,

he has repeatedly insisted, is not a rational phenomenon to be comprehended by logical analysis; it is "a matter between the imagination and the feelings." Expressed with the utmost economy of means, often compressed into an arresting sensory image, each emotional unit or suggestion in Bergman's theater seeks to reach the spectator spontaneously and directly, through the medium of the senses, without an intermediary landing in the intellect.

With these general observations in mind, then, let the reader examine for himself a practical demonstration of Bergman's method in his editing of the hypnotic third-act scene in which Hedda finally destroys her former lover. Both overt symbolism (vine leaves) and expository explanation ("you looked down its barrel once") have been stripped away to reveal the emotional core of close, unspoken violence in the scene. First, the text as it was played at Dramaten, showing the cuts in square brackets:[23]

HEDDA: What will you do now?

LØVBORG: Nothing. I just want to put an end to it all. As soon as possible.

HEDDA *(takes a step towards him)*:   Eilert Løvborg, listen to me. Do it– beautifully!

LØVBORG: Beautifully? [(*Smiles*) With a crown of vine leaves in my hair? The way you used to dream of me–in the old days?]

HEDDA: [No. I don't believe in that crown any longer. But–do it] (B)eautifully[, all the same]. Just this once. [Goodbye.] You must go now. And don't come back.

LØVBORG: Adieu, madam. Give my love to George Tesman. *(Turns to go.)*

HEDDA: Wait! I want to give you a souvenir to take with you. *(She goes over to [the writing table, opens the drawer and] the pistol case, and comes back to Løvborg with one of the pistols.)*

[LØVBORG *(looks at her)*:   This? Is this the souvenir?]

HEDDA *(nods slowly)*:   You recognize it? [You looked down its barrel once.]

LØVBORG: You should have used it then.

(Bergman direction: Pause. Hand-kiss.)

[HEDDA: Here! Use it now!]

LØVBORG *(puts the pistol in his breast pocket)*:   Thank you.

HEDDA: [Do it] (B)eautifully, Eilert [Løvborg. Only] promise me that!

LØVBORG: Goodbye, Hedda Gabler.

And in the Munich revival the final beat of this scene, as Løvborg takes the pistol from Hedda, became even more terse and more brutal:[24]

LØVBORG: This? Is this the souvenir?

LØVBORG *(puts the pistol in his breast pocket)*:   Thank you.

HEDDA: Beautifully, Eilert Løvborg. Promise me that!

LØVBORG: Goodbye, Hedda Gabler.

After her move to destroy Løvborg himself, Hedda's burning of his manuscript seals her own fate, by finalizing her willful rejection of the future and her election of the past and of death. This action – perhaps the most intense emotional gesture in Bergman's productions of the play – was positioned by him at the very center and forefront of the stage. Facing the audience directly, Hedda slowly knelt before the hooded prompter's box itself, which then became the "stove." As a result, every slight nuance of facial expression was remorselessly disclosed in the searching light that flooded the stage at this point. With icy determination, her face now frozen in an immutable masklike expression, she fed the "fire" with page after page of Løvborg's manuscript – his vision of the future, his and Thea's spiritual child. Just when her act of wanton destruction had been completed, Bergman added a startling touch that exemplifies his extraordinary gift for compressing the essence of a situation into one eloquent visual image. The sorrowing figures of Tesman and the black-clad and veiled Miss Tesman, in mourning for her dead sister, appeared behind her, and at a single stoke the image of physical death merged with the image of Hedda and the motif of death-in-life, emotional sterility, and inhumanity that she embodies.

In this interpretation Hedda's implacably exposed public suicide, which Bergman considers "the most consequent of any in dramatic literature," became as logically inevitable as the solution to a mathematical problem. Nothing was permitted to mitigate the harshness or obscure the clarity of this final scene. The "frenzied dance melody" that Hedda plays on the piano in Ibsen's text was reduced to a few dissonant, nonmusical chords hammered out in frustration. As she stood before the mirror and quietly prepared to put a bullet through her head, her husband and the self-possessed Thea Elvsted sat motionlessly at the other end of the stage, totally absorbed in their absurd task of reassembling the dead Løvborg's notes – a deadly picture of hollow people trying to paste together a vision whose spirit they do not comprehend, clinging to a meaningless past that completely overshadows both the present and the future.

Hedda's last act before withdrawing into the ultimate isolation of death was to remove her high-heeled shoes carefully, in a final irrational attempt to control and transcend a reality that had become a nightmare. "The only thing she wants is to die a beautiful death," Bergman has been prompted to explain. "She has rehearsed the last gesture before the mirror. She knows how to use the pistol so that it becomes aesthetic. Perhaps she also takes into consideration that she wants to fall nicely. It is an uncontrollable moment that she subconsciously tries to control by taking off her shoes."[25]

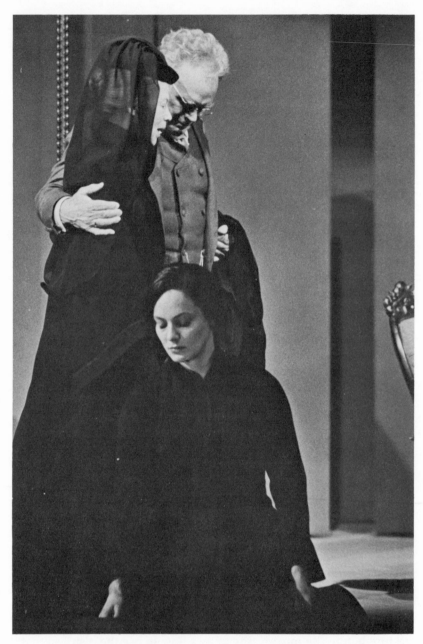

The sorrowing figures of Tesman (Kurt Meisel) and his Aunt Julle appear behind Hedda just as she has burned Løvborg's manuscript. Residenztheater, 1979.

Judge Brack had the last word, as of course he does in Ibsen, in all three of Bergman's productions of the play. In Munich, however, his line was reinforced by an astonishing gesture of sheer brutality. Standing nonchalantly over Hedda's outstretched corpse, Brack seized her roughly by the hair and lifted her head, as though to assure himself that she was dead, before pronouncing his cynical verdict that "people don't do such things!" Like Eilert, Hedda had found only a harsh and unlovely end. "The irony in all this," Bergman remarks, "is that she dies such an ugly death anyway – that she ends up lying there with her rump in the air."

AN ACTORS' THEATER

In some respects, the staging of Bergman's brilliant revival of Ibsen's *The Wild Duck*, which began its lengthy run at Dramaten on March 17, 1972 and was subsequently seen on tour in six other European countries, bore a distinct resemblance to the novel scenographic style that he had adopted for *Hedda Gabler*. In this new production, both of the detailed naturalistic environments described in the stage directions were condensed into deliberately incomplete settings that consisted of isolated elements on an otherwise empty stage. Simple, stylized wall screens were again used to denote the contours of these two interiors. Each of them was confined to a relatively shallow area at the front of the revolving stage, with the result that beyond it one saw only an encircling black void that was sometimes pierced by abstract projections. The atmospheric interplay of light and shadow within the setting itself heightened the semireal effect.

The "expensive and comfortably furnished study" of Haakon Werle in the first act was a relatively cold, green-tinted room of angles and corners, defined only by a back screen and completely open at the sides. An aristocratic fireplace with poker and tongs stood at one end of the room, with no wall behind it. Four upholstered chairs and an ornate writing table were the only other furnishings. A pair of tall ornamental candelabra placed in either corner, just outside the actual setting, added a note of elegance and opulence. Only one striking addition was actually made by Bergman and his designer (Marik Vos) to Ibsen's specifications for this interior – a richly framed portrait of a woman, presumably Werle's late wife, occupied a conspicuous place on the wall above the writing table. In his various productions of *Hedda Gabler*, as we know, Bergman had eliminated the portrait of General Gabler precisely because it belongs to that category of over-simplified, deterministic "explanation" that obscures the true complexity of the central character's situation – a woman who is *not* a mere product or victim of social or hereditary circumstances, but who has consciously chosen – in an existential and also a quite coincidental manner – her own hell. In Bergman's production of *The Wild Duck*, meanwhile, the interpolated portrait was not at all this kind of closed naturalistic symbol – although at least one bedeviled commentator professed to see in it "the symbol of Gregers' Oedipal complex." Rather, it seemed a concrete but completely open image that manifested the irrevocable presence of the past in the play, the awareness that old sins cast long shadows and that, ultimately, "the forest will have its revenge."

The forest was indeed very much a part of Hjalmar Ekdal's humbler and more comfortable studio in the acts that followed. Here the

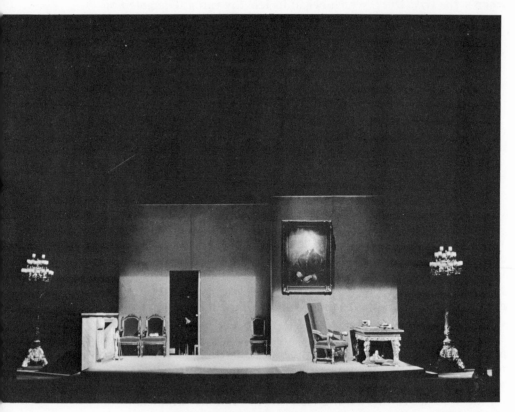

The study of Haakon Werle, designed by Marik Vos, for the first act of *The Wild Duck*. Dramaten, 1972.

most striking pictorial addition was a large screen depicting an old-fashioned woodland scene – virtually a vision of the great forest about which Old Ekdal warns us so often – which the director introduced, with characteristic logic, as a conventional prop of the kind that one might very naturally expect to encounter in the modest studio of a portrait photographer. Where the pair of stately candelabra had stood in Werle's study, dried-out old spruce trees could now be glimpsed (the "four or five withered Christmas trees" that are, as Relling remarks, the same to Old Ekdal as "the great, fresh forests of Høydal"), reinforcing the impression of a "waking reality" suspended in a void, "an island in the sea of flight from reality" (*Göteborgs Handels– och Sjöfartstidning*). Even the rectangular screen used to demarcate one corner of the room carried, in its faintly flowered wallpaper, a tantalizing hint of this motif of the encroaching dream forest.

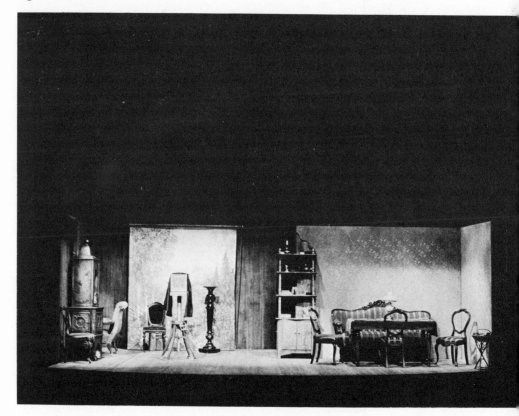

The studio of Hjalmar Ekdal in *The Wild Duck*. Dramaten, 1972.

Other sharply defined contrasts to the more patrician Werle establishment were suggested with deft economy through the strategic placement of the sparse furnishings. The position occupied by the elegant fireplace in the previous setting was now taken by an old iron stove. At the opposite side of the stage from it, in the area formerly occupied by Werle's commanding desk, a dilapidated sofa and table arrangement served both as a work place for the none-too-energetic Hjalmar and as the center of domestic warmth where the various (indispensable) meals in the play could be served. Here in this warmly illuminated area the Ekdals gathered – frequently watched closely by Gregers, "the outsider who intrudes in order to influence the life of the family" and who hence often sat "as far removed as possible from the dining-room table, the natural gathering place of the family, with his back towards the audience so that he shared his watching attitude with them."[26]

"Here rule the night and the dreams." Gregers's first visit to the attic, as it was conceived in Bergman's production of *The Wild Duck*.

For those familiar beforehand with the specific details of *The Wild Duck*, Bergman's most unexpected innovation was doubtless his relocation of the attic in the Ekdal studio – although, once accomplished, his daring reversal of the play's perspective seemed, to informed and unsuspecting viewers alike, both completely consistent and disarmingly self-evident. Previous productions of the play have traditionally sought to fulfill Ibsen's familiar stage directions more or less to the letter, attempting to reproduce the "long and irregularly shaped loft" that lies beyond the rear wall, "full of dark nooks and crannies, with a couple of brick chimney-pipes coming through the floor. Through small skylights bright moonlight shines on to various parts of the loft, while the rest lies in shadow."[27] In Bergman's hands this fateful and fleetingly perceived interior loft, the abode of the maimed wild duck and the realm of illusion and entertainment for three generations of Ekdals, was transformed into a magical ghost-attic located in the no-man's-land between the audience and the stage. "Without stage properties and with only the aid of the lighting and the art of the actors, Bergman creates, before the eyes of the audience, that fantasy world that Hjalmar and Old Ekdal have built up around themselves," wrote Leif Zern in *Dagens Nyheter*. "Here rule the night and the dreams, in scenes of such intensity and poetry that I have never witnessed their like."

In this ingenious arrangement, characters entered the "loft" through a side door in the stage-right wall of the studio – with the interesting result that they did not thereby disappear from view but were instead seen to draw nearer, both physically and metaphorically, to the audience itself. Bergman "has with a resolute touch burst the bounds of the perspective box by placing the imaginary loft almost where the spectators are sitting," recorded Henrik Sjögren in *Kvällsposten*. "Accordingly they can observe every one of the characters who turns toward the wild duck [whose 'basket' was the prompter's box]." Only the facial expressions of the actors and projections of roofbeams on the stage floor and on the black background above them served to indicate where they were and what it was they saw in this kingdom of the imagination. The resultant sense of immediacy was truly startling. "More than in any other production of Ibsen's play that one recalls," one reviewer wrote of the touring production, the attic became "an image of that secret fantasy life that these escapists and losers have not been strong enough or courageous enough to realize for themselves. The small living room of Hjalmar Ekdal becomes a doll's house of eternal childhood above which, in the scenes with the wild duck, the roofbeams soar like the lofty vaults of a cathedral, while from afar one hears the surge of the wind."[28] The withered Christmas trees, obscured in any conventional performance by the backs of those characters who, at various times, peer into the mysterious attic at the rear, were now, for the first time, brought forward to form a profoundly expressive component of the Ekdal environment. As a result the thematic bond between studio and forest was strengthened; time present and time past were fused together in a fluid but indissoluble concurrency. "The symbolic essence of the play thus becomes central and more securely welded to the clockwork mechanism of the dramatic action than I have ever experienced it before," Sjögren concluded.

Once again, then, Bergman's technique of bringing forward exposed, close-up glimpses of peripheral or implied offstage action added an entirely new dimension to the audience's mode of perceiving the realistic action of Ibsen's drama. In this respect, similarities to his innovative staging of *Hedda Gabler* seem fairly obvious – although one basic difference between these two productions must also be recognized. In *Hedda Gabler* the "inner room" of the central character was still seen as a place. Regardless of how stylized or abstractly conceived it was, it was still furnished with recognizable physical objects – the piano and stool, Hedda's chair, the mirror. In *The Wild Duck,* however, the "interior loft" had no independent existence of its own. Its reality was created *solely* through the medium of the actor's art. As such, this production epitomizes a cardinal principle of Bergman's theater poetics – the subordination at all times of the technical dynamics of staging to the creative presence of the living actor. "Once you agree that the only important things are the words, the actors, and the audience, then it isn't the setting that matters," he argues when talking about *The Wild Duck.* Moreover, his thinking in this regard is fundamentally "simple" and practical, uncomplicated by abstract theoretical considerations. "The actors must materialize, before the eyes of the audience, the magic of the attic. And they cannot do that at a distance; with their eyes, their way of walking and standing and moving, they create it in front of you. So you can see it. That is the magic of the theater."

Indeed, no other Bergman production has more persuasively reaffirmed that unique and most important gift of his – as a director of actors, with a mesmeric ability to ignite a performer and extract hidden resources from his cast. ("Perhaps the truth is," Bibi Andersson once remarked, "that when Ingmar is creating something, he radiates such hypnotic persuasiveness and intensity that one is in-

toxicated and overwhelmed.") His capacity for forging an unbreak-
able ensemble is, of course, directly related to his fabled talent for
choosing exactly the right actors – a talent that, in turn, presupposes
an intimate familiarity with his players. "We are all closely involved
with each other. I know how many parts each carries with him," he
told an interviewer shortly after his production of *The Wild Duck*.
"Sometimes the actors themselves don't know that they can play [a
certain part]. But without actually telling me, they show me the
parts they contain."[29] During the great Dramaten years of the early
1970s, even relatively minor roles in a production such as *The Wild
Duck* were filled by leading members of the familiar Bergman "company": Anders Ek was available to depict a powerful and commanding Haakon Werle; Harriet Andersson created a stately, gracious
Mrs. Sørby devoid of any trace of vulgarity; Holger Löwenadler was
Old Ekdal, "a grandiose ruin of someone who was once a human
being"; and even Erland Josephson was called upon to impersonate
one of the stuffy guests at Werle's dinner party.

At the hub of this superb ensemble was the quartet of characters
around whom the action of the play revolves – a quartet carefully
selected and finely tuned by Bergman to reveal a subtly shaded
lattice of tensions and contrasts, rooted in Ibsen's own character
descriptions and articulated by the director in terms of a distinctive
rhythm of movements, gestures, facial expressions, and vocal nuances. "The figures reveal themselves in every subtle detail of voice
and movement, and they do so with formidable logic until they
stand there etched into our consciousness, lit through to the bare
skeleton," Tord Baeckström declared in *Göteborgs Handels–och
Sjöfartstidning*. With cameralike sharpness, Bergman's direction
seemed to cut through the restrictive limits of realism to seek out
and lay bare the inner essence of each character. "Driven to its
fullest consequence, realism becomes unreal," Baeckström continued. "The X-ray vision suddenly exposes not living and vaguely
contradictory human beings, but rather psychological constructs in a
laser-sharp, two-dimensional projection."

Hjalmar Ekdal (Ernst-Hugo Järegård) and Hedvig (Lena Nyman)
seemed, to many observers, less like father and daughter and much
more "like two children of the same age, a loving brother and sister."[30] "Incestuous" was the spurious adjective attached by one or
two critics with an inflexibly Freudian cast of mind – but a powerful
sense of genuine domestic warmth and tenderness, rather than any
suggestion of incest, was the real thematic point at issue here. Their
eager embraces and natural displays of affection in the earlier,

lighter scenes deepened the sense of Hedvig's naive, almost animalistic dependency on her father. "The warmth in the Ekdal home stems from her hunger for life," commented Leif Zern–and hence the effect of Hjalmar's abrupt rejection of her love, as he tore himself loose from her embrace in the fourth act, acquired added dramatic clarity and poignancy. Järegård's uncomplicated Hjalmar was a totally unsentimentalized, tragicomic figure–a happy egoist in constant need of encouragement from his surroundings, a natural actor "whose family is the most grateful public any performer could wish for," as Zern put it: "even his self-pity is a role he plays, as everyone well realizes." His open cherubic face, his curly hair, and his soft velvet attire all bespoke the charming and much-adored child, who was even assisted in putting on his slippers by a wife and daughter who literally got down on their knees for him. Accordingly, the earthy, maternal Gina of Margaretha Krook played "mother" to both these children, and their simple, helpless dependency on her foretold their defenselessness against the revelations with which Gregers Werle, the outsider, destroys their childish fantasy world forever.

Yet Gregers, the fourth member of the quartet, was in this instance neither the convinced fanatic nor the unsympathetic villain that he can often become in the theater–alone Bergman's choice of Max von Sydow for the role precluded such a result. The character created by von Sydow–"an idealist whose good intentions one cannot doubt for a moment" (*Svenska Dagbladet*)–was in physical terms the diametrical opposite of Hjalmar Ekdal. A very tall man who assumed a stooped, cramped posture, his short nervous laugh and his habit of crossing his arms over his chest to hide his hands under his armpits ("as though he were trying to tie himself into a straitjacket," thought one observer) suggested, to many of the critics, deep inner anxiety and insecurity. "He complains more than he accuses," remarked *Sydsvenska Dagbladet*, and in the two extremely effective scenes with his father–of whom he appeared utterly terrified–"his attacks [were] as shaky and powerless as his gestures and posture; he seems to be ready to run away at any time." Between Gregers and Hjalmar there seemed, despite their physical differences, to be a shared lack of self-knowledge and self-assurance: "they suffer from the same disease, even though the symptoms are different," Leif Zern argued. "Gregers, too, goes outside himself to find the solution to his problems. Precisely like Hjalmar–and like Peer Gynt, for that matter–he assumes a role that does not express his true self." Critics sought—as critics are wont to seek—sinuous explanations for the behavior of this untraditional Gregers. Thus he was seen variously as being beset by a severe Oedipus complex, conducting a sublimated father-rebellion, or even representing the failed political revolutionary in the class struggle. But, here as elsewhere, Bergman's aim was not to offer an ideological or a psychological comment on Ibsen's play but rather to amplify, in concrete theatrical terms, the matrix of dynamic emotional relationships upon which the play builds. In these terms, the effect of this new and more complex characterization of Gregers was to intensify and enrich the dramatic impact of his confrontations with Haakon Werle, his relationship to Hjalmar, and, above all, the three crucial conversations he holds with Hedvig on the subject of the wild duck.

Left, Gregers Werle (Max von Sydow) in the third-act scene with his father, played here by Anders Ek. Dramaten, 1972.

By electing to bring the attic forward and "materialize" it before the eyes of the audience, Bergman inevitably also focused more tightly on the process by which Hedvig comes to take her life, and on Gregers's implication in that process. This became the prism through which all the other events in the drama were refracted and assimilated. In their first, oneiric scene alone, as the plain, shy, snub-nosed little girl told Gregers about the "different world" of the loft, with its strange collection of old paintboxes, old picture books, and old clocks that no longer run, she acquired a radiance "as if sunlight and soft shadows moved across this childish face, dreaming about that that will never come to pass" [Zern]. The second of their scenes together – transferred by Bergman to the shadowy precincts of the "attic" itself, where the actors could now face the audience directly – strengthened the sense of mutual understanding and even comradeship between these two childlike dreamers. As Gregers implanted the suggestion of sacrificing the duck to appease Hjalmar, his movements to draw Hedvig close to him and her response carried implications of a mesmeric, even an erotic seduction of her will. An incisive cut to eliminate the anticlimax of Gina's return at the end of this scene allowed the fourth-act curtain to fall on the line with which Hedvig seemed to signal her compliance: "I'll do it tomorrow morning" (with the reference to "the wild duck" deleted).[31] In the third step (in all fairy tales the final and conclusive one), the process of psychological suasion was completed, as Gregers – without resorting to the exclamatory exhortations contained in Ibsen's text and using only one simple line ("But I still believe in you, Hedvig") – recalled her to her blunted purpose.

Perhaps the darkest and most fascinating aspect of Bergman's interpretation of *The Wild Duck* was the fact that never for an instant was the audience in real doubt about the deliberate and premeditated nature of Hedvig's suicide. On the one hand, small but telling cuts – in particular the deletion of the short scene in which Old Ekdal lectures the child about how to shoot ducks properly – tended to strengthen the impression that the wild duck never *had* actually been intended by Hedvig as the target of her revolver. Moreover, the chance that she might have made a mistake and had killed herself by accident – surely one of the least fortunate of all the ambiguities in Ibsen's drama – now no longer existed as a logical possibility. As Hjalmar, already warming to his new role and calling histrionically for his notes and the draft of his "memoirs," ordered Hedvig from his presence, she slipped out quietly, pistol in hand – only to reappear on the forestage moments later. The projection of the roofbeams rose above her head, while behind her the other characters continued their unwitting discussion in the background. The audience thus experienced these last terrifying minutes through her consciousness, saw them through her eyes. As the dialogue between the overwrought Gregers and the self-centered Hjalmar proceeded, she took aim, hesitated, and fired. "We see her listening to the conversation that makes her shoot herself," observed one reviewer. "And the voluntary sacrifice of her tragic death thereby became, to an even greater degree, a judgment upon the intractable childishness of the adults."[32]

Following the shot, the suspense generated in Ibsen's play by the ensuing confusion over who had actually fired at what deepened into irony, because the audience of this production knew what the characters themselves did not yet realize. Then, as Relling and the parents gathered around the crumpled form on the darkened forestage, Bergman added a bold visual stroke that heightened the oppressive sense of finality and ultimate futility created by Hedvig's suicide. Juxtaposed with the shadowy group in the foreground was the startling image of Old Ekdal, seated before the photographer's forest backdrop in his old lieutenant's uniform, still intoning his favorite refrain: "The forest will have its revenge – but I'm not afraid at any rate." Perhaps only Gregers was truly afraid, for he recognized the terrible finality of the judgment that had been passed on them – and as he left the Ekdal home, he held in his hand the revolver that Hedvig had used on herself.

The precisely coordinated, rhythmical orchestration of visual and aural impressions that rendered the closing moments of Bergman's production of *The Wild Duck* so moving and poignant reflect perfectly that uniquely "musical" way in which he goes about translating a play's "score" into the syntax of the theater. Max von Sydow has described Bergman's practice of providing the actor with "a rhythmic outline of the role" that will serve as a suggestive stimulus to his own creative powers: "To watch Ingmar planning the arrangement of an entire act of a play is very fascinating, I find, because it is not simply a matter of moving someone geographically through space – settling down here, standing up there, crossing to this or that piece of furniture, sitting down in that chair, and then saying your line – but also always includes an indication of roughly the tempo and the rhythm with which it should happen." Musical comparisons occur to von Sydow because, as he says "somewhere or other in the back of your head you hear musical expressions and

The arrangement of Hedvig's suicide on the shadowy forestage, juxtaposed with the image of Old Ekdal (Holger Löwenadler) seated in his uniform before the photographer's forest backdrop. Dramaten, 1972.

know approximately how many beats to count on for a move or before introducing an accentuation. If you understand the first direction provided during Ingmar's blocking, then you have grasped the essence of his idea about the role. As a result, as an actor I feel immensely free."[33]

The creative freedom of the actor, as an independent artist in his own right, is in general a cardinal precept of Bergman's method as a director. It would indeed be difficult to name another modern director for whose work the actor has had greater or more direct significance as a truly collaborative artist. "One of the great things about Ingmar Bergman is that he supports the actor's own intuition," remarks Gertrud Fridh who, like Max von Sydow, is among the numerous Bergman artists who have been outspoken in their recognition of his unique ability to build an atmosphere that incites the actor to become an active partner in the creative process. "He sets his stamp on a production, but you nevertheless have the feeling of having created something you yourself can and will stand up for. With his affectionate way of listening, he stimulates the actor to boldness and freedom."[34]

"Puppet-master" is one of those foolish popular epithets that has attached itself to Bergman on occasion – as it has done with almost every strong, creative director in this century. Yet nothing could be more alien to Bergman's method than a view of the actor as a marionette or a medium to be exploited for the director's own purposes. "In principle, today, it is rare that anything happens during the rehearsal process that I have not foreseen and prepared," he admits – but he also hastens to add that the actors' creative involve-

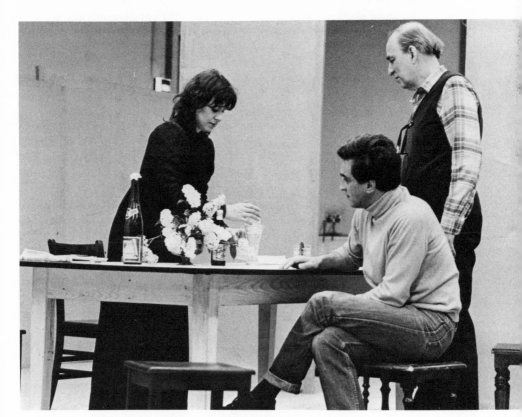

Bergman rehearsing his new production of *Miss Julie:* "After all, I am one of them. I am the complementary part."

ment in rehearsals can nonetheless readily alter his plans for any given scene.[35]

Hence, an instruction or a decision that makes no immediate emotional sense to an actor is rarely either explicated or insisted upon by Bergman – it is simply changed to something else that does communicate itself more clearly to the performer. Instances of such creative changes abound, both in his film work and in his stage productions. As one typical example, he first intended the title character in his 1980 production of Witold Gombrowicz's grotesque, fairy tale fantasy *Yvonne, Princess of Burgundy* to wear a mask, in order to amplify the significance of her extreme ugliness and otherness. Instead, Andrea-Maria Wildner, who played the role of this silent and unspeakably loathsome woman who is arbitrarily chosen by the disillusioned Prince to be his bride, wished to discard the idea of a mask and attempt to convey the sensation of ugliness in her own way, using her own features and movements. The end result was a miraculous feat of creative physical transformation – a hunched, rubber-faced,

Rehearsing *The Misanthrope*: "The actor has an intense need for a correcting and controlling ear and eye."

Rehearsing *The Three Sisters:* "Someone must set the march tempo."

uncoordinated marionette of a woman whose intense and uncom-
promising repulsiveness was a mirror in which those around her
saw their own spiritual deformities hideously reflected.

Bergman has always steadfastly refused to discuss his rehearsal
methods in either intellectual or mystical terms. "An immense
amount goes on between the actors and me on a level that cannot be
analyzed," he says simply. "That is how it often is in relations with
the actors. After all, I am one of them. I am the complementary
part." The creative actor is, as he has frequently observed, also the
exposed actor who, at the moment he exhibits himself and his spiritual life on a stage or before a camera, has "an intense need for a
correcting and controlling ear and eye that will follow him continually." It is in this respect that he refers to the director as "more like

Rehearsing *The Wild Duck:* "I must give the actor completely distinct,
clear technical directions."

an atmosphere: a sensitive source of confidence, an animator, and, to a certain extent, the one who holds everything together. And if something has jammed, one doesn't hammer or grind or pull at it – you help to loosen the knots." With the artistic integrity of the actor clearly before him, the director exists to provide the assistance, inspiration, and guidance that will effectively liberate the actor's own creative imagination. Someone, as Bergman puts it, must set the "march tempo" and must then ensure that everyone is marching together in the same direction – "that everyone agrees, is making an effort to preserve the style, and is striving in common to achieve a good result." Ghita Nørby, Bergman's Célimène in the Copenhagen production of *The Misanthrope*, has summed up the psychological and creative impact of his technique with succinctness and honesty: "His demands were the greatest conceivable and his strictness was the greatest conceivable, and he took it as a matter of course that his demands would be met because he made you feel that you – in this entire world – were the best conceivable choice for this particular role. And, as a result, you could not help but grow – you became better than you were."[36]

To provide the necessary creative stimulus by means of rhythmically precise technical instructions – that is the essential core of Bergman's method of directing actors. "I can not hand out emotional rubbish to an actor, then he's got me in an instant. I must give him completely distinct, clear technical directions." The identification of the actor with his role "should be regarded as resembling an easily assumed piece of clothing. Protracted meditation, dogged emotional discipline, violent excitation are completely unjustifiable. The actor must be able in a completely technical manner (perhaps aided by the director), to put on and take off his identification like clothing. Psychological hysteria and prolonged overstraining of the will represent death to expressiveness." Lengthy discussions, conferences, or explanations – all forms of overtly intellectual theorizing, in fact – only serve to cloud the clarity and vitiate the exactitude of the "rhythmic outline" that Bergman endeavors to establish in the simplest possible technical terms. "You work with suggestions, incitements, and let the audience do the rest," he told one actor who, during rehearsals for *Woyzeck*, questioned this insistence upon conscious exactitude. "Your vocal inflections have been decided upon beforehand. If they are conscious and exact, then the text and the audience will carry you as though on a wave. You leave an opening to be filled by the audience's need to engage itself in the drama. It is for this reason that the scene [of Marie's murder] has to be so simple and straightforward. It won't do to clog it with feelings. You must know what you are doing."[37]

In the final analysis, Bergman's method hinges on the recognition that the exposed and creative actor is also the magical actor. The one fundamental similarity between his work as a film maker and his work in the theater is, in his own opinion, the overriding necessity of arranging the actors, in relation to each other and in relation to the spectator (camera), in such a way that their persuasive charisma ("the magic of their faces and their movements") communicates itself as forcefully and unambiguously as possible. The "theater of circumstances," with its "busy" management of scenery, lighting, and sound effects that ultimately only serve to detheatricalize the presence of the living actor, has long since been put behind him. Instead, he has sought to restore the actor to his rightful place in the theatrical framework, in just relationship to the two other elements that, in Bergman's experience, are required to create that which we call theater – the words the actor speaks and the actively engaged audience he reaches out to encounter.

A great director expresses approval at rehearsal.

6   Talking about tomorrow

Early in the spring of 1980, we had the opportunity to return to Geiselgasteig for another conversation with Ingmar Bergman. By this time, shooting of *Aus dem Leben der Marionetten* had been completed, and Bergman was deeply engrossed in the demanding task of cutting his new picture. The ten weeks of rehearsal needed for his stage production of Gombrowicz's *Yvonne* were to begin shortly at the Residenztheater in Munich. Yet, in the midst of this rush of current activity and doubtless because of it, our talk soon focused upon tomorrow – upon the new plans and the new challenges that lay ahead, and that always seem to fill this remarkable man with the pleasure of keen anticipation.

At the time, Bergman's next project was to have been a new production of *A Dream Play* – his fourth – that he had planned to stage at the National Theatre in Oslo. The role of Indra's Daughter was intended for Liv Ullmann, whose only previous appearance on a Bergman stage to date has been as the Step-Daughter in Pirandello's *Six Characters in Search of an Author*, which he directed in Oslo in 1967.

As it turned out, however, this project was ultimately shelved in favor of a far bolder and more radically experimental idea, the germ of which, as the reader will discover, was already present in Bergman's mind when the conversation that follows took place. This was his ambitious Project Bergman – the simultaneous production, on different stages of the Bayerisches Staatsschauspiel in Munich, of Ibsen's *A Doll's House*, Strindberg's *Miss Julie*, and a new stage adaptation of his own television film *Scenes from a Marriage*. Seen side by side (and actually intended to open on the same evening before going into the regular repertory rotation), Bergman's parallel productions of these three works would form not a trilogy but what he calls, with a touch of irony, a "triangle," reflecting three facets of the relationship between man and woman and the effect upon it of the society that they inhabit.

IB.   *A Dream Play* is a work that is very, very close to me. I love it. Liv Ullmann and I have talked about making *A Dream Play* together for a very long time – as early as 1968, I think, I said to her

that she must play Indra's Daughter. And now we have decided
we must try it.

FJM.   Would you perform the play in the same way again – dividing
Indra's Daughter and Agnes as two separate characters?

IB.   No. The next time I will not use two actresses for Indra's
Daughter. Slowly I have discovered . . . in all three of my *Dream-
plays* I have made cuts, you know . . . because I couldn't fit the
passages in correctly. I didn't understand them, they were too
strange to me. But next time I will try to perform the entire play –
except the prologue, of course. That was written later, and it's
made of different stuff – just as the third part of *To Damascus* is
completely different from the first two parts. The Stockholm
Dreamplay is one of the productions that is closest to my heart. But
I think that my cuts in that production were very brutal.

FJM.   I don't agree. They were superb. [Laughter.]

IB.   Yes, but – [chuckles] you know, there *is* something very sentimental, very overaesthetical about *A Dream Play* at times. Much
too much *Jugendstil* for our own time. Do you know what I mean?

LLM.   Yes.

IB.   Strindberg had a corner in his home and there he had three
palm trees – and in these palms colored bulbs were hung. He had
an armchair in this corner, and when his sister visited him and
played Beethoven for him, he would sit there and flick on those
colored bulbs. Sometimes I get the feeling in *A Dream Play* that we
are very close to that corner. And yet you must find a means of
approaching it, you know, because that way of enjoying beauty is
also wonderful. That sentimental, not very tasteful way. I think
that my *Dreamplay* in Stockhom was very pure and, in a way, very
dogmatic. A little too pure, I find.

FJM.   One thing is the aestheticism you describe, but another aspect entirely is the whole machinery of Eastern mysticism in the
play. You wouldn't reintroduce that without modification, would
you?

IB.   Yes, because it is very essential for Strindberg. I will try next
time to find a way – a very theatrical way. I won't talk more about
it now, because I think I will change my mind many times. But I
will find a way.

FJM.   The one version of *A Dream Play* that neither of us has seen is
your 1963 television adaptation.

IB.   I'm very happy that you haven't seen it. [Laughter.] We were
strangled by technical problems. Completely. I think that, in all,
perhaps four or five minutes of that production are acceptable.

That was the first time we were able to tape, you see. They had just invented the videotape recorder, so parts of it could be taped but they didn't know how to cut. They had to go to Denmark, where they had a machine – and a very imprecise machine at that. It was terrible. And the fire scene at the end – God help us! You couldn't mix sound at that time. You would add sound, but you couldn't take it away again. Oh God, it was terrible. But I think it was Strindberg's revenge. [Laughter.]

FJM.   It has often been said about *A Dream Play* that it would make a splendid film. Have you ever wanted to make a film of it?

IB.   A part of it, a small part of it might make a wonderful picture. But that play belongs to the theater. The magic of that play is that it belongs to the stage, to the magic of the stage.

LLM.   Especially so in Scandinavia, where there is such a strong and unbroken tradition of Strindberg performance. I know you don't like to be called an innovator – someone who reshapes a tradition – but what you have done with Strindberg is so totally different from the work of, say, Olof Molander. You seem not to be influenced at all by what you have seen.

IB.   But I *am* very influenced. I am extremely influenced. Oh yes, I am. I am very influenced by Molander's productions, but that doesn't mean that I try to reproduce them. Molander's point of view was always very religious, very moral. But to me, Strindberg's religious mind was very primitive. To me, the most fascinating thing about Strindberg is that enormous awareness that everything in life, at every moment, is completely amoral – completely open and simply rooted.

FJM.   Always extremely concrete and specific, isn't he?

IB.   Yes, yes, yes. Very concrete and very precise. With Ibsen, you know, you always have the feeling of limits – because Ibsen placed them there himself. He was an architect, and he built. He always built his plays, and he knew exactly: I want this and I want that. He points the audience in the direction he wants it to go, closing doors, leaving no other alternatives. With Strindberg – as with Shakespeare – you always have the feeling that there are no such limits.

FJM.   You like Strindberg better than Ibsen, don't you.

IB.   No, that isn't so. Strindberg is closer to my heart. He's more familiar. Ibsen can sometimes seem very strange to me. We have just been discussing a production of his last play, *When We Dead Awaken*. I reread it a few weeks ago – and of course it is a sort of *Ghost Sonata*. But how to perform it, I don't know. It's a very, very difficult play, and here in Munich we don't have the proper stage for it. The stage in this big beer hall [Residenztheater] is too large. The small one – Theater im Marstall – is too small. The difficulty with the Cuvilliés-Theater is that it's beautiful but it's not intimate enough. There are more than 450 seats, and I feel that the audience is very far away. And we're prevented by the fire regulations from building things.

LLM. In *Hedda Gabler,* for instance, you succeeded in creating a very intimate atmosphere in the "beer hall," though.

IB. [Laughing] Yes, we had to rebuild the whole thing. It was a tremendous job because we had to reconstruct the entire stage. No, the play by Ibsen I would like to do sometime is *A Doll's House.* I don't know why, but I have such a soft feeling for that play.

FJM. But can you break out of that setting? Could one eliminate the realistic framework?

IB. I don't find it necessary, it isn't necessary at all. It's a question of what you can bring to the play. Most productions of it start from the beginning and go on to the end, and then the end collapses, suddenly. But if you produce *A Doll's House,* you must start at the end – you must *know,* you must move from the end to the beginning with your souls. When you rehearse it, you must start at the end with the actors. Then, when they do come to start from the beginning, they will have that ending very clearly in mind. What you almost always see with productions of *A Doll's House* is a lack of awareness of the enormous difficulties facing the actors. An insensitivity to the beauty of the last scene. How important it is today to be aware of the tragedy of Helmer – that is even more important than the drama of Nora, for Helmer's tragedy is that he is bound and imprisoned in his role of being the man, the husband. And he collapses under it. He plays his part because it is the only one he knows and understands. And then he suddenly finds himself face to face with this furious woman. She leaves, and he is left there without knowing what has happened.

LLM. Are you going to stage that here in Munich, then?

IB. What I would like to do sometime is a simultaneous production of *A Doll's House* and Strindberg's *Miss Julie* – perhaps on the same evening on two different stages or else on the same stage on alternate evenings, I don't know. Because those plays are so contradictory, and just to have them together and let them interact would be very, very strange. Nora – who is everyone – was born in 1879, more than a hundred years ago, and Miss Julie was, I think, born about ten years later. And while Miss Julie is sacrificed under the pressure of her father and her social conditions, Nora has the strength to go out and attempt to create a new world. It makes a very interesting contrast. And so I have this intense desire, you see, to do these plays at the same time, to show how dimensions suddenly suggest themselves and materialize when you see the plays right beside each other. How entirely new and fascinating tensions are created.

LLM.   And you would see the chief tension between the plays arising from the differing situations of the two women?

IB.   I want to challenge people to make comparisons. When these plays are seen together, an interesting discussion might arise. What does our society – political, religious, and pedagogical – do to the relationship between man and woman? Why does it cripple men and women to such an extent that when they try to live with one another the result is, for the most part, a catastrophe?

Nora and Julie are, in a way, sisters. Nora is an anarchist – almost all of Ibsen's women are real anarchists – and she is tremendously strong. She breaks out of her social milieu. Julie, on the other hand, is crushed by hers. By her upbringing and by circumstances. Then, a hundred years later, Nora and Julie have a sister in Marianne [in *Scenes from a Marriage*] – and Marianne sits there trying to figure out what Nora has already told us a hundred years before. A change has only begun to set in – just the beginnings of a change. Marianne hasn't come much further. She searches for a new role and begins to find her own identity. She is in a very precarious situation. How the future will work out for her we really don't know.

FJM.   With your long record of Strindberg productions, it seems surprising that you haven't thought of staging *Miss Julie* before.

IB.   I have intended for years to produce *Miss Julie*. For twenty years, or something like that. But I have wanted the perfect couple for it, you see. At times I have been just about to do it – I wanted Liv [Ullmann] to play Miss Julie, but I didn't have the right man for it at the time. We talked about playing it on Broadway . . . but they give you only four weeks for rehearsal, you know, and that's absolutely impossible with a play like that.

FJM.   Would you make changes in it?

IB.   I would play every word of it, every single word. I wouldn't change a thing. But with *A Doll's House* I would cut out the children [laughs], the maid . . .

LLM.   And the trimming of the Christmas tree?

IB. Out, out! I'd take away all that realistic stuff – and that would make the play extremely beautiful. Sometimes you get the feeling, you know, that the actors become strangled by all that stuff – all those objects and furnishings and I don't know what else. Just take everything away – and then you find out how *fantastic* the shape of this play really is. It doesn't need all those things.

FJM. Couldn't we persuade you to come to Canada and stage one of these Ibsen or Strindberg projects there?

IB. [Boisterous laughter.] No, I'll tell you why. I'd love to, you know, but there are two things. I don't know the actors – although I have seen a lot of Canadian films by now, and I can see that you have a great many wonderful actors there – and I wouldn't be given the time I need to rehearse. Besides which, you know, there is another great difficulty that doesn't exist here. British actors and North American actors, too, have a very, very strange way of performing plays from abroad. They always seem to play them in a special sort of British rhythm that is very fast – fahst – bubbub- bubbubupt! Especially Ibsen. – It was extremely difficult to do Ibsen in London [in 1970]. Terrible.

LLM. That particular production of *Hedda Gabler* is really very un- representative of your work on that play, isn't it.

IB. Oh yes. I felt very uncomfortable – in my relations with Lau- rence Olivier. I always admired him as an actor, but as the head of the theater he was . . . it was awful. And the whole theater was a mess. I disliked it very much. And I didn't know the actors at all.

LLM. Had you cast the actors yourself before coming to London?

IB. No, Laurence Oliver cast them. I didn't know their actors, and I had no time to come there and look at them. And he – it began very strangely, you know, because he – didn't really want me to come. He wanted my idea for the play, and then he wanted to take over and stage it himself, in my choreography.

LLM. But that's absurd.

IB. Of course it was a silly idea, but he was very charming and he . . . succeeded in convincing me. And then I . . . regretted it very much. So the time in London was one of my most unhappy periods.

LLM. What finally did happen?

IB. I came and talked to the actors, and the actors wanted me to stay. We had some very strange rehearsals together, with Lau- rence Olivier sitting there watching us. I stayed fourteen days or something like that, then I had to go away.

FJM.   Before the opening?

IB.   Yes, I had some mixing to do or something–I don't know–so I had to go back to Sweden. I had to promise the actors that they could work on alone, without me, for two or three weeks. I promised to come back for the last seven days or so.

FJM.   Did you come back?

IB.   Yes, I did. I did, but it was very unsuccessful.

FJM.   That has been your only English-language production to date. Could you be tempted to do another? *Rosmersholm*, for example?

IB.   Liv [Ullmann] and I have often discussed a production of *Rosmersholm*, but we can't find a Rosmer. It's very difficult. Because it is the most passionate of Ibsen's plays–the last act is one of the most erotic scenes ever written for the theater. The erotic element is uppermost throughout the play. Rebecca is obsessed with Rosmer, but he has never touched her. He must be magnetic, charismatic, but at the same time totally passive and remote. And without a convincing Rosmer, a production of the play can never succeed. The perfect Rosmer is Max von Sydow; if you think of Max von Sydow, he is a hundred percent perfect for that part. And to try to find someone else is all wrong.

LLM.   Can't von Sydow do it? Is he too busy now, or . . .

IB.   It's impossible, because he is Swedish and she's Norwegian and we can't speak each other's language. It's absolutely impossible. And to perform with them in English–we have now been invited to play *Rosmersholm* on Broadway, you see, but I have said "No, thank you"–because it would be completely ridiculous.

LLM.   Wouldn't you find the artistic conditions there intolerable?

IB.   Only four weeks of rehearsal. And they always depend on having a star, or two stars. I think the conditions there are absolutely terrible.–No, I have learned now to work–in the German language. And it has begun to go smoothly. After four years I know my actors very well, so that by now I think I have the basis I need to proceed on. I'm very aware that this must be the basis for me: to be familiar with the actors, to be familiar with the surroundings, and to be in a position to develop my own atmosphere, a creative atmosphere–[chuckles] and to know the language.

FJM.   Perhaps the most fascinating problem of all is, of course, the whole question of your method in working with actors. When asked in the past which method of directing actors you prefer, you have invariably replied: "my own." But going back to our remarks

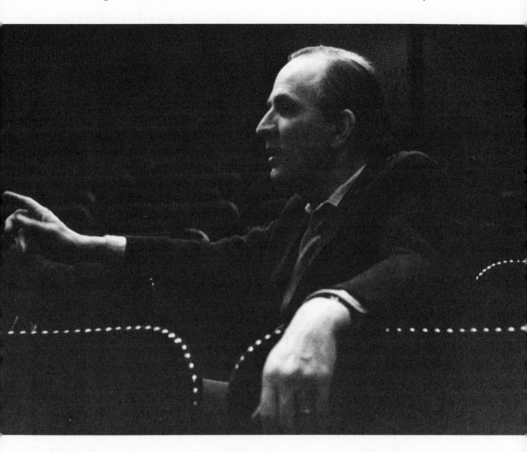

just now about the American theater, it seems very clear that you would find the extreme psychological motivation of much American acting completely alien to your style. Your approach is obviously very different.

IB. Liv also told me that it was very, very difficult for her to play together with American actors, because her education was of another sort entirely.

FJM. The interesting thing about you, though, is that you are certainly not the product of a Scandinavian acting school either. You have created your own personal method.

IB. Yes.

FJM. One that is totally independent of the established *elevskole* [acting school] tradition as well.

IB. Yes, yes, of course it is. Because I have never acted – or rather I have acted very, very little. But when I did act, it was a very good experience for me, because it taught me how vulnerable the actor is and how extremely dependent he is on someone who exists outside himself. Just as the ballet dancer has the mirror and the musician has his tape recorder. Someone who watches him very objectively but very sympathetically.

LLM.   Did you find any difference between the Swedish actors and the actors you are working with here in Germany?

IB.   No.

LLM.   At the outset, I mean – not now, because by now you have to some extent trained them.

IB.   There is one difference, and that is a tragic one. The actors here are of the highest standard, but somehow they are destroyed mentally. The climate here is so very, very tough for actors. There are many theaters and naturally there is lots of work to be found, but the way they are treated by the directors and by the critics and by the audience is terrible.

LLM.   The German critics are a difficult lot in general, aren't they?

IB.   Oh yes, they are . . . a little bit nastier and meaner than the Swedish ones, I think. But the critics here are very experienced; they know a lot and they have seen a lot and generally they write very well. And if they hang you, you will not be hanged in silence. [Laughter] I must say I like that very much: I like reactions. Even if they are tough and even if sometimes they are very silly, I like reactions very much.

LLM.   You don't become angry at them?

IB.   No, no, no. The only time – the *only* time I became angry at a critic was when a Swedish critic insisted, as a matter of principle, on writing humiliating things about the actors. If he wants to write about me, I don't care. But if he writes nasty things, unfair and very personal things about my actors, I think he is a poison and has to be destroyed.*

FJM.   I agree with you.

IB.   Because the actors themselves have no opportunity to respond, to fight back. They are also too frightened, too insecure. They always think: This time perhaps he writes ill about me, but let me not make an enemy of him because next time perhaps he will write well about me.

---

*The offending critic, Bengt Jahnsson of *Dagens Nyheter,* gained sudden fame when he was assaulted by Bergman at an open rehearsal of *Woyzeck.* Bergman was subsequently charged and fined S.Kr. 5,000 (about £625). Reportedly, he paid the fine with pleasure.

LLM. But to come back to the question of your method of directing actors . . .

IB. That was a question, was it? [Laughter.]

LLM. Don't you feel very strongly opposed to Stanislavski and his method, for example?

IB. I don't care for Stanislavski. Stanislavski was very good for the Russian theater, but I think he has been completely misunderstood by Lee Strasberg and others. A friend of mine, a very clever girl named Bibi Andersson, joined the Strasberg school in New York for some weeks, and when she came back she told us she had almost fainted from laughter. It was the biggest bluff in the world, she said, because it was all built on some sort of strange, psychological, suggestive magic.

FJM. The psychological identification of the actor with his role.

IB. Yes. Some sort of – some sort of masturbation. Now I must say I have nothing against masturbation, but when one comes upon it in the theater, when they all sit there together masturbating their souls, I find it . . .

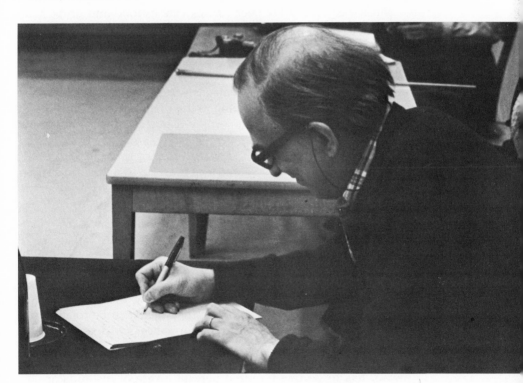

LLM.   Self-indulgent?

IB.   Yes, exactly. No, I must say I have no method at all.

LLM.   But if you were to advise a young actor, what would you say
to him? What kind of training would you tell him to get? Or
wouldn't you tell him to get any training?

IB.   No. When we work together – when I work with young actors –
or with any sort of actor – very slowly we try to discover the meaning of the play, what we are going to think at this particular
moment, what we are going to feel at that particular moment.
Very precisely. And the movement must correspond precisely to
the emotions and the rhythm of these moments. Everything in life
is rhythm, and when we create art we must also discover the
rhythm of what we are attempting to do. This must be the basis,
then: First of all the meaning of the play; then absolutely to know
at every moment, at every second, what to think, what to feel –
the movements, the tune, the key, the rhythm.

LLM.   The terms you employ to describe it suggest that it would be
almost impossible for you to work with an actor who was unmusical.

IB.   Music has all my life been just as vital as food and drink. One
of the important basic inspirations, perhaps even the most important. Music is a great source of strength. And most actors *are*
musical. Sometimes they may not know it, and then you have to
exercise their ability. For instance, the German actors are generally
so used to playing their parts on their own, in isolation, that they
aren't very interested in listening to their fellow actors. They don't
know how to listen. Of course they listen, but they don't know
how to listen. When you are acting a part, you are not an I, you
are always a you. You must concentrate not on yourself but always on your fellow actors. And you must do so all the time, even
when you are not on the stage. The actors must not drift off to the
canteen; they must remain there on the stage. Usually I tell the
actors: Stay on the stage; and I try to make the setting so simple
that no stagehands or electricians or others are needed. Because
whenever they take away a setting, they always take something
more with them. So I try to keep them out of it, to find a solution
that is so simple that we won't need any stagehands.

LLM.   What do you tell your actors concerning the audience? Are
they aware of the audience, or are they meant to be totally unaware of its presence during the performance? Or does it have to
do with the particular play?

IB.   I believe that every actor, even if it may seem that he is not
aware, has to be one hundred percent aware of his audience, at

every moment. He must never forget the audience for a moment, because if he does he retreats into some sort of private solitude. And then it's all over, you know, then it becomes completely uninteresting. So we always try, in all our work, to find our way to the audience – to discover how it will react to this thing or that.

LLM. Then if the actors are aware at all times of the presence of an audience, do they adjust themselves to its reactions during the course of the performance – or don't you think that matters? Do they in fact control the audience's reactions?

IB. Yes, I think they do. In the beginning, the first time somebody is sitting there, their nerves begin to work. But slowly they learn to rule – both their own nerves and the audience. The actor must make sure at all times that the audience is never allowed to become passive, but remains active.

FJM. Viewed from the audience's side, though, the effect created by a technique such as the continued visible presence of the actors on stage is very decisive.

IB. Oh yes.

FJM. In other words, you say that you do this for the sake of the actors, as a means of maintaining their involvement. Seen from the audience's point of view, however, it then creates a very consciously theatricalized experience.

LLM. Do you regard this device – keeping your actors seated on stage throughout a performance – as something that focuses audience attention more sharply on the stage, or do you feel that, on the contrary, it serves to distance the audience – that it reminds the audience that it is watching a performance?

[Long pause]

IB. The real theater always reminds – the real theatrical creation always must remind the audience that it is watching a performance. I believe that if you try to depart from that rule, you will very soon collapse. Because the function of the spectator – if we talk about an ideal spectator watching the ideal performance – is that he continually undergoes changes of mind, changes in his concentration. From being completely involved at one instant, he is in the very next instant aware of being in the theater. The next second he is involved again, completely involved; then after three seconds he is back again in the theater. And that is a part – and a very, very important part – of his being a participant in the ritual. – Because that word *verfremdung* [alienation] is a complete misunderstanding. The spectator is always involved and he is always outside, at one and the same time.

LLM. Theater is very different from film in that respect, isn't it?

IB.   Oh yes. In film, you see, the spectator is hypnotized – because he is also in the position of someone who is being hypnotized. As you know, when you are being hypnotized the mesmerist very often uses a small lamp, a spot of light, and says: "Follow this with your eyes." [Demonstrating.] Then he moves the spot of light up there, on the ceiling – and you look at it, he says, and you concentrate on that. With film it is exactly the same. You sit comfortably, I hope, with light in front of you, in the dark, very silent, very far from other people.

LLM. We saw your *Magic Flute* again recently and I was just wondering whether you consider that filmed theater or theatricalized film? For example, I'm thinking of the way in which you stress certain themes by letting the spectator read the text of what is being sung. Which is a wonderful device, to be sure. But is the intended effect something in between theater and film?

IB. It's not a film – it was made as a television play, and that's different. The spectator's perception of a TV play is completely different from his perception of a motion picture. The spectator is placed in three completely different situations, sitting in the theater, sitting at home watching a TV play, or sitting in a movie theater. They represent three entirely different ways of perceiving something. And when you make a TV play, you must of course continually bear that fact in mind – the situation of the spectator and his particular manner of perceiving.

Of course you can show a television play like *The Magic Flute* in a movie theater – as you know, you can also watch a movie on your television screen. But very often you'll notice that, when you do watch a very beloved picture at home on your television set, you sit up and think: good heavens, what's wrong!

FJM. Don't you like the idea of your own films being shown on television, then?

IB.   Oh, I love it. Yes, because even if the conditions of perception are not very good and certainly not ideal, I think it's marvellous that suddenly hundreds of thousands of people . . .

FJM. Yes, I understand.

IB.   And let's say that out of them a hundred or two hundred or three hundred people liked it or suddenly found that it was something worth watching . . . I think that's lovely.

And now I'm sorry, but I must go back to my work. I'm cutting my picture now.

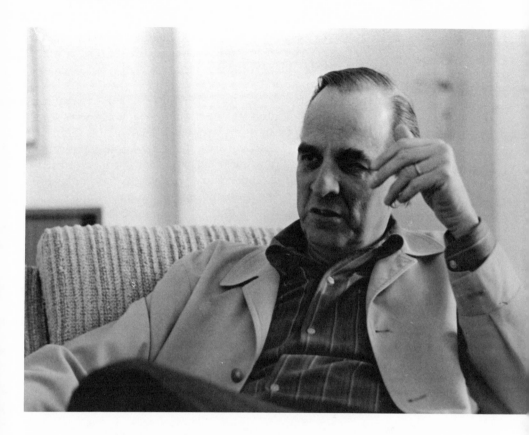

LLM. May we ask you – are you pleased with your new picture? Or are you too much in the midst of it to say?

IB. [Laughing] You have written a picture and you have shot the picture and now you are cutting it; and then you have to mix it, and then you must go through that long period of waiting to see the first print. You don't judge any longer. No, once you begin the shooting of a particular film, you stop judging.

LLM. The process of cutting one of your films must be an extraordinarily difficult one.

IB. To cut? No, it's a nice job. I like that very, very much.

LLM. You don't find yourself too close to it.

IB. No, no, you have to be very objective. You must simply look at it as though someone else had made it. From the beginning of shooting, the writer is dead; you are the director, and your job is to direct the material you have got. You must bring it to life in your own way. It's completely a Dr. Jekyll and Mr. Hyde proposition. Of course if you have made a bad picture, cutting it makes for a very unhappy time. You don't feel very well while you cut it.

FJM.   But if it's a good one – then it's exciting?

IB.   It's never a question of good or bad – it's only a matter of whether a picture still interests you. Sometimes, you know, something very, very unpleasant can happen: While you are shooting a picture, you suddenly discover that the material no longer interests you – and that is the worst of all. Whether it's good or bad – it doesn't work that way, because you always try to do your best. So that isn't the problem. The problem can be that it ceases to interest you. And all I can say now is that – at least at this point – I am still interested in cutting my picture. [Laughter.]

Geiselgasteig, February 1980

7   Bergman's world: a chronology

This annotated chronology is intended to be a guide to Ingmar Bergman's stage productions. (His earlier nonprofessional productions are not included.) Its focus is on Bergman's work in the living theater, and only the more significant of his many radio and television productions have been included. Nor is a complete filmography to be found here, although dates of his major motion pictures have been provided. However, illustrating the breadth of Bergman's repertory over nearly four decades in the professional theater, this guide bears persuasive witness to his extraordinary productivity and to the astonishing versatility of his art.

1944

With his appointment as artistic director of the Hälsingborg City Theatre, Ingmar Bergman began, at the age of twenty-six, to attract widespread public notice. During the hectic autumn of his first season, which also saw the production of his first screenplay, *Torment*, under the direction of Alf Sjöberg, the young director staged:

Aschebergskan på Widtskövle, a regional folk comedy by Brita von Horn and Elsa Collin, opened on September 21;

Hvem er Jeg? [Who Am I?], a Freudian satire by the Danish dramatist Carl Erik Soya (already staged by Bergman as a student production the year before) followed on October 10;

Macbeth, presented as an anti-Nazi drama, opened on November 19.

1945

Kriss-Krass-filibom, a satirical revue subtitled "some things in two acts by Scapin, Pimpel, and Kasper," appeared on New Year's Day (Bergman's interest in Kasper and the *Kasperl* tradition was already established: *Kasper's Death*, one of the earliest of his own plays, had been staged by him as a student show three years earlier);

Sagan [The Legend], by Hjalmar Bergman, opened on February 7 as the first of three different productions of this bittersweet fantasy;

235

Reducera moralen [*Morality Reduced*], a new comedy by Sune Bergström, appeared in April.

The war was over when *Jacobowsky and the Colonel,* Franz Werfel's popular anti-Nazi "comedy of a tragedy" opened the new season on September 12. "Our theater must be a touchstone for our ability to criticize ourselves," the director declared in a program note. The premiere on November 1 of *Rabies* by Olle Hedberg ("much more unpleasant than any of Bernard Shaw's most unpleasant plays") served notice that Bergman meant to keep the implied promise.

The Pelican, Opus IV of Strindberg's Chamber Plays, opened under Bergman's direction, as a guest production, at the Malmö City Theatre's Intimate Stage on November 25. "Great demands are placed on him. But next time he'll do it," remarked Herbert Grevenius in *Stockholms–Tidningen.*

1946

February 26: Bergman's first independent motion picture, *Crisis,* is released by Svensk Filmindustri (SF);

March 6: *Rekviem,* a new Swedish play by Björn-Erik Höijer, is Bergman's ninth and last directing assignment in Hälsingborg;

September 12: He directs one of his own early plays, a "morality" entitled *Rakel och biografvaktmästaren* [*Rachel and the Cinema Doorman*], for the Malmö City Theatre's Intimate Stage;

November 9: *It Rains on Our Love,* his next feature film, is released.

In the autumn, Bergman took up new duties as resident stage director (under the firm hand and watchful eye of manager Torsten Hammarén) at the larger and more demanding Gothenburg City Theatre. The first of his ten productions here, an explosive presentation of Camus's *Caligula,* opened on November 29.

1947

Bergman directed G. K. Chesterton's comic fantasy *Magic* on March 29 and two of his own "moralities," *Dagen slutar tidigt* [*Early Ends the Day*] on January 12 and *Mig till skräck* [*To My Terror*] on October 26 for the Gothenburg City Theatre's experimental studio. He was also deeply involved in film making, both as a screenwriter (*Woman Without a Face*), as a director (*Music in the Dark*), and in his customary double role as writer and director (*A Ship Bound for India*); and he directed the first of numerous radio productions of Strindberg's plays, *Playing with Fire* and *The Dutchman*.

1948

February 8: The premiere of *Dans på bryggan* [*Dance on the Wharf*] by Björn-Erik Höijer opens in the Studio at Gothenburg;

March 12: Bergman's second production of *Macbeth* appears on the main stage;

September 11: He directs Jean Anouilh's "rose" comedy, *Thieves' Carnival*, on the Studio stage;

October 18: *Port of Call*, Bergman's Gothenburg-inspired waterfront film, is released by SF;

November 4: His radio production of Strindberg's short play *Mother Love* continues the Swedish seaside theme.

December 8: *Kamma noll* [*Draw Blank*], the only Bergman stage play *not* first directed by its author, opens in Hälsingborg.

1949

His films, *Prison* (also known as *The Devil's Wanton*) and *Three Strange Loves* (or *Thirst*), were released. In Gothenburg he directed Anouilh's early "black" play, *La Sauvage*, at the Studio on February 11, then concluded his three-season engagement with an impressive production on the main stage (March 1) of Tennessee Williams's *A Streetcar Named Desire*. "With it Ingmar Bergman has created his masterpiece, and with it he leaves Gothenburg," declared *Stockholms–Tidningen*. The remainder of the year was devoted to film work.

1950

Bergman returned to Gothenburg in February with a guest production of Ramón María del Valle-Inclán's savage and erotic "tragicomedy of village life," *Divine Words*.

Two more Bergman pictures, *To Joy* and *This Can't Happen Here*, came out; and the first "summer" film, *Summer Interlude* [or *Illicit Interlude*, as it was titled in the United States], was completed during the spring and summer, but only released more than a year later.

Meanwhile, he was engaged by Lorens Marmstedt to direct at his Intima teatern in Stockholm – but presented only two programs: *The Threepenny Opera*, the sole Brecht work in his career, opened on October 17; and *En skugga* [*A Shadow*], one of Hjalmar Bergman's "marionette plays," and Anouilh's one-act version of Euripides' *Medea* appeared as a double bill on December 28.

"Everything went to hell during this period," Bergman recalls. "There was only one thing that mattered, and that was to make something the public liked."

1951

During the shutdown of the Swedish film industry to protest the heavy entertainment tax, Bergman staged two guest productions:

Det lyser i kåken [*Light in the Hovel*], his third Björn-Erik Höijer drama of life in northern Sweden, opened at Dramaten (Lilla scenen) on April 19; this was the first of many major productions at the Swedish national theater.

The Rose Tattoo, his second Tennessee Williams production, was given a free, imaginative interpretation at the municipal theatre in Norrköping on November 15.

Bergman's experimental radio drama, *Staden* [*The City*], was broadcast on May 9.

1952

Bergman began his richly creative six-year association with the Malmö City Theatre as its artistic director, after a guest production on February 14 of his own controversial drama, *Mordet i Barjärna* [*The Murder at Barjärna*], in the 204-seat experimental studio theater (Intiman).

On November 14 he presented a simplified production of Strindberg's folk play *The Crown-Bride* on the main stage. (He also found time to direct five radio productions, including two other Strindberg plays, *Crimes and Crimes* and *Easter*, and Garcia Lorca's *Blood Wedding*.)

As soon as the film embargo was lifted, Bergman also completed two major films in quick succession, *Waiting Women* and *Summer with Monika*.

1953

Gycklornas Afton (renamed *The Naked Night* in the United States and, even more awkwardly, *Sawdust and Tinsel* in Britain) was released on September 14;

The theme of humiliation and the concern with the artist's place in the world link the film to the play with which Bergman elected to begin his first full season as artistic director at Malmö – Pirandello's *Six Characters in Search of an Author* (Intiman, November 21); *The Castle,* adapted from Kafka's novel by Max Brod and presented by Bergman on a virtually bare stage, opened at Intiman four weeks later.

A new radio production of Strindberg's *The Dutchman* was also directed by Bergman on October 9.

1954

The Ghost Sonata, the third and best-known of Strindberg's Chamber Plays, opened on the main stage at Malmö on March 5;

With his sparkling production of Franz Lehár's *The Merry Widow* (October 1), Bergman displayed a command of the musical theater that called forth critical comparisons with Reinhardt's famous staging of *Die Fledermaus;*

Three days later *A Lesson in Love,* a Bergman comedy, was released by SF.

1955

This important year in Bergman's career began with his vigorously ironic rendering of Molière's *Don Juan* at Intiman (January 4). John Patrick's commercial success, *Teahouse of the August Moon,* followed on the main stage one month later. In March, he returned to Intiman with *Trämålning* [Painting on Wood], a one-act play that he wrote as an exercise for the acting students at Malmö – and that quickly became the inspiration for one of his most important films, *The Seventh Seal.* His production of the popular Swedish novelist – dramatist Vilhelm Moberg's biblical drama *Lea och Rakel* [*Leah and Rachel*], opened at Intiman on October 27.

On the screen, *Dreams* (British title: *Journey into Autumn*) was released in August, followed at the end of the year by *Smiles of a Summer Night*.

1956

Full international recognition came when *Smiles of a Summer Night* was awarded a Special Prize at the 1956 Cannes Film Festival; during the same year, he completed work on *The Seventh Seal* – in an astonishing thirty-five days! Meanwhile, his absorption in theater work continued unabated. ("It was a theater existence that was totally unneurotic, and it was sheer joy to make theater, a kind of theater vitality.")

The Poor Bride, Alexander Ostrovski's bitter satire of human pettiness and narrowmindedness, opened at Intiman on January 28;

Cat on a Hot Tin Roof, Bergman's third Tennessee Williams production, was seen in his starkly simplified mise-en-scène on October 19;

Erik XIV, Strindberg's demanding historical drama, came to Stora scenen only seven weeks later.

1957

During the year of *So Close to Life* and of the internationally acclaimed *Wild Strawberries*, Bergman still found time to present two of the most important productions of his career on the main stage at Malmö: Ibsen's *Peer Gynt* on March 8, Molière's *The Misanthrope* on December 6. Max von Sydow, fresh from his triumph in *The Seventh Seal*, acted both Peer and Alceste.

Bergman also directed his first television production, Hjalmar Bergman's *Herr Sleeman kommer* [*Mr. Sleeman is Coming*] (April 18) – just over two years after the official inauguration of television transmission in Sweden. "Television cannot demand so much of its audience," he told an interviewer. "My films are constructed much more symphonically, like music, with five or six or more motifs. But that won't work with television – there only one motif is found" (*Kvällsposten*, January 5, 1958).

1958

Bergman directed two more television productions: *The Venetian*, an anonymous sixteenth-century piece, on February 21; a revival of Olle Hedberg's play *Rabies* on November 7.

His last three productions at the Malmö City Theatre displayed three distinct facets of his directorial range:

With *The Legend,* which he now staged for the second time, he reaffirmed his preoccupation with the symbolic fantasies of Hjalmar Bergman (Intiman, April 12);

Goethe's *Ur-Faust* (Stora scenen on October 17) was a daring classical reinterpretation in which Mephistopheles was seen as the diabolical, ever-present mirror image of Faust;

Värmlänningarna [*The People of Värmland*], F. A. Dahlgren's traditional nineteenth-century folk play, was given a scrupulously loyal and uncaricatured revival on December 19, and with it Bergman took leave of his Malmö public.

One week later Bergman's motion picture, *The Face* (called *The Magician* in the United States), was released.

Although he had been engaged by Dramaten in Stockholm as its chief director, he was occupied almost exclusively with film work during the next two years.

1959

Bergman directed nothing new for the theater. He found it necessary to withdraw from a production of Molière's *Amphitryon* planned for the Malmö City Theatre in March (Lars-Levi Læstadius, the theater's managing director, took over the project). The 1958 production of Hjalmar Bergman's *The Legend* was revived at Intiman on March 14, and was later seen at the Théâtre Sarah Bernhardt in Paris. Bergman's production of *Ur-Faust* was also on tour to London during the same Spring.

The principal motion pictures to emerge from this prolonged period of theatrical inactivity (1959–60) were *The Virgin Spring* and *The Devil's Eye.*

1960

Bergman's production of *Storm Weather,* Opus I of Strindberg's Chamber Plays, was telecast throughout Scandinavia on January 22; his production of Strindberg's one-act comedy *First Warning* was also broadcast on August 11.

1961

January 6: A decade after his first directing assignment at Dramaten, Bergman returns with a controversial production of Chekhov's *The*

Seagull ("a tired, lax production," he later called it: "I wasn't happy in the theater and felt that everything went wrong");

January 22: His new production of Strindberg's grim one-act comedy, *Playing with Fire,* is broadcast;

April 22: Bergman's brilliant staging of the Stravinsky–Auden opera *The Rake's Progress* at the Royal Opera in Stockholm marks a pivotal highpoint in his directing career;

October 16: *Through a Glass Darkly* ("a theater piece in disguise," Bergman remarks, on which his direction of *The Seagull* "also had its influence") is released by SF.

1962

During the eighteen months that followed *The Rake's Progress* – when the film trilogy of *Through a Glass Darkly, Winter Light,* and *The Silence* was completed – Bergman directed nothing for the theater.

1963

On January 14, Bergman was chosen to succeed Karl Ragnar Gierow as head of Sweden's national theater at the end of the season. His first, much-awaited production in this new capacity, an explosive rendering of Edward Albee's commercial success, *Who's Afraid of Virginia Woolf?,* opened on October 4. Hjalmar Bergman's *The Legend* – revived for the third time in his career – followed at Lilla scenen, Dramaten's 350-seat studio stage, on December 20. During the same year Bergman also directed a television adaptation of Strindberg's *A Dream Play* (May 2).

1964

Tre knivar från Wei [Three Knives from Wei], a historical saga of cruelty in seventh-century China by the Swedish poet Harry Martinson, was given its first production by Bergman on June 4. Three days later, Bergman's first color film, the farcical comedy *Now About These Women,* appeared. Neither venture prospered.

Success quickly followed, however, with his radically simplified performance of Ibsen's *Hedda Gabler* (October 17), unquestionably one of the most remarkable stage productions of his career.

1965

February 24: Molière's *Don Juan*, which Bergman had directed exactly ten years before at Malmö, is revived by him as a school
production. (The performance was also broadcast for educational
television.)

December 4: Albee's *Tiny Alice*, which Bergman took on when the
play's scheduled director fell ill, is seen in a sexually explicit production at Lilla scenen.

1966

Bergman's stark "sonata for two," *Persona* – his first major motion
picture since *The Silence* – came to the screen, and he resigned his
full-time position at Dramaten. His final production as administra-
tive director was a "theater of fact" presentation of Peter Weiss's
documentary "oratorium" *The Investigation*, on February 13.

On November 20 Bergman returned to Dramaten with a controversial production of Molière's *The School for Wives* that a number of
the critics found disappointingly "abstract." *The Criticism of the
School for Wives* was presented as a provocative prologue to the production, with Erland Josephson, Bergman's successor as the head of
Dramaten, cast in the role of Dorante, Molière's spokesman for critical common sense and "the Approbation of the Pit."

This production seemed at the time to represent Bergman's dis-
gruntled retirement from the Swedish theater scene and its vicissitudes.

1967

Much of this year was devoted to film work. The manuscript for *The
Shame* was finished by Bergman in the spring, and the production of
it began in September. *The Rite*, a highly charged "artist" drama that
he wrote and produced independently for television, was completed
in July. (It was telecast on March 25, 1969.)

On April 1, however, he again staged Pirandello's *Six Characters in
Search of an Author* – this time at Nationaltheatret in Oslo. This production – Bergman's first outside of Sweden – marks a turning point.
Although its director seems to have called it a "farewell performance," it has in reality turned out to be the beginning of a continu-

ing series of guest productions that he has staged at theaters
throughout Europe.

His earlier production of *Hedda Gabler*, which traveled to Helsing-
fors in June, opened the new season at Dramaten in September and
played to enthusiastic audiences in Berlin the following month.

1968

The Hour of the Wolf and *The Shame* came to the screen, but Bergman
directed no new major stage production. However, his *Hedda Gabler*
opened for a brief but significant run of guest performances at the
Aldwych Theatre in London in June.

1969

Happily, Bergman's "retirement" from Swedish theater was brief.
On March 12 his arena-style production of Büchner's *Woyzeck*, for
which he had introduced the practice of open, public rehearsals,
was given its first official performance at Dramaten. Three days later
he had already begun work on *Fårö–dokument*, an eighty-minute
documentary film about the sheep-raising society on his island retreat in the Baltic. The color film *Passion*, generally regarded as a
continuation of *The Shame*, was released by SF and Cinematograph
on November 10.

1970

Strindberg's *A Dream Play*, adapted by Bergman as a chamber play,
opened at Dramaten's studio stage on March 14;

An English version of his *Hedda Gabler*, performed by members of
the National Theatre Company, opened at the Cambridge Theatre in
London on June 30;

Reservatet [*Sanctuary*], "a tragicomedy of banality" written by Bergman but directed by Jan Molander, was telecast on Eurovision on
October 28.

1971

March 20: *Show*, a new work by the Swedish lyric dramatist Lars
Forssell, becomes Bergman's fourteenth production at Dramaten;

April 19: His *Dream Play* opens at the Aldwych Theatre in London as part of the World Theatre Season;

June 6: *The Touch*, Bergman's first film in English, is seen at the Berlin Film Festival.

1972

The Bergman production of Ibsen's *The Wild Duck*, regarded by many as one of his finest achievements in the theater, had its premiere at Dramaten on March 17.

Cries and Whispers, his harrowing film study of the process of death, stems from the same year. (Released March 5, 1973.)

1973

During this important and astonishingly productive year in his career, Bergman directed two very demanding works taken up from his earlier repertory at Malmö. Strindberg's *The Ghost Sonata*, which had been in rehearsal for two and a half months, opened at Dramaten on January 13. After barely a month's pause, he traveled to Copenhagen to begin rehearsals for a new production of Molière's *The Misanthrope*, which opened at the Danish Royal Theatre on April 6.

Meanwhile, London audiences saw his production of *The Wild Duck* during Peter Daubeny's tenth and final World Theatre Season at the Aldwych. Even New York audiences had a small taste of Bergman, albeit much diluted, when Stephen Sondheim's musical *A Little Night Music*, based on *Smiles of a Summer Night* (and inspired by "a desire to produce a waltz musical"!) reached Broadway.

Bergman's popularity touched a high point when his six-part television film, *Scenes from a Marriage*, was seen in weekly episodes on Swedish television (April 11–May 16). (In the United States, the film's subsequent moviehouse distribution was hailed as his "most successful attempt yet at moving a mass audience.")

1974

Bergman's by now customary annual production at Dramaten, an adaptation of Parts I and II of Strindberg's *To Damascus*, opened on February 1. On May 10, a national telecast of the Copenhagen production of *The Misanthrope* was seen on Danish television. The production came to Dramaten for four guest performances later in the same month.

1975

On New Year's Day, Bergman's television production of Mozart's opera *The Magic Flute*, filmed during the preceding spring to commemorate the fiftieth anniversary of the Swedish Broadcasting Company, was seen throughout Scandinavia.

With his production of *Twelfth Night*, which opened at Dramaten on March 7 and ran through the summer, Bergman returned to Shakespeare for the first time since his *Macbeth* productions of the forties.

His preoccupation with the television medium continued with the making of *Face to Face*, a hallucinatory, psychoanalytical television film in four parts that was released the following year.

1976

On January 30, 1976, Swedish police questioned Bergman in connection with alleged tax irregularities. The charges were subsequently disproven and withdrawn, but the incident made a deep impression. On April 25, he announced to *Expressen*, Scandinavia's largest newspaper, that he was leaving Sweden, and since that time he has resided in West Germany. In August, he told a Frankfurt audience during his acceptance of the Goethe Prize: "I can no longer live in a land where my honor is publicly and unjustly impugned."

1977

Two very different but equally uneven works emerged as the first products of Bergman's new surroundings. *The Serpent's Egg*, concerned with the violent upheavals in Germany during the chaotic weeks of November 1923, became his thirty-ninth feature film – and the first to be made entirely outside of Sweden. At the Residenztheater in Munich, his new home, he directed *A Dream Play*, which opened on May 19.

1978

During the year that brought *Autumn Sonata* to the screen, Bergman's second German-language production, a provocative reinterpretation of Chekhov's *The Three Sisters*, opened at the Residenztheater in Munich on June 22, following an unusually intensive rehearsal period of nearly fifteen weeks. The production continued to appear in repertory and on tour in Germany during the following season.

Rehearsals for Strindberg's *The Dance of Death*, which had been interrupted by the police in 1976, were resumed at Dramaten in August, but they were once again broken off when Anders Ek, who was to have played the Captain, fell ill.

Nonetheless, when Bergman celebrated his sixtieth birthday in Fårö on July 14, he could look back on an astonishingly productive career: some sixty-five major stage productions and forty films in thirty-four years of professional activity.

1979

Tartuffe, Bergman's sixth production of a Molière comedy, opened at the Residenztheater on January 13 and appeared as part of the Bregenzer Festspiele in July.

A German revival of *Hedda Gabler,* Bergman's third approach to this play, had its premiere at the Residenztheater on April 11.

Twelfth Night was revived at Dramaten during July, the first Bergman production to be seen in Sweden in four years.

1980

Bergman's stark, rigorously stylized rendering of Gombrowicz's tragifarce *Yvonne, Princess of Burgundy* opened in Munich on May 10 to enthusiastic critical accolades in the German press.

Aus dem Leben der Marionetten [*From the Life of the Marionettes*] had its first public screening in July at a small film festival in Oxford. It had its official premiere in Paris on October 8.

Fårö Document '79, an expansion of his earlier study of the island community, was screened in New York on October 30.

Twelfth Night, one of the brightest examples of Bergman's theater art, was summoned to Paris in November to add its lustre to the celebrations marking the tercentenary of the Comédie Française.

1981

Nora und Julie, Bergman's simultaneous production of Ibsen's *A Doll's House* and Strindberg's *Miss Julie,* opened at the Residenztheater on April 30. The third part of the "trilogy," his stage adaptation of *Scenes from a Marriage,* opened on the same evening at the intimate Theater im Marstall.

The production of *Miss Julie* made a guest appearance at Dramaten in May, as part of a Strindberg festival.

Notes

2. FIRST SEASONS

1. Nils Beyer, *Teaterkvällar* (Stockholm, 1953), p. 46. Interestingly enough, Beyer's portentous review bore the title "Gycklarnas afton"—the same title Bergman gave to his film masterpiece (*The Naked Night* in English) in 1953. All translations in this book are by the authors, unless otherwise indicated.

2. Interview in *Expressen* (Stockholm), February 18, 1974. The "psychobiographical" school of Bergman criticism, with which the present study is not directly concerned, draws heavily on childhood experiences described in this interview and in Jörn Donner's film interview, "Three Scenes with Ingmar Bergman" (1975). Cf. Martin Drouzy, "Barnet i klædeskabet. Arbejdsnoter til en undersøgelse om Ingmar Bergman og hans film," *Kosmorama*, 13 (Spring 1978), 30–4, and Marianne Höök, *Ingmar Bergman* (Stockholm, 1962).

3. "Dialog med Ingmar Bergman" in Henrik Sjögren, *Ingmar Bergman på teatern* (Stockholm, 1968), p. 295. [Hereafter called "Dialog".]

4. Stig Björkman, Torsten Manns, and Jonas Sima, eds. *Bergman om Bergman* (Stockholm, 1970 & Copenhagen, 1971), p. 13.

5. Sjögren, "Dialog," pp. 302–3.

6. Cf. Henrik Sjögren, "Ingmar Bergman's teater–rörelser i rummet" in *Perspektiv på teater*, eds. Ulf Gran and Ulla-Britta Lagerroth (Stockholm, 1971), p. 122.

7. Cf. Per Bjurström, *Teaterdekoration i Sverige* (Stockholm, 1964), pp. 145–6.

8. Sjögren, "Dialog," p. 299.

9. Björkman, Manns, and Sima *Bergman om Bergman,* p. 38.

10. Ibid., p. 59.

11. Sjögren, "Dialog," p. 298.

12. For further details, see Frederick J. Marker and Lise-Lone Marker, *The Scandinavian Theatre: A Short History* (Oxford, 1975), pp. 262–4.

13. Interview in *Helsingborgs Dagblad,* February 2, 1973.

14. Sjögren, "Dialog," p. 295.

15. For some discussion in English of Bergman's early plays (which are not a principal concern in this study), see, for example, Vernon Young, *Cinema Borealis: Ingmar Bergman and the Swedish Ethos* (New York, 1972), pp. 48–51 et passim.

16. Jean-Paul Sartre, "Forgers of Myths" in *Playwrights on Playwriting,* ed. Toby Cole (New York, 1961), p. 118.

17. Another Swedish production opened in Malmö on the same night (March 1, 1949); Olof Molander's production opened in Stockholm a few weeks later; a very successful Danish production (subtly renamed *Omstigning til Paradis* or *Transfer to Paradise*) opened at the Royal Theatre in Copenhagen on September 1.

18. A. Gunnar Bergman, quoted in Sjögren, *Ingmar Bergman,* p. 70.

19. The design for the Jo Mielziner backdrop is found in his *Designing for the Theater: A Memoir and a Portfolio* (New York, 1965), p. 144.

20. "Conversation with Bergman" in John Simon, *Ingmar Bergman Directs* (New York, 1972), p. 33.

21. Reprinted in his *Avsidesrepliker: Teaterkritik 1961–1965* (Stockholm, 1966), pp. 146–7.

22. Sjögren, "Dialog," p. 314.
23. Sjögren in *Perspektiv på teater*, p. 124.
24. Höök, *Ingmar Bergman*, pp. 120–1.
25. Carl Cramér in *Ny Tid*, February 4, 1950.
26. Sjögren, "Dialog," p. 307.
27. Per Lindberg "On Building a Theatre" (1933), quoted in Henrik Sjögren, *Stage and Society in Sweden*, trans. P. B. Austin (Stockholm, 1979), p. 19.

3. THE STRINDBERG CYCLE

1. See Simon's "Conversation with Bergman" (p. 17) and Björkman, Manns, and Sima, *Bergman om Bergman*, p. 26.
2. See, for example, Young's *Cinema Borealis* (pp. 31–3) and Marilyn Johns's brief summary, "Kindred Spirits: Strindberg and Bergman," in *Scandinavian Review*, 3 (1976), 16.
3. The comparisons are found, respectively, in Simon "Conversation with Bergman," (pp. 299–300), Young, *Cinema Borealis* (pp. 276–7), Jörn Donner, *The Films of Ingmar Bergman*, trans. Holger Lundbergh (New York, 1972), p. 153, and Stig Ahlgren, "Riset bakom spegeln," *Vecko-Journalen*, 47 (November 24, 1961).
4. Björkman, Manns, and Sima, *Bergman om Bergman*, p. 124.
5. See Fritiof Billquist, *Ingmar Bergman: teatermannen och filmskaparen* (Stockholm, 1960), pp. 18–30.
6. Simon, "Conversation with Bergman," p. 19.
7. Hansingvar Hanson in *Stockholms–Tidningen*, March 6, 1954.
8. *Scenen*, January 1, 1921.
9. Siegfried Jacobsohn, "Vignettes from Reinhardt's Productions" in *Max Reinhardt and His Theatre*, ed. Oliver M. Sayler (New York, 1924), p. 325.
10. *Svenska Dagbladet*, January 21, 1949.
11. August Strindberg, *The Chamber Plays*, ed. Evert Sprinchorn (New York, 1962), p. xxiv.
12. Cf. Gunnar Ollén, *Strindbergs dramatik* (Stockholm 1961), pp. 356–8.
13. Sjögren, *Ingmar Bergman*, p. 128.
14. Discounting its eight-meter (26 ft) removable forestage, the main stage at the Malmö City Theatre measures 24 m (78 ft) both in depth and in height, making it slightly shallower than the Paris Opera (26 m) or the Royal Opera House Covent Garden (27.1 m). But its maximum proscenium width of 22 m (71.2 ft) is more than half again as great as in either of these two theaters, and when – as Bergman did for the final scene of *The Crown-Bride* – the stage is opened to its full width (36 m or 117 ft) it is one-third wider than the Covent Garden stage, and nearly twice the width of the stage of the Aldwych in London.
15. Vagn Børge, *Strindbergs mystiske teater* (Copenhagen, 1942), p. 175.
16. Sjögren "Dialog," pp. 311–12. A film of *The Crown-Bride* had actually been planned with Nordisk Tonefilm, but, given the conclusions about simplification that Bergman had reached, it is not hard to imagine why he lost interest in this project.
17. Ollén, *Strindbergs dramatik*, p. 322.
18. Quoted in *Directors on Directing*, eds. Toby Cole and Helen K. Chinoy (Indianapolis, 1963), p. 297.
19. Quoted in Billquist, p. 226.
20. Björkman, Manns, and Sima, *Bergman om Bergman*, p. 152.
21. Sprinchorn, *Chamber Plays*, p. 207.
22. Egil Törnqvist, *Bergman och Strindberg* (Stockholm, 1973): The misleading title

promises more than it holds, however, for the book deals only with the subject defined by its subtitle, *Spöksonaten–drama och iscensättning, Dramaten 1973*, and not with the Bergman–Strindberg relationship in general. The book is valuable chiefly for the full transcription it provides (pp. 115–75) of the production script for the 1973 performance. Törnqvist's short English summary of his book, entitled "Ingmar Bergman directs Strindberg's 'Ghost Sonata' " *Theatre Quarterly* 3 (July–September 1973), 3–14, does not contain this script.

23. Ibid., p. 98.
24. Sjögren, *Ingmar Bergman*, p. 146.
25. Quoted in Törnqvist, *Bergman och Strindberg*, p. 226.
26. Ibid., p. 100.
27. Ibid., p. 157. The actual dialogue here is in Evert Sprinchorn's translation. It is perhaps worth recording that Vernon Young, who has written enough nonsense about Bergman and Strindberg to disqualify three critics, proposes a fatuous parallel between the dinner party given by Johan Borg's demons in *Hour of the Wolf* (a film Young neither likes nor appears to understand) and the ghost supper in *The Ghost Sonata* – "itself so far over the edge that it can only be viewed without a quaver if you check your risibilities at the cloakroom. . . . Naima Wifstrand removing her rubber face [the old woman in the film removes her hat in order to hear the music better, and her face – identity – comes off with it] is only funnier in a desolate way than Strindberg's Mummy who lives in a closet and talks like a parrot." (*Cinema Borealis*, pp. 298–9)
28. Quoted in Törnqvist, *Bergman och Strindberg*, p. 102.
29. Quoted ibid., p. 107.
30. Typed production script, marked *Scenen*, p. 40 (Kungliga dramatiska teatern). This script and the copy of the production stage manager (Arne Hertler) supply all light, sound, and projection cues.
31. Törnqvist, *Bergman och Strindberg*, p. 151.
32. Ollén, *Strindbergs dramatik*, p. 474.
33. Molander's fascinating descriptive argument first appeared in *Göteborgs–Posten*, September 12, 1946. The building itself has unfortunately since been torn down.
34. Hansingvar Hanson suggests these associations in his review in *Stockholms–Tidningen*, March 6, 1954.
35. Henrik Sjögren, *Regi: Ingmar Bergman* (Stockholm, 1969), p. 20. Again, the title of this book makes it sound more general than it actually is; the subtitle, "Dagbok från Dramaten 1969," conveys its true scope.
36. Quoted in Törnqvist, *Bergman och Strindberg*, p. 186.
37. Björkman, Manns, and Sima, *Bergman om Bergman*, p. 47.
38. Quoted in Törnqvist, *Bergman och Strindberg*, p. 192.
39. Quoted ibid., pp. 97–8.
40. Quoted in Törnqvist's "Bergman directs Strindberg's 'Ghost Sonata'," 8.
41. Törnqvist, *Bergman och Strindberg*, p. 198.
42. Quoted ibid., p. 102.
43. Gunnar Brandell, "Vad har Bergman gjort av Strindberg?" [What has Bergman done with Strindberg?], *Dagens Nyheter*, February 19, 1974.
44. In a letter questioning Törnqvist's method and quoted by him (p. 11). In reality, Bergman's private reaction to this book's characteristically literary manner of approaching and evaluating a theatrical production is far more negative than this quotation alone might suggest: "His approach to the whole miracle of the production, the creation of the play, was completely intellectual – in a bad way, not in a good way," he has said in an interview.
45. Törnqvist, *Bergman och Strindberg*, p. 167.

46. Quoted ibid., p. 192.
47. Quoted ibid., p. 108.
48. Sjögren, "Dialog," p. 293.
49. Rehearsals began on December 9, 1969, and a total of fifty-six were held, including four public previews.
50. Michael Meyer's translation of the Bergman text, Strindberg, A Dream Play, Adapted by Ingmar Bergman (New York, 1973), follows the typed production script exactly. However, the stage directions contained in this translation are not Bergman's and are, in many cases, quite misleading. We have taken floor plans and other details about the staging from the production script, marked Scenen (76 pp., Kungliga dramatiska teatern). Other relevant items in the Dramaten library include a ring binder containing some of the director's rehearsal notes.
51. Quoted in Sjögren, Regi: Ingmar Bergman, p. 19.
52. A special production script for Daniel Bell contains a list of music cues. In general, the character of Bergman's musical selections for A Dream Play – a simple barrel organ melody, piano or cello music, occasional harp tones, and the like – affords an interesting contrast to the more grandiose, "operatic" style of musical accompaniment usually adopted by Olof Molander. For instance, the script for Molander's 1940 production of the play in Copenhagen describes an extremely complex pattern of musical cues. Most of the prologue in heaven was spoken to music from Ravel's ballet Daphnis et Chloé, while during the remainder of the play an orchestral potpourri composed of a Beethoven quartet, Chopin's Funeral March, Ravel's ballet, and his orchestral suite Rapsodie espagnole, Bach's Toccata con Fuga No. 10 (Strindberg's choice), a little Mozart, and much else provided an almost continual symphonic accompaniment. (The Molander script is in the Royal Theatre Library, Copenhagen.)
53. Although these two attributes of the Stage-Door Keeper – stjärntäcket and schalen – are quite distinct, they are for some reason translated with the same word ("shawl") in the Meyer edition (p. 11).
53. Interview in Berlingske Tidende (Copenhagen), January 1, 1975.
55. Face to Face, trans. Alan Blair (New York, 1976), p. vii.
56. Typescript, with copious handwritten notations, marked Regiexemplar (118 pp., Kungliga dramatiska teatern). Supplementary information about this production is contained in the production script of the director's assistant, Kari Sylwan, and in the separate scripts for sound, lighting, and projection cues.
57. Letter dated May 24, 1898. More information in English about the first production of To Damascus I is found in Marker and Marker, The Scandinavian Theatre, pp. 188–93.
58. Svenska Dagbladet, January 21, 1899.
59. Henrik Sjögren in Arbetet (Malmö), February 2, 1974.
60. In a letter to Gustaf af Geijerstam, dated October 17, 1898.
61. Carl Hammarén in Nerikes Allehanda (Örebro), February 2, 1974.
62. Jarl W. Donnér in Sydsvenska Dagbladet (Malmö), February 2, 1974.
63. Regiexemplar, p. 70. Translation by the authors.
64. Ibid., p. 85. The passage is also a good example of Bergman's skillful cutting.
65. Leif Zern seemed unaccountably puzzled by the deliberately ironic mode of the production. In an American interview, he objected to the choice of Jan-Olof Strandberg for the part of the Unknown because he is not "a psychological actor. He presents a role instead of playing a character. . . . He is an actor with a great sensitivity for the theatrical and comical, with a feeling for space; a physical actor." Though these would appear to be the very qualities Bergman was seeking, Zern evidently intended the comment as a negative one: "As a result, his

Stranger became a rather comic figure; it gave the production an ironic tone, and I wasn't sure that was intended." In the light of the evidence, the conclusion to which this critic is led seems little short of astounding: "One might almost think Bergman didn't take the play seriously, or at any rate did not take the character of the [Unknown] really seriously." *Scandinavian Review*, 3 (1976), 22–3.
66. *Regiexemplar*, pp. 117–18.
67. Lars Törnqvist in *Sundsvalls Tidning*, February 2, 1974.

4. A THEATER FOR MOLIÈRE

1. Interview in *Aktuelt* (Copenhagen), February 13, 1973.
2. Björkman, Manns, and Sima, *Bergman om Bergman*, p. 31.
3. Interview in *Helsingborgs Dagblad*, February 2, 1973.
4. Louis Jouvet, *Conferencia*, 18 (September 1, 1937), quoted in Jacques Guicharnaud, ed., *Molière: A Collection of Critical Essays* (Englewood Cliffs, N.J., 1964), p. 12.
5. *Helsingborgs Dagblad*, February 2, 1973.
6. *Theater Rundschau*, 25 (March 1979), 8.
7. Production script, marked *Scenen* (156 pp., Kungliga dramatiska teatern), p. 154.
8. *Dagbladet* (Ringsted), February 13, 1973.
9. Quoted in Sjögren, *Regi: Ingmar Bergman*, p. 14.
10. Ibid., p. 132.
11. Ibid., pp. 104–5.
12. *Journal 27. maj 1971–72 okt. 1976* (ms. volume, Royal Theatre Library).
13. *Aktuelt*, February 13, 1973.
14. Sjögren, *Regi: Ingmar Bergman*, p. 157.
15. Sjögren, "Dialog," p. 300.
16. Sjögren, "Ingmar Bergmans teater – rörelser i rummet," *Perspektiv på teater*, p. 121.
17. Hans Ruin in *Sydsvenska Dagbladet Snällposten*, December 7, 1957.
18. Alceste's time-honored attire as "the gentleman with green braids" was deliberately altered by Bergman to unrelieved black. The line was changed to match the alteration.
19. Ulf Ekman in *Information*, December 7, 1957.
20. Sjögren, *Ingmar Bergman*, p. 196.
21. Sjögren, "Dialog," p. 308.
22. The actual text used by Bergman was the rhymed and splendidly playable Danish translation of the play by P. Hansen. The translation quoted here and other lines quoted in this chapter are taken from Richard Wilbur's version of *The Misanthrope* (1955).
23. This point is emphasized in Jytte Wiingaard's *Teatersemiologi* (Copenhagen, 1976), a book which uses Bergman's *Misanthrope* as a clinical example in the author's discussion of the "language" of signs and gestures in the theater.
24. Jarl W. Donnér, "Herre mot strömmen," *Svenska Dagbladet*, December 7, 1957.
25. Documentation for specific details of placement, movement, and line interpretations in this production have been drawn not only from the director's own script but also from the very meticulous record of the performance compiled by his assistant, Ulla Elmquist. In addition, videotapes made available through the courtesy of Danmarks Radio have been immensely useful in substantiating personal recollection.
26. Bibi Andersson, "Ingmar Bergman," in the Royal Theatre program for the production (unpaginated, n.d.).

27. *Sydsvenska Dagbladet Snällposten,* December 7, 1957.
28. Wiingaard, *Teatersemiologi,* p. 95.
29. *Berlingske Tidende,* December 26, 1972.

5. THE ESSENCE OF IBSEN

1. Tord Baeckström in *Göteborgs Handels–och Sjöfartstidning,* March 9, 1957.
2. Carsten Nielsen in *Berlingske Tidende* (Copenhagen), March 10, 1957.
3. Cf. Lise-Lone Marker and Frederick J. Marker, "Ibsen's Theatre: Aspects of a Chronicle and a Quest," *Modern Drama,* 21 (1978), 354–5. A Norwegian analysis of the Nilsen production is found in Hans Midbøe, *Peer Gynt, teatret og tiden,* II (Oslo, 1976).
4. Baeckström in *GHT.*
5. Billquist, *Ingmar Bergman,* p. 229.
6. Sjögren, *Ingmar Bergman,* p. 190.
7. Ebbe Linde in *Dagens Nyheter,* October 18, 1958.
8. Per Erik Wahlund in *Svenska Dagbladet,* March 9, 1957.
9. Nils Beyer in *Morgon–Tidningen,* March 9, 1957.
10. Sjögren, "Dialog," p. 310.
11. Quoted in Billquist, *Ingmar Bergman,* p. 232.
12. Siegfried Melchinger in *Theater heute,* 10 (1967), 8.
13. Jeremy Kingston in *Punch,* 77 (July–September 1970) and Ronald Bryden in *The Observer,* July 5, 1970.
14. Quoted in Randolph Goodman, *From Script to Stage: Eight Modern Plays* (New York, 1971), p. 67.
15. Tord Baeckström in *Göteborgs Handels–och Sjöfartstidning,* October 18, 1964.
16. The device of the half-raised curtain, which conveyed its own strong suggestion of oppressiveness, caused its share of difficulties when this popular production toured through Sweden, Finland, and Germany. The tale is told that in the small town of Växjö, in southern Sweden, the local theater manager was beseiged at intermission by complaints that part of the audience could not see the stage at all because of the curtain. Entreaties to raise it to alleviate the situation were rebuffed by the director, however, and complainers were told that those wishing their money returned could take it and leave.
17. Sjögren, "Dialog," p. 312.
18. Lennart Josephson in *Sydsvenska Dagbladet* (Malmö), October 18, 1964.
19. Quoted in Vilgot Sjöman, *L 136: Diary with Ingmar Bergman,* trans. Alan Blair (Ann Arbor, 1978), p. 212.
20. Detailed information about this scene and about Bergman's instructions to the Residenztheater cast is derived from the script of *regieassistent* Johannes Kaetzler, whose generous help is gratefully acknowledged.
21. Francis Fergusson, *The Idea of a Theater* (Princeton, 1949), p. 93.
22. *Four Stories by Ingmar Bergman,* trans. Alan Blair (Garden City, N.Y., 1977), pp. 86, 87.
23. Cuts based on the stage manager's script, marked *Scenen* (247 pp., Kungliga dramatiska teatern), and on the director's own script. The translation is by Michael Meyer (published Garden City, N.Y., 1961); Meyer supplied the text for Bergman's London production.
24. From Heiner Gimmler's excellent German translation, mimeographed typescript (178 pp., Residenztheater), pp. 149–50.
25. Quoted in *Kvällsposten* (Malmö), October 18, 1964.

26. Björn Samuelsson in *Folket* (Eskilstuna), March 24, 1972.
27. Quoted from Michael Meyer's translation of *The Wild Duck* (Garden City, N.Y., 1961), p. 180.
28. Jens Kistrup in *Berlingske Tidende* (Copenhagen), April 27, 1973.
29. Charles Thomas Samuels, "Ingmar Bergman: An Interview," in *Ingmar Bergman: Essays in Criticism*, ed. Stuart M. Kaminsky (Oxford, 1975), p. 106.
30. Kistrup in *Berlingske Tidende*, April 27, 1973.
31. All information about cuts is taken from the prompter's copy, marked *Sufflörexemplar* (161 pp., Kungliga dramatiska teatern).
32. Kistrup in *Berlingske Tidende*, March 18, 1972.
33. Quoted in Henrik Lundgren, "Bergman og skuespillerne," *Kosmorama*, 13 (Spring 1978), 43.
34. In *Svenska Dagbladet*, January 22, 1973.
35. Quoted in Törnqvist, *Bergman och Strindberg*, pp. 99–100.
36. Bergman quotations in this paragraph are from : Björkman, Manns, and Sima, *Bergman om Bergman*, pp. 57–8; ibid., p. 18; Törnqvist, *Bergman och Strindberg*, p. 99; *Bergman om Bergman*, p. 228; and Sjögren, "Dialog," p. 300. Nørby's remark appeared in *Politiken* (Copenhagen), August 17, 1980
37. Quotations in this paragraph are from: Björkman, Manns, and Sima, *Bergman om Bergman*, p. 96; Billquist, *Ingmar Bergman*, p. 250; and Sjögren, *Regi: Ingmar Bergman*, pp. 40–1.

Selected bibliography

Andersson, E. *Tjugofem Säsonger 1926–51*. Gothenburg, 1957.
Arpe, Verner. *Das schwedische Theater*. Gothenburg, 1969.
Beijer, Agne. *Dramatik och teater*. Lund, 1968.
Bergman, G.M., ed. *Svensk teater: Strukturförandringar och organisation 1900–1970*. Stockholm, 1970.
Bergman, Ingmar. *Autumn Sonata*, trans. Alan Blair. New York, 1978.
   "Each Film is My Last," *Drama Review* T–33, vol. 11 (Fall 1966), 94–101.
   Face to Face, trans. Alan Blair. New York, 1976.
   Filmberättelser. 3 vols. Stockholm, 1973.
   Four Screenplays, trans. Lars Malmström and David Kushner. New York and London, 1960.
   Four Stories, trans. Alan Blair. Garden City, 1977.
   Jack hos skådespelerna. Stockholm, 1946.
   Moraliteter: Tre pjäser. Stockholm, 1948.
   Persona and Shame, trans. Keith Bradfield. London, 1972.
   The Serpent's Egg, trans. Alan Blair. New York, 1977.
   Three Films by Ingmar Bergman, trans. P. B. Austin. London, 1967.
   Trämålning: En moralitet. Stockholm, 1956
Bergman om Bergman, eds. Stig Björkman, Torsten Manns, and Jonas Sima, Stockholm, 1970; Copenhagen, 1971.
Bergom-Larsson, Maria. *Ingmar Bergman and Society*, trans. Barrie Selman. London and South Brunswick, N.J., 1978.
   Ingmar Bergman och den borgerliga ideologin. Stockholm, 1976.
Bergström, Beata. *Teater: ögonblickets konst, fångad i bilder*. Stockholm, 1976.
Beyer, Nils. *Teaterkvällar 1940–53*. Stockholm, 1953.
Billquist, Fritiof. *Ingmar Bergman: teatermannen och filmskaparen*. Stockholm, 1960.
Bjurström, Per. *Teaterdekoration i Sverige*. Stockholm, 1964.
Brunius, Niklas, Göran O. Eriksson and Rolf Rembe. *Swedish Theatre*. Stockholm, n.d.
Børge, Vagn. *Strindbergs mystiske teater*. Copenhagen, 1942.
Cole, Toby, ed. *Playwrights on Playwriting*. New York, 1961.
Cole, Toby and Helen K. Chinoy, eds. *Directors on Directing*. Indianapolis, 1963.
Cowie, Peter. *Sweden 2*. New York, 1970.
Donner, Jörn. *The Films of Ingmar Bergman* (earlier title: *The Personal Vision of Ingmar Bergman*). New York, 1972.
Dyfverman, Henrik, ed. *TV-teatern tio år, 1954–1964*. Stockholm, 1964.
Fergusson, Francis. *The Idea of a Theater*. Princeton, 1949, rept. Garden City, N.Y., 1953.
Goodman, Randolph. *From Script to Stage: Eight Modern Plays*. New York, 1971.
Gran, Ulf and Ulla-Britta Lagerroth, eds. *Perspektiv på teater*. Stockholm, 1971.
Grevenius, Herbert. *Offentliga nöjen*. Stockholm, 1946.
   Dagen efter. Stockholm, 1951.
Guicharnaud, Jacques, ed. *Molière: A Collection of Critical Essays*. Englewood Cliffs, N.J., 1964.
Holm, Ingvar. *Drama på scen*. Lund, 1969.

Höök, Marianne. *Ingmar Bergman*. Stockholm, 1962.
Kaminsky, Stuart M., ed. *Ingmar Bergman: Essays in Criticism*. Oxford, 1975.
Lagerroth, Ulla-Britta. *Regi i möte med drama och samhälle*. Stockholm, 1978.
Marker, Frederick J. and Lise-Lone Marker. *The Scandinavian Theatre: A Short History*. Oxford, 1975.
Meyer, Michael, ed. and trans. *Strindberg: A Dream Play*, adapted by Ingmar Bergman. New York, 1973.
Mielziner, Jo. *Designing for the Theater: A Memoir and a Portfolio* New York, 1965.
Ollén, Gunnar. *Strindbergs dramatik*. Stockholm, 1961.
Rydeberg, Georg. *Ridån går alltid ned*. Stockholm, 1970.
Sayler, Oliver M., ed. *Max Reinhardt and His Theatre*. New York, 1924.
Simon, John. *Ingmar Bergman Directs*. New York, 1972.
Sjögren, Henrik. *Ingmar Bergman på teatern*. Stockholm, 1968.
  Regi: Ingmar Bergman. Dagbok från Dramaten 1969. Stockholm, 1969.
  Stage and Society in Sweden, trans. P. B. Austin. Stockholm, 1979.
Sjöman, Vilgot. *L 136: Diary with Ingmar Bergman*, trans. Alan Blair. Ann Arbor, 1978.
Sprinchorn, Evert, ed. and trans. *August Strindberg: The Chamber Plays*. New York, 1962.
Strømberg, Ulla and Jytte Wiingaard, eds. *Den levende Ibsen*. Copenhagen, 1978.
Teater i Göteborg 1910–1975. 3 vols. Stockholm, 1978.
Thalia, 25 –et kvartsekel med Malmö Stadsteater, ed. Ragnar Gustafson. Sydsvenska Dagbladets Årsbok, 1970.
Törnqvist, Egil. *Bergman och Strindberg: Spöksonaten –drama och iscensättning, Dramaten 1973*. Stockholm, 1973.
Wahlund, Per Erik. *Avsidesrepliker: Teaterkritik 1961–1965*. Stockholm, 1966.
  Scenväxling: Teaterkritik 1951–1960. Stockholm, 1962.
Wiingaard, Jytte. *Teatersemiologi*. Copenhagen, 1976.
Wood, Robin. *Ingmar Bergman*. New York, 1969.
Young, Vernon. *Cinema Borealis: Ingmar Bergman and the Swedish Ethos*. New York, 1972.

Index

Adolphson, Kristina, 104
Ahlbom, Martin, 57
Albee, Edward (*see also* under individual titles), 45, 73
Anderberg, Bertil, 25
Andersson, Bibi, 39, 53, 162, 206, 229
Andersson, Elis, 42, 43, 45, 46
Andersson, Harriet, 51, 53, 207
Anouilh, Jean (*see also* under individual titles), 41, 44
Antigone (Anouilh), 44
Arlésienne, L' (Daudet), 29
Årlin, Georg, 71, 77, 106, 109
Aronson, Boris, 46
Atzorn, Robert, 139
Aus dem Leben der Marionetten, 5, 220

Baeckström, Tord, 207
Balanchine, George, 13
Barrault, Jean-Louis, 29
Benktsson, Benkt-Åke, 68, 71, 75
Benrath, Martin, 191
Bergman, Hjalmar (see also *Legend, The*), 32, 53, 132
Bergman, Ingmar: on actors and acting, 8–9, 12, 15–16, 83–4, 212–18, 226–8, 229–31; amateur productions of, 31–2, 69; early productions in Gothenburg, 35–40, 41–7, 49–52; on film making, 6–7, 24–5, 232–4; on French theater, 27–30, 49, 133; on German theater, 18–19, 223, 228, 230; in Hälsingborg, 32–5; influence of Hammarén on, 38–40; influence of Molander on, 23, 55–7, 69–70, 222; on lighting, 17–18; open rehearsals adopted by, 14–15, 143–4; production style at Malmö City Theatre, 16, 52–3, 57–63, 64–5, 80–2, 172–8; at rehearsal, *xiii – xiv*; theatrical career, summary of, 1–2; works: *Aus dem Leben der Marionetten*, 5, 220; *Cries and Whispers*, 197; *Early Ends the Day*, 41; *Face to Face*, 113; *Fanny and Alexander*, xiv; *Murder at Barjärna, The*, 60; *Naked Night, The*, 43, 50; *Passion, A*, 54; *Persona*, 1, 25, 54, 66; *Scenes from a Marriage*, xiii, xiv, 220, 224; *Serpent's Egg, The*, 21; *Seventh Seal, The*, 1, 25, 47, 50, 173; *Silence, The* 1, 66; *Smiles of a Summer Night*, 1, 63; *Summer with Monika*, 51; *Through a Glass Darkly*, 1, 54, 66; *To Joy*, 63; *To My Terror*, 41; *Torment*, 32, 33; *Twilight Games*, 13; *Wild Strawberries*, 1, 54; *Winter Light*, 1, 66
Bergstrand, Allan, 79
Beyer, Nils, 31, 60, 82, 180, 186
Bizet, Georges, 29
Blue Bird, The (Maeterlinck), 31
Böcklin, Arnold, 85
Borchsenius, Hanne, 152
Børge, Vagn, 61
Bosch, Hieronymus, 175
Bosse, Harriet, 80, 123
Brandell, Gunnar, 92, 96
Brod, Max, 64
Brodin, Helena, 120
Buchegger, Christine, 182, 185, 187
Burke, Kenneth, 197

Caligula (Camus), 41–4, 49, 127
Camus, Albert (*see also* under individual titles), 41, 44
Castle, The (Kafka), 84
Cat on a Hot Tin Roof (Williams), 45, 65
Cézanne, Paul, 193
Chekhov, Anton (*see also* under individual titles), 2, 10, 12, 22
Corneille, Pierre, 153
Craig, Edward Gordon, 85
Cries and Whispers, 197
Crimes and Crimes (Strindberg), 54, 63
Criticism of the School for Wives (Molière), 11, 133, 136
Crown-Bride, The (Strindberg), 51, 54, 59–63, 65

Dagen slutar tidigt, see *Early Ends the Day*
Dam, Inge, 154
Dance of Death, The (Strindberg), 2, 22–3, 55

259

Daudet, Alphonse (see also *Arlésienne,*
    L'), 29
Divine Words (Valle-Inclán), 49–52, 60
Dohm, Gaby, 134, 140
Doll's House, A (Ibsen), xiv, 172, 220,
    223–5
Dom Garcie de Navarre (Molière), 27
Don Juan (Molière), 133, 135, 136, 137
Dörfler, Walter, 21, 110
Dream Play, A (Strindberg), 2, 3, 41, 54,
    59, 85, 90, 114, 128, 220; Bergman
    comments on, 21–2, 220–2; Molan-
    der productions of, 55–7; produc-
    tion analysis of, 97–113
Dutchman, The (Strindberg), 54, 64

Early Ends the Day, 41
Easter (Strindberg), 54, 63–4
Edwall, Allan, 108
Ek, Anders, 43, 45, 55; Bergman on, 22,
    23, 38; roles, 37, 42, 43, 44, 53, 58,
    63, 70, 76, 78, 124, 125, 207, 209
Ek, Malin, 104
Ekerot, Bengt, 11
Ekman, Härje, 174
Eliot, T. S., 53
Engberg, Harald, 152
Erichsen, Svend, 163
Ericsson, Sune, 34
Erik XIV (Strindberg), 54, 65–6

Faber, Erwin, 141, 143
Face to Face, 113
Fagerström, Allan, 176
Falck, August, 21
Falk, Per, 61, 65
Fall, The (Camus), 44
Fanny and Alexander, xiv
Faust [*Ur-Faust*] (Goethe), 18, 175, 176,
    178
Fergusson, Francis, 197
Feydeau, Georges, 28
First Warning, The (Strindberg), 54
Fledermaus, Die (Strauss), 65
Flemming, Charlotte, 135, 137
Fridh, Gertrud, 22, 53, 63; on Bergman,
    212; in *The Ghost Sonata*, 70, 91, 93,
    94, 95; in *Hedda Gabler*, 185, 186,
    190; in *The Misanthrope*, 162–3

Ghosts (Ibsen), 58
Ghost Sonata, The (Strindberg), 2, 3, 54,
    222; Bergman on, 22, 67, 75; earlier
    productions of, 55–7; production
    analysis of, 67–96
Gierow, Karl Ragnar, 36

Gimmler, Heiner, 9
Goethe, J. W. von (see also *Faust*), 53
Gombrowicz, Witold (*see also* under in-
    dividual titles), 2, 139
Grabow, Carl, 123
Grandinson, Emil, 114
Grevenius, Herbert, 34, 36, 42, 49, 52,
    58, 80
Grieg, Edvard, 172, 173
Grillparzer, Franz, 19
Guth, Klaus, 140

Hagman, Gerd, 60
Hamlet (Shakespeare), 19
Hammarén, Torsten, 25, 38, 40, 52
Harrie, Ivar, 71
Hedberg, Olle, 32
Hedda Gabler (Ibsen), 2, 3, 15, 41, 172,
    201; Bergman on, 154; London pro-
    duction of, 179, 225–6; Munich pro-
    duction of, 9, 17–18, 180, 223; pro-
    duction analysis of, 178–201
Hedeby, Kerstin, 145, 147
Henrikson, Mathias, 91, 95
Hetz, see *Torment*
Hjortsberg, Lenn, 26
Höijer, Björn-Erik, 32, 41
Horn, Brita von, 32
Horváth, Ödöm von, 19

Ibsen, Henrik (*see also* under individual
    titles), 2, 3, 5, 41; Bergman com-
    ments on, 15, 18, 75, 154, 178, 186,
    197, 223–4; excision of overt sym-
    bolism in, 178, 225; place in
    Bergman's career, 132, 172
Impromptu de Versailles, L' (Molière), 27,
    165

Jacobsohn, Siegfried, 56
Jahnsson, Bengt, 115, 228
Järegård, Ernst-Hugo, 207, 208
Johansson, Ulf, 121, 130
Josephson, Erland, 207
Josephson, Ragnar, 59
Jouvet, Louis, 28, 29, 133, 139, 142

Kavli, Karin, 45, 51, 60
Kazan, Elia, 46, 75
Kjellson, Ingvar, 189, 190
Kragh-Jacobsen, Svend, 70, 71, 82, 154
Krook, Margaretha, 208
Kruse, Jens, 157

Lagerkvist, Pär, 31
Leah and Rachel (Moberg), 64

Legend, The (Hjalmar Bergman), 41
Lindberg, Per, 23, 53, 56, 117
Lindblad, Gunnar, 33
Lindblom, Gunnel, 53, 176, 178
Linde, Ebbe, 43, 47, 60, 62, 65, 83, 135, 175
Londemann, Gert, 138
Long Day's Journey into Night (O'Neill), 15
Lorca, Federico Garcia, 60
Löwenadler, Holger, 105, 207, 212
Lucky Per's Journey (Strindberg), 31, 55, 114
Lundgren, Henrik, 149, 157

Macbeth (Shakespeare), 32–7, 37–8, 41, 44
Maeterlinck, Maurice (see also *Blue Bird, The*), 31, 57
Magic Flute, The (Mozart), 112–13, 232
Magnusson, Georg, 48
Mago [Max Goldstein], 180, 181, 185
Marivaux, Pierre de, 15
Master Olof (Strindberg), 31
Meisel, Kurt, 10, 189, 200
Melchinger, Siegfried, 179, 186, 188, 193
Merry Widow, The (Lehár), 65
Meyer, Jean, 28
Meyerhold, Vsevolod, 43
Mielziner, Jo, 46
Mig till skräck, see *To My Terror*
Misanthrope, The (Molière), 2, 133, 214, 217; Bergman on, 11, 26–7, 28; Copenhagen production of, 11–12, 17, 132, 139, 142; production analysis of, 145–71
Miss Julie (Strindberg), xiv, 55, 213, 220, 223–4
Molander, Olof, 32, 87, 98, 106; Bergman comments on, 23, 55, 222; on Reinhardt, 56, 57; Strindberg productions of, 56–7, 58, 69–70, 79–80
Molière [Jean-Baptiste Poquelin] (*see also* under individual titles), 2, 3, 5, 19, 27, 28, 41; Bergman comments on, 11, 15, 19, 49, 132–3, 154, 157; theatrical heritage of, 133, 134, 135, 137–8, 148, 161
Moritzen, Henning, 151, 152, 154, 158, 167
Mørk, Erik, 165
Mörk, Lennart, 102, 105
Mother Love (Strindberg), 54
Munch, Edvard, 181
Murder at Barjärna, The, 60

Naked Night, The, 43, 50
Naur, Robert, 149, 151
Nestroy, Johann, 19, 134
Nilsen, Hans Jacob, 172
Nilsson, Maj-Britt, 63
Nørby, Ghita, 163, 217
Nyman, Lina, 207

Olivier, Laurence, 225
Ollén, Gunnar, 79
Olsson, Gunnar, 64
Open Letters to the Intimate Theatre (Strindberg), 66
Osborne, John, 152

Palme, August, 123
Palmstierna-Weiss, Gunilla, 37, 38
Passion, A, 54
Pawlo, Toivo, 66, 70, 75, 78, 176, 178
Peer Gynt (Ibsen), 127, 172–6, 177, 178, 208
Pelican, The (Strindberg), 54, 65, 66, 91; Bergman's production of, 55, 57–9; earlier productions of, 56, 57
Perlström, Åke, 86, 92, 98, 128, 174
Persona, 1, 25, 54, 66
Pirandello, Luigi (see also *Six Characters*), 88, 185
Playing with Fire (Strindberg), 54
Prince of Homburg (von Kleist), 18

Racine, Jean, 133
Rangström, Ture, 62
Reinhardt, Max, 3, 63, 65, 175; eclecticism of, 64; Strindberg productions of, 56, 57, 69, 79
Ringheim, Lise, 165
Rode, Ebbe, 158, 159
Rose Tattoo, The (Williams), 45
Rosmersholm (Ibsen), 226

Saeverud, Harald, 173
Saga of the Folkungs (Strindberg), 55
Sartre, Jean-Paul (see also *Unburied Dead, The*), 25, 44
Sauvage, La (Anouilh), 44
Scenes from a Marriage, xiii, xiv, 220, 224
Schmidinger, Walter, 134
Schnitzler, Arthur, 19
School for Wives, The (Molière), 11, 85, 133, 138
Schwab-Felisch, Hans, 181
Seagull, The (Chekhov), 22
Serpent's Egg, The, 21
Seventh Seal, The, 1, 25, 47, 50, 173

Shakespeare, William (*see also* under individual titles), 2, 19, 21, 31, 41
Sherlock Holmes (Gillette), 95
Shollin, Christina, 22
Silence, The, 1, 66
Simon, Alfred, 156
Simon, John, 47
Six Characters in Search of an Author (Pirandello), 220
Sjöberg, Alf, 32, 41
Sjögren, Henrik, 5, 61, 71, 151, 205, 206
Skawonius, Sven Erik, 136
Skymningslekar, see *Twilight Games*
Smiles of a Summer Night, 1, 63
Smith, Maggie, 179
Sprinchorn, Evert, 58
Stanislavski, Constantin, 229
Steen, Peter, 165
Stenberg, Gaby, 83, 84
Storm Weather (Strindberg), 54
Stråât, Hans, 106
Strandberg, Jan-Olof, 117, 123
Strasberg, Lee, 229
Streetcar Named Desire, A (Williams), 45–7
Strindberg, August (*see also* under individual titles), 2, 5, 15, 19, 31, 132, 196; artistic kinship of Bergman with, 3, 54–5, 66–7, 130–1; attitude toward *The Crown-Bride*, 62–3; Bergman comments on, 8, 19, 221, 222; defines chamber play, 66–7; identification of his presence in his plays, 56, 57, 79–80, 90–1, 98; and Intima teatern, 21, 69; resides at Karlavägen, 40, 80; on sciopticon projections, 114; on *To Damascus*, 114, 115, 119
Ström, Carl-Johan, 35, 36, 41, 42, 43, 51
Strömberg, Martin, 173
Strömstedt, Bo, 98
Stronger, The (Strindberg), 54
Summer with Monika, 51
Sundquist, Folke, 81, 83, 84
Swanwhite (Strindberg), 55, 59
Sydow, Max von, 53, 212; Bergman on, 173, 226; comments on Bergman, 211; in *A Dream Play*, 108, 111; in *Faust*, 176; in *The Misanthrope*, 151–2, 153, 162; in *Peer Gynt*, 173, 174, 175, 177; in *The Wild Duck*, 208, 209

Tartuffe (Molière), 9, 10, 18, 133, 141; Bergman on, 10, 134; Bergman's production of, 26, 28–9, 134, 135–8, 141

Teahouse of the August Moon (Patrick), 64
Terselius, Lil, 39
Thoor, Alf, 114, 115
Three Sisters, The (Chekhov), 22
Through a Glass Darkly, 1, 54, 66
Thulin, Ingrid, 53, 173, 177
Tiny Alice (Albee), 45, 48
To Damascus (Strindberg), 2, 22, 54, 66, 96; Bergman on, 23, 221; Molander production of, 23, 55; production analysis of, 113–31
To Joy, 63
To My Terror, 41
Torment, 32, 33
Törnqvist, Egil, 73, 76
Tristan und Isolde (Wagner), 197
Twelfth Night (Shakespeare), 2, 9, 37, 38, 39, 41
Twilight Games, 13

Ullmann, Liv, 25, 220, 224, 226, 227
Unburied Dead, The (Sartre), 25

Valle-Inclán, Ramón Maria del (*see also Divine Words*), 49, 50
Vos, Marik, 85, 89, 114, 122, 123, 201, 202

Wagner, Richard (*see also* under individual titles), 197
Wahlund, Per Erik, 48, 61, 62, 80, 82, 98, 109, 180, 188
Wegener, Paul, 69
When We Dead Awaken (Ibsen), 222
Who's Afraid of Virginia Woolf? (Albee), 15–16, 45, 47, 48
Wifstrand, Naima, 53, 60, 71, 72, 178
Wild Duck, The (Ibsen), 2, 15, 172; Alceste compared to Gregers in, 152, 154; Bergman on, 20; production analysis of, 201–11
Wild Strawberries, 1, 54
Wildner, Andrea Maria, 142, 214
Williams, Tennessee (*see also* under individual titles), 44, 75
Winter Light, 1, 66
Woyzeck (Büchner), 14, 83, 102, 103, 143, 217

Yvonne, Princess of Burgundy (Gombrowicz), 2, 138–42, 214, 220

Zern, Leif, 79, 93, 96, 98, 103, 108, 205, 208, 210